D1543027

BUYING AND SELLING
A BUSINESS...
SUCCESSFULLY

BUYING AND SELLING A BUSINESS... SUCCESSFULLY

A PROVEN GUIDE FOR ENTREPRENEURS

Arnold S. Goldstein

Dow Jones-Irwin
Homewood, Illinois 60430

© RICHARD D. IRWIN, INC., 1990

Dow Jones-Irwin is a trademark of Dow Jones & Company, Inc.

All rights reserved. No part of this publication may be
reproduced, stored in a retrieval system, or transmitted,
in any form or by any means, electronic, mechanical,
photocopying, recording, or otherwise, without the prior
written permission of the publisher.

This publication is designed to provide accurate and
authoritative information in regard to the subject matter
covered. It is sold with the understanding that the
publisher is not engaged in rendering legal, accounting, or
other professional service. If legal advice or other expert
assistance is required, the services of a competent
professional person should be sought.

*From a Declaration of Principles jointly adopted by a Committee
of the American Bar Association and a Committee of Publishers.*

Sponsoring editor: Jim Childs
Project editor: Joan A. Hopkins
Production manager: Ann Cassady
Designer: Mike Finkelman
Compositor: Caliber Design Planning, Inc.
Typeface: 11/13 Century Schoolbook
Printer: R.R. Donnelley & Sons Company

Library of Congress Cataloging-in-Publication Data

Goldstein, Arnold S.
    Buying and selling a business—successfully : a proven guide for
entrepreneurs / Arnold S. Goldstein.
      p.   cm.
    Includes index
    ISBN 1-55623-162-8
    1. Business enterprises, Sale of—United States. 2. Business
enterprises—United States—Purchasing I. Title.
HD1393.25.G637 1990
658.1'6—dc20   89–7736
                                         CIP

Printed in the United States of America

1 2 3 4 5 6 7 8 9 0 DO 6 5 4 3 2 1 0 9

PREFACE

Buying or selling a business is usually a once-in-a-lifetime experience. And if you're like most people, you're about to buy or sell for the very first time. A frightening prospect? Probably. That's why I wrote *Buying and Selling a Business . . . Successfully*. With this guide at your fingertips, you can move ahead intelligently, confidently, and successfully on this most important undertaking.

This essential guide steers you through each phase of the buy-sell process, showing you the proven ways to avoid costly errors, dangerous pitfalls, and common mistakes while obtaining the best deal possible. In the following chapters, you'll find the right way

- To plan the acquisition or position the business for a fast, profitable sale
- To find the best opportunities or qualified buyers
- To investigate and evaluate each phase of the acquisition
- To negotiate the purchase or sale on terms most favorable to yourself
- To structure the transaction advantageously for the optimum tax and business benefits
- To finance the acquisition to your advantage whether you are a buyer or seller
- To protect yourself with essential but commonly overlooked contract terms
- To ensure a smooth and orderly ownership transition

Comprehensive, *Buying and Selling a Business . . . Successfully* tackles all the troublesome questions and situations you are likely to encounter, providing the clear, step-by-step answers and strategies you need.

Whether you are planning to buy or sell a small retail shop or a large manufacturing firm or have interest in a special situation such as a franchised company or turnaround opportunity, this book puts years of experience right at your disposal.

Buying and Selling a Business . . . Successfully is not just for buyers and sellers. It also belongs on the desktops of accountants, attorneys, business brokers, lenders, appraisers, acquisition consultants, and other professionals who can benefit their clients by sharing with them the wealth of information this guide features.

This book has been designed not only to tell you how to profitably buy or sell a business but also to provide you with the essential tools. As a complete "action kit," this valuable handbook includes numerous sample forms, checklists, worksheets, correspondence, contracts, agreements, and documents to save you time and money throughout each step of the transfer. You'll also discover the handbook to be a resource-rich companion listing numerous sources of assistance for any buyer or seller.

Buying or selling a business can be quite complex, as there are various legal, accounting, and tax matters to consider. Therefore, no book can, or should, take the place of your attorney or accountant in providing you with the right advice for your specific situation. But we *do* encourage your advisers to review this book. We are confident they will recommend it as a most valuable armchair adviser for making those important business decisions.

A book is rarely the creation of its author alone, and this book is no exception. I wish to acknowledge gratefully the assistance of several individuals who have enthusiastically contributed to it. I wish particularly to thank Kevin Harrington, president of Franchise America, who provided valuable insights into the field of franchise acquisitions. My good friends Ray Miles and Ken MacKenzie of the Institute of Business Appraisers offered an expert perspective on business valuations. Last, but certainly not least, I am indebted to my wife Marlene for her tireless efforts in editing and typing the manuscript. Without her efforts, this book would still be but an idea.

Arnold S. Goldstein

CONTENTS

CHAPTER 1

BEFORE YOU BUY A BUSINESS

Will you be one of the nearly 300,000 Americans who will buy a business this year?

Who are these new entrepreneurs? They come from every age group, background, and walk of life. Women and minority groups are increasingly joining the ranks. What these people have in common is the dream of becoming independent and the opportunity to use their talents to build a better future as owners of their own business.

When do they decide to go into business for themselves? When they get tired of the corporate rat race, when they get fired, when they are pushed into it by an ambitious spouse, or when they finally realize business ownership is the only way to reach their goals.

What will they buy? Every size and type business from ice cream stands to publishing firms, from shoeshine parlors to semiconductor firms. Some will be nothing more than part-time, work-at-home enterprises, whereas others will become formidable Fortune 1000 corporations. The businesses acquired are as varied as their buyers.

How do they go about it? Business ownership typically begins with a vague idea, becomes a dream, progresses through several formative stages, and finally emerges as a reality. Such deliberate buyers may spend months—even years—learning, exploring, examining, researching, and finally jumping. Others close their eyes and quite suddenly plunge right in. No matter how they go about it, virtually all will tell you that the decision to buy is at the same time both exhilarating and frightening. You welcome the chance to build a better life, yet the future remains unchartered as you leave behind a secure past. You have made the one important decision that you want a business of your own, but you realize this one decision spawns countless other decisions.

- Why do I want to buy?
- Why type of business should I buy?
- How will I raise the money?
- Should I start a new business instead?
- Do I need a partner?
- Who can help me make these decisions?

Of course, these just highlight the many important questions that illustrate what the decision to buy is really all about. However, decisions are more easily reached if you carefully plan the acquisition. Assess your goals and then logically sift through the various alternatives available best to satisfy those goals.

1,001 REASONS TO BUY

Many rewards and benefits come from owning your own business. Many people believe that money is the most rewarding aspect of business ownership. Surprisingly, more buyers report greater satisfaction from the *process* of achieving success than they do from financial success itself. The emotional payoff from operating your own business must be substantial to compensate adequately for the enormous amount of time and energy needed to create and maintain a successful enterprise.

Independence is also considered by many to be a major benefit. The ability to put your ideas to work, free of the interference or restraint imposed by a boss, is indeed satisfying. For once, you can do things "your way." Then there's pride of ownership, a powerful reward in itself. The ability to boast "This business is mine!" can greatly enhance your self-esteem.

However, the reality is that you probably won't buy a business for one reason alone; rather, you will have several motives. And it's vitally important to understand those hidden motives if you are to look for the opportunity to best achieve those goals. Ask yourself which of these reasons are most important to you.

1. Owning a business will offer greater income opportunities than available through employment, or the business will

be purchased as an investment to supplement employment income.

2. Ownership offers greater security than employment, or you come from the ranks of the unemployed and you see a business as a way of regaining financial stability.
3. Ownership is viewed as a way to build financial equity and to create future wealth and retirement income.
4. The particular type business allows you the opportunity to engage in more self-satisfying work than is available through employment.
5. You are attracted by the many tax advantages or the many perks and benefits of business ownership.
6. You are motivated to buy, recognizing that you are not suited to work for others or that you are uncomfortable within a large organization.
7. Ownership will enhance your ego or self-image.

Rank each objective on a 1–10 scale. How important is each? What are the trade-offs? Are you willing to sacrifice more enjoyable work for the prospects of a higher income? You see the idea. The goal is to understand clearly in your own mind what you expect from your business. Only when this goal is intelligently and objectively achieved can you begin to look for opportunities or to assess how each available opportunity will satisfy what it is you expect from your business.

Owners of existing businesses and larger corporations seeking new acquisitions are usually motivated more by financial objectives than by the personal or emotional reasons more common with the first-time buyer; however, like the novice buyer, the veteran owner must also focus clearly on his or her own acquisition objectives.

1. The buyer with an existing business may look at expansion as the only way to obtain the buying or advertising leverage necessary to compete with larger companies.
2. The existing company may want to diversify to achieve a broader-based operation to reach new markets, offer additional product lines, or enjoy a stronger earnings base.
3. An acquiring company may be attracted by a seller's cash reserves or undervalued assets that will improve the buyer's own financial position.

4. A company with cyclical cash flow may benefit from a match with a business that can stabilize its own cash flow with more steady income.
5. The buyer may have excess plant capacity, and thus the seller's operation can be advantageously merged, achieving greater economies of scale.
6. The buyer may consider a seller's growth prospects as more favorable than its own and therefore see the acquisition as a way to expand more rapidly.
7. A seller may represent an attractive source of raw material or offer access to exclusive product lines not otherwise available.
8. The seller's business may represent a ready outlet for the buyer's products or enhance the buyer's marketing, sales, or merchandising programs.
9. The selling company may have a particularly capable management or technical staff unobtainable by the buyer on the open employment market.
10. The selling company may have a special process, invention, or piece of unique machinery available to the buyer only through acquisition.
11. The acquisition may feature a valued name or reputation that will enhance the buyer's existing market image and add to its goodwill.
12. The seller may have substantial tax losses which may be useful to shelter the buyer's own future profits from taxes.
13. The acquisition may be a distress sale that the buyer may acquire at a fractional value and—once turned around—either sell for short-term gain or hold for long-term profitability.

Existing companies are generally attracted to "middle-market" firms in the $2 million to $20 million range. Buyers primarily recognize the profit potential and economic advantages of acquiring an established business that has both positive cash flow and strong potential for growth. Today's middle-market buyers range from large public and private corporations to private investor groups. Foreign buyers, taking advantage of favorable currency rates, represent a growing trend in the middle market, with foreign buyers acquiring about 20 percent of all such companies. Indeed, there is no limit to the many reasons so many businesses are purchased every single day.

SO WHAT'S HOLDING YOU BACK?

Surprisingly, while there are countless people who want to buy or start their own business, only a very small percentage ultimately achieve it. What holds so many people back? Five major obstacles may block your way.

The Financial Obstacle

Is lack of money a problem? If so, how much capital do you *think* it will take to buy your business? How do you know? What efforts have you made to test the market and determine the actual cash requirements for your size and type of business? What efforts have you made to raise the capital or save the down payment?

The first question tests the reality of your perception. First-time buyers may easily overestimate or underestimate the capital required to buy a particular type of business. You never know how much cash is needed until you check the market and scout and negotiate a few opportunities. Only then will you have a fair idea of what it will take.

The last question really separates those who dream from those who do. For over five years, one of my closest friends aspired to buy a small luncheonette. How much cash would he need? Probably $15,000 to $20,000. How much has he saved? Zero! You'll find my friend at the bowling alley most evenings; he could have achieved his goals two or three years ago if only he had spent his time moonlighting at a second job rather than wasting his time. Buying a business demands commitment. If you lack sufficient commitment to scrape together the down payment somehow, it's unlikely you'll have the commitment to succeed in a business of your own. Why not add up your financial scorecard? It's not difficult to prepare a personal balance sheet to check your net worth (Figure 1–1). You may be wealthier than you think!

FIGURE 1-1

PERSONAL BALANCE SHEET

Assets:		Liabilities:	
Cash in Bank	____	Loans at Banks	____
Stocks or Other		Loans to Others	____
Negotiable Securities		Real Estate Loans	____
(Market Value)	____	Other Debts	____
Notes Receivable	____	_____	____
Value of Real Estate:		_____	____
(Market Value)		Credit Cards	____
Home	____	Retail Stores	____
Other	____	TOTAL LIABILITIES	____
Automobiles	____		
Cash Value of			
Life Insurance	____	TOTAL NET WORTH	____
Personal Assets	____	(Assets Less Liabilities)	
Other	____		
TOTAL ASSETS	____		

Capital Available
For Business Investment

SOURCES OF CASH: AMOUNT:

(e.g. savings, stocks, friends,
relatives, equity in property, etc.)

_____	_____
_____	_____
_____	_____
_____	_____
TOTAL	_____

Collateral Available
(Market Value)

Real Estate	_____
Stocks and Bonds	_____
Other	_____

The Security Obstacle

Owning your own business can be frightening if the idea of leaving behind a steady paycheck bothers you. But ask yourself how much job security you have now if your employer fails or suddenly decides to fire or replace you.

There are several steps you can take to reduce concerns over security. First, set aside a reasonable contingency fund so that you can support yourself for a reasonable time, should your venture not work out. Second, consider whether your spouse can help work the business with you while you hold on to your job until you're satisfied that the business demands and justifies your full-time efforts. Finally, determine whether you are interested in a type of business that may be operated on a part-time basis; if so, then confine your search to such a spare-time venture.

The Self-Confidence Obstacle

A surprising number of prospective buyers admit that they lack the self-confidence necessary to buy a business. But ask yourself if you are as capable of running your own business as are the thousands of others who will buy a business this year—or the approximate 14 million people who already own a business. Perhaps you can or maybe you can't, but since you'll never know until you try, making the effort is the all-important first step.

To the uninitiated, successful business ownership may appear to demand superhuman skill and managerial brilliance. In truth, successful entrepreneurship requires little more than a dose of common sense, a dash of commitment, and tons of hard work.

You'll develop more self-confidence if you stay with the type of business you know and have experience with. You may also consider a partner. Partnerships often provide insecure people with the opportunity to bolster each other for support. Another way to build confidence is to work in the business before buying it. Accept increased responsibility. Grow into all areas of management. Gradually accept fuller responsibility if the situation allows. You'll probably find that running a business is not so difficult, once you're actually doing it.

The Fear-of-Failure Obstacle

You may fail in business. In fact, most small businesses *do* fail, although you will have considerably less chance of failure buying an existing business than initiating a new start-up venture. But what will happen should you fail? Yes, you'll lose some money, you'll have a bruised ego, and you'll also learn from your errors and become a sharper businessperson the next time around. No,

FIGURE 1-2

ENTREPRENEURIAL CHECKLIST

Select the answer which best
assesses your capabilities:

	Good	Fair	Poor
Determination to own your own business	————	————	————
Willingness to risk capital	————	————	————
Self-confidence	————	————	————
Attitude toward people	————	————	————
General management ability	————	————	————
Knowledge of the particular business	————	————	————
Willingness to accept failure	————	————	————
Commitment to work required hours, etc.	————	————	————
Work habits	————	————	————
Common sense on business matters	————	————	————
Ability to cope with problems	————	————	————
Realistic outlook on business earnings and demands	————	————	————

---

your objective is not to avoid risk—for that's impossible—but to have the potential rewards that far outweigh the risks.

I speak from experience. I've had my share of successes, but I've also suffered a few humiliating failures. My winning episodes provided more fun and profit, but my losing ventures taught me considerably more and have proved to be more valuable experiences.

Many of today's most successful businesspeople have failed once, twice, or even several times before they reaped the rewards of a successful business. Ask these persistent entrepreneurs about failure and they'll tell you just how therapeutic failure can be. This doom-and-gloom talk isn't intended to scare you but to help you look at the risk of failure from a new perspective. Perhaps the best perspective is always to remember that without the risk of failure there can be no possibility of success.

The Family Obstacle

Many buyers are discouraged from fulfilling their ambitions by spouses who resist the idea. Your spouse may face many of these obstacles even if you don't. If husband and wife don't share the same goals, failure practically becomes inevitable. Communicate. Explain your reasons for wanting the business. Try to compromise to resolve concerns. Make the experience a family affair.

Other obstacles to buying can exist, but regardless of the hurdles to clear, resolution can best be defined by one word: *commitment*. Do you really have a commitment to owning your own business, or will you be blocked by one of the many obstacles that stand in your way?

Test your entrepreneurial aptitude (Figure 1–2). How would you rate yourself? What are your strengths and weaknesses? In what areas do you need support? Don't be too self-critical. Even the most successful businesspeople have managerial deficiencies. The objective is to assess your talents candidly and answer honestly whether business ownership is for you.

MATCHING YOU TO THE RIGHT BUSINESS

Are you interested in a retail business or service business, factory, or franchise? Take you pick. But before you do, remember that the most important step in the entire acquisition process is correctly deciding upon the business opportunity that's right for you.

Where do you begin? The first place to start is with *you*, as you are the one most important factor in selecting the "right" business. Certainly, you want to choose a business that will be successful and provide the income you need to support you and your family; but just as critical, you also want a business that matches your interests, needs, and personal objectives.

In turn, you must also understand what you can bring to the business, because for the business to succeed, it will need an owner who can provide management, capital, and perhaps most important, the necessary enthusiasm.

Some people are particularly well-suited to owning their own business but, for a variety of reasons, buy a business that's wrong for them. Usually, these people select their business for its profit potential alone and never consider whether it's the type of business they can most effectively and comfortably operate.

When is a business *right* for you?

- When you can *enjoy* the business
- When you can *manage* the business
- When you can *earn* sufficient income from the business
- When you can *afford* the business

Will You Enjoy the Business?

Motivation and enjoyment in operating the business are essential. It simply makes no sense to buy a business you dislike running, when so many exciting opportunities exist.

Remember, when buying a business, you may find it a perfect opportunity to start a rewarding new career or occupation totally different from your past work. Primarily consider the nature of the work. For example, if the business involves selling, then a strong sales aptitude is essential. Career counselors call this the "chemistry test": Your aptitudes should be compatible with the business, *but* the business should provide you a comfortable feeling as well.

There are many factors that can make a business more or less enjoyable, and each plays an important role in leading you to your right opportunity. A franchise, for example, affords you less control, or a partner may intrude on decision making, thus showing how relationships can influence your enjoyment of the business. Location, travel requirements, and working hours must also be considered. Before you decide how happy you'll be with your business choice, look carefully at the work you'll do, with whom you'll work, and where and when the work will be performed.

How do you decide on the type of business you'd enjoy? It may be the type of work you're presently involved in. In addition to work-related activities, consider social, hobby, and even educational interests. You may see a pattern emerge. Don't speculate on whether you'll enjoy a particular business. Perceptions can be far different than the reality. Try working a similar business first, even if it's on a part-time basis, and then you'll know whether it's for you.

Can You Manage the Business?

Anyone can manage a business, provided it's the right business. Very few people, however, can effectively manage any business. The objective, then, is to find the business *you* can manage properly.

What is your experience in the business you are considering? Even the simplest business has its tricks of the trade that can spell the difference between failure and success. Even with long experience in the business, you may have only the narrow, limited experience your particular job demanded. Ownership, on the other hand, requires broad management skills to cover all phases of operation. Your management skills can also be decisive in determining the condition of the business. For example, a financially troubled company will require turnaround skills not required in the profitable, more stable business.

Be objective when measuring your management capabilities. Decide beforehand whether you need more experience, a partner to supplement your abilities, or perhaps a seller who will remain and teach you the business. Statistics prove that buyers who attempt to learn the business *after* they buy suffer a far greater failure rate than experienced buyers. Learn the tricks of the trade at someone else's expense. Your new business cannot afford expensive on-the-job training.

Can You Earn Sufficient Income from the Business?

Next, test the earning power of the business you have in mind.

Start by asking yourself about the earnings you require. If you need $30,000 a year, objectively define the size of the business that can comfortably provide that income. Consider the limited income the business can provide in the earlier years when note payments must be made and earnings reinvested for future growth. A common and dangerous error is to drain excessive salary from a newly acquired business that cannot afford it. First-time buyers suddenly exposed to an overflowing cash register often lack the personal discipline to limit their salary to what the business can safely afford. This is usually the result of overestimating what a business can afford to pay its owner.

The question of earnings helps define the size of the business rather than the type of business. Don't, however, blindly assume you can rapidly build a business to provide the income you need. Buyers usually discover that success doesn't happen as rapidly or easily as they had hoped, leaving them with less income than anticipated. Also keep this in mind if you have partners or investors involved. They have their own minimum income expectations from the business, which may differ from yours.

Can You Afford the Business?

What you may desire in a business and what you can afford may be two entirely different matters. Many buyers set their sights too high and ambitiously look for a business too large or costly for their pocketbook. Unable to find such a business at a price they can afford, they never buy.

What you can afford will depend on three factors: the down payment, the available financing, and your negotiating ability. Your first step is to calculate the down payment you can raise from personal assets. Keep adequate cash in reserve for personal needs. Determine not only what you can invest but what you can safely and comfortably invest. Determine prices and down payment requirements for the type of business you're interested in by testing the market. You'll soon have a sense of what you can realistically afford. Lower your sights and look for a more modest business if that's all you can initially afford, provided it can still satisfy your minimum income needs. Once the smaller business is fully paid for, you can use it as a springboard to one that matches your goals. As a first-time buyer, starting on a smaller scale will also give you a chance to prove your management abilities and thus serve as a proving ground for the bigger opportunities more easily financed by lenders with increased confidence in you.

FORMULATING THE ACQUISITION CRITERIA

Once you objectively consider the various factors for selecting a business, you should have a reasonably precise idea of what your target acquisition will look like.

A buyer may say, for example, "I'm looking for a card and gift store grossing over $200,000 annually, located in the Chicago area," or another may say, "I want a hi-tech firm with a sales potential of at least $5 million annually, located anywhere on the East Coast." As another example, a buyer may express an interest "in any type of wholesaling firm in the Boston area," pinpointing a specific geographic area and business activity but with flexibility as to industry.

How would you define the acquisition that would be best for you with these points in mind?

- Business activity (manufacturing, distribution, retail, service)
- Industry
- Size (or sales volume)
- Geographic area
- Financial condition
- Price range (or down payment requirements)

Keep several additional points in mind. First, you probably won't find a business that precisely matches the criteria you set. Don't expect to. So establish flexible boundaries. If you can't find a hobby shop, will you accept a toy store instead? Would a family-style restaurant be an acceptable alternative for a gourmet restaurant? Would you consider a desirable business 25 miles away when you hoped to find an opportunity within 15 miles?

Scout several months for the business you had your sights on; but if you can't find a business close to fulfilling your criteria, you are probably working with unrealistic goals. Many buyers have too rigid requirements, and their lack of reasonable flexibility or objectivity assessing what may be available prevents them from buying a business. Conversely, there are buyers with so little idea of the business they want that they never appear to be serious buyers to either brokers or sellers. Nor can someone else really tell you what you should look for. A broker, for example, can help define the size of restaurant that would match your pocketbook, but a buyer who as willingly considers a restaurant as a gas station must begin to ask some hard questions about whether sufficient thought was given to the choice of business and whether he or she is ready to buy after all.

WHY NOT START A BUSINESS?

Countless people start new businesses each year when buying would have been far wiser. Conversely, quite a few buyers would have fared better starting from scratch.

The decision whether to buy or start your business must be made, but the decision shouldn't be made until you have thoroughly tested the market to determine the availability and price of existing businesses against which to measure the economics of a start-up.

Some types of businesses clearly should be started from scratch, but these usually feature unique products or services. The choice becomes more difficult when planning the more common and readily available businesses such as a hardware store or a travel agency. Then again, your entrepreneurial instincts may be the deciding factor. Many people will consider only a start-up, excited by the challenge of building a new business from the ground floor. Others apparently prefer being handed the keys and, although comfortable operating a business, can't muster what it takes to design a successful business from thin air.

Assuming no strong preference exists, consider these additional factors.

1. The acquired business has a track record. You know its sales and profits, so you know what the business should earn for you. In contrast, a start-up offers only financial speculation. Therefore, the acquired business is ordinarily a safer investment because it has future predictability.
2. The takeover of a profitable business is more easily accomplished. You have customers, employees, suppliers, and physical plant in place. Conversely, it takes considerable effort to put a start-up together and get it off the ground.
3. You should obtain better financing for an acquisition. The existing business has a track record to satisfy lenders, available collateral to pledge, and the possibility of seller and other forms of internal financing.
4. A start-up may be considerably less expensive, as you don't have to pay for a seller's "goodwill." Against this, a start-up may lose considerable money until it reaches break-even sales and may thus prove even more costly in the long run

than an already profitable acquisition sporting a higher initial price tag.

5. One major advantage of a start-up is that you can create precisely the business you want. Size, layout, merchandising, image, and location are all under your control. Whether the business you create from scratch ultimately becomes more successful than an existing business would remain the important question only you can answer.

JOIN THE FRANCHISE BOOM?

Over 2,000 franchise systems now flourish in the United States. Franchisers boast over a half a million retail and service outlets and generate close to 50 percent of all retail sales. And the franchise industry, whether it be motels or landscape services, continues to grow at an astounding rate.

Since franchise companies hold such a dominant position on the business scene, the possibility of acquiring a franchised business cannot be ignored. Later chapters discuss the investigation and analysis of the franchised operation and help guide you toward a safe franchise opportunity; but for now, consider whether you would do best operating a franchised business instead of becoming a rugged individual operating on your own.

Assuming a solid business franchise is available in your field, consider both the advantages and disadvantages it offers. The major advantage is that you greatly reduce your risk of failure. Operating under an established business concept, statistics show that the failure rate of franchised businesses is now below 5 percent. Compare this with the 50 percent failure rate for independent businesses and you understand why so many people do buy franchises. To help ensure your success, you'll receive training, assistance, supervision, and a blueprint for successfully operating the business. This is an important benefit for buyers lacking managerial experience or confidence in their ability to operate a business on their own successfully. Perhaps of greatest importance, your business is identified with a recognized name, which ordinarily translates into higher sales and profits than you could generate on your own.

On the other side of the coin, franchising is expensive with the more successful franchised businesses, such as McDonald's, selling for several times the price of a comparable independent business. There are also continuing royalty payments of 2 to 4 percent of sales to cope with. So joining a franchise family can be costly. Still, a franchise may be cost-justified when the higher expenses associated with the franchise are counterbalanced by the higher sales and increased profits a franchise affiliation will likely produce.

Under the watchful eye of the franchiser, you may feel more like an employee than your own boss. When you do purchase a franchise, you necessarily adopt the company's name, layout, merchandising, pricing, and operating policies. In other words, you operate by the franchiser's strict rules. While this can be viewed as an advantage to those who welcome close managerial support, a franchise is not for the more entrepreneurial or independent individual who wants to run the business his or her own way and without the constraint of a franchiser's rules.

THE PARTNERSHIP QUESTION

Another question to contend with is whether you should buy a business with a partner or journey into business on your own. You might consider your answer much as you would the franchise question, for in reality a franchise is similar to a partnership.

A partner can offer certain advantages: He or she may provide the confidence and psychological support needed to take the entrepreneurial plunge. As stated before, a partnership is oftentimes nothing more than an arrangement whereby two or more individuals muster their collective courage to do what each fears to do independently. The right partner, properly selected to balance your management skills and interests, can strengthen the overall management of the company. The best partnerships create a "synergy" where far more is accomplished together than could be accomplished by the two partners operating alone. A partner's capital can also be important. Added funding allows you to substantially improve the business, build it faster, and acquire a still-larger business than you could probably afford on your own.

Partnerships, however, are not always rosy. Partnership success depends chiefly on the ability of the partners to get along and develop a good working relationship. Since this is easier said than done, this remains one big drawback of a partnership. It is extremely difficult to avoid conflict when working together closely, and it becomes nearly impossible to maintain harmony if more than two active partners are involved. Moreover, a partnership adds financial strain to the smaller business unless the partnership allows for the purchase of a larger "two-paycheck" business.

So, is a partnership a good idea or a bad idea? Summarily, a partnership is no better or worse than the partner you select. Therefore, never accept an active partner on the basis of financial need alone. A partner should be considered only when you are confident you have found the individual you totally trust, have complete confidence in, enjoy working with, and share a vision of your future business with.

GATHER YOUR PROFESSIONAL TEAM

When you consider your many options and decisions that must be made, early guidance from your professional advisers can be an exceptionally wise investment.

The time to line up your professional team is *before* you actively begin your search for a business. You may not have time to locate advisers that are right for you once you do come across a good opportunity; so you will want your team ready to go to work well in advance. In addition, your advisers can help you plan your acquisition strategy and provide objectivity when deciding many of the issues raised in this chapter.

Consider several factors when choosing your accountant and attorney. First, you are selecting advisers not only to handle the acquisition but to work closely with you long after the acquisition. Therefore, choose professionals who have the time and talent to do the job and grow with you. Match yourself to the professional within the firm with whom you work best, as a comfortable relationship with your adviser is essential if the relationship is to succeed. Discuss fees candidly. When starting out, you want advisers you can afford and advisers who know the priorities and can give you the best value for every dollar spent.

Select an accountant with experience in small business operations. Ideally, your accountant has experience within your industry, as an accountant thoroughly familiar with your industry will be able to assist you on many operational decisions and will prove far more valuable than one who has little understanding of how your type of business functions.

A certified public accountant (CPA) is not necessary unless your bank requires certified statements. Franchised accounting services such as Comprehensive Business Services or General Business Systems have low-cost computerized accounting services and are excellent for the smaller firm. I highly recommend these services because they provide financial controls specifically designed for the small business at surprisingly reasonable cost.

It may be costly to overly economize on your accountant's services. You need more than tax preparation. Adequate professional assistance means help in forecasting, budgeting, expense control, and financial management. Rely on your accountant to be your financial navigator, as you will need this support and guidance, particularly in your first years when you have yet to develop the solid experience needed to operate the business.

Although there are over 600,000 lawyers in this country, finding a good one to handle small business matters is seldom easy. Law has become increasingly specialized, so look for a business or corporate law specialist. Lawyers who represent commercial banks are usually a good choice for business owners because banks insist on high professional standards, their attorneys routinely handle the type of work your business needs, and most bank attorneys have broad experience in handling business transfers. Locate an attorney within the town the business is located, particularly if your business may be involved in zoning or licensing problems and your attorney has local influence.

A message repeated throughout this book is: Never sign a contract or offer to purchase without your attorney's approval.

But also expect your attorney to incorporate your business, negotiate and draft leases, obtain licenses, review your organization to ensure legal compliance, and help keep your business out of trouble.

Why not add a small business consultant to your professional team? Unfortunately, very few new entrepreneurs use business consultants, partly because they don't know such experts exist, or they don't know where to find them or mistakenly believe they cannot afford them. Once you finish reading this book, I'm sure you'll recognize the complexity of the seemingly endless business decisions that must be made. A consultant can safely steer you through this entrepreneurial minefield. Fees will run from expensive to free. For instance, the Small Business Administration's (SBA's) SCORE (Service Corps of Retired Executives) group, found through your local SBA office, provides valuable help absolutely free of charge. If you feel uncomfortable using your hard-earned capital to buy your own business because the process seems overwhelming, then consider discussing the project with a small business consultant familiar with your type of operation found in the yellow pages under "Management Consultants" or "Business Consultants."

Inexperienced in the type of business under consideration? Try to hire someone successful from within the industry to act as your consultant on a per diem basis. An experienced eye will more accurately gauge the true potential of the business, detect hidden problems, and generally assess the value of the enterprise and decide what must be done to make it more successful.

In one of our recent transactions, for instance, a prospective buyer of a large clothing store hired a very successful New York clothing merchandiser to review the business. The consultant alarmingly pointed out that the store's major supplier, an exclusive manufacturer, intended to discontinue operations. With the foreseeable loss of this vital supplier, the buyer wisely turned the business down. Without the knowledge of this seasoned veteran, my client would have lost a small fortune. Unless you are thoroughly familiar with the industry, you'll need someone who is. Inquire within the industry and hire someone who'll spend two or three days helping you make all the right decisions. It's the best investment you can make.

SUMMING UP

1. Try to understand precisely why you want a business of your own. It will help you select the right business.
2. You'll face many obstacles to business ownership. The challenge is to conquer them one by one.
3. Set your sights on a business you can effectively manage and would enjoy operating.
4. A franchised business is usually safer, but remember that you forfeit much of your independence.
5. Buying a business involves complex decisions and specialized skills. Put together your professional team before you start.

CHAPTER 2

HUNTING YOUR PERFECT OPPORTUNITY

Lace up your hunting boots! With nearly 14 million businesses of every size and description, you'll find no shortage of good opportunities. Although there are countless businesses for sale, very few will be the right one for you. To find your best opportunity, you will need plenty of determination, time, patience, and the help of the strategies found in this chapter.

PREPARE ADEQUATELY FOR THE SEARCH

Before you can intelligently start the search for your ideal business, you should keep six important points in mind.

Be Patient

Don't get discouraged if you don't quickly find what you're looking for. It can frequently take a year or more, and contact with hundreds of businesses for sale, before you locate the right opportunity.

Develop Experience

Consider the search a learning experience to look at as many businesses as possible to thus sharpen your judgment, develop a feel for the market, and spot a bargain when you see it. So don't rush in and buy until you have checked sufficient opportunities and sharpened your ability to measure comparative values.

Think Competitively

You are not the only buyer in search of a good business. In fact, there are many more qualified buyers than there are good, reasonably priced businesses for sale. Therefore, you need a comprehensive, innovative, and aggressive search strategy by which you'll be first to reach the best deals as they come on the market.

Explore Every Opportunity Source

Never rely on one source of leads. As you proceed through this chapter, you will discover many possible ways to find businesses for sale. Although some sources tend to be more effective than others, you never know where or how you will find your perfect deal; so leave no stones unturned.

Stay Flexible

You may start your search with a reasonably good idea of the business you're looking for, but stay flexible and keep your options open. With flexibility, you may come across an opportunity far better than what you originally hoped to buy.

Be Organized

A systematic, well-organized search is essential to a successful search. Start by setting goals. How many leads will you obtain each week? How many businesses do you plan to visit or investigate each week or each month? Develop and stay with your action plan. Keep a notebook and record the information on each lead so you'll have information about each business at your fingertips. Figure 2–1 provides a helpful format for a business profile. Follow up and stay in continuous contact with your sources. You never know when your perfect business will appear.

COLD CANVASING FOR HOT LEADS

From my own experiences, I have discovered the very one best way to find good opportunities is to approach directly owners of the type of business you are interested in. This strategy is pre-

FIGURE 2-1

BUSINESS PROFILE

BUSINESS NAME AND ADDRESS	OWNER'S NAME AND ADDRESS
TELEPHONE HOURS OWNER REACHABLE	TELEPHONE HOURS OWNER REACHABLE

BUSINESS DESCRIPTION	LOCATION COMMENTS

ASKING PRICE	TERMS

YEAR ENDING GROSS SALES GROSS PROFITS PRETAX NET AFTER TAX INCOME OWNER'S SALARY BENEFITS	TOTAL BOOK VALUE INVENTORY FURNITURE, FIXTURES,& EQUIPMENT: ORIGINAL COST CURRENT VALUE ACCOUNTS RECEIVABLE

FORM OF BUSINESS	YEAR FOUNDED	YEARS PRESENT OWNER	HOURS	NO. OF EMPLOYEES	AVERAGE EMPLOYEE WAGE

MONTHLY RENTAL	MONTHLY UTILITIES	LEASE EXPIRES ON: RENEWAL OPTION:	TAXES: PERSONAL PROPERTY INVENTORY REAL ESTATE

DESCRIPTION OF PREMISES (INCLUDING PARKING AND SQUARE FOOTAGE)	REASON FOR SALE

---

cisely how business brokers obtain their listings, yet very few buyers consider using this same valuable strategy to find businesses on their own.

The obvious advantage of this direct approach is that you are likely to find very good opportunities *before* they are actively placed on the market. There are quite a few owners who have some interest in selling but, for one reason or another, have not actively advertised or placed the business for sale with a broker. Your inquiry may be both timely and profitable, as you'll be well ahead of the pack of competing buyers.

Use a dual approach to reach business owners. Start with a direct-mail campaign. You can obtain mailing lists through the yellow pages, trade associations, or mailing list brokers.

Personalize your inquiry letter to draw increased attention. The primary message of the letter is simply to let the owner know you are a ready and able buyer for his or her type of business, outlining your general acquisition criteria. Figure 2–2 is an example of an inquiry letter that has proved effective and can be readily modified to your situation.

Follow up within two weeks with a telephone inquiry. An owner may not respond to your letter but may be receptive to discussing the possibility of selling, once engaged in direct conversation. Don't press for information over the phone except simply to inquire whether the owner has interest in selling. Further information should be left for a subsequent meeting.

If you are too timid to cold canvas, or have too little time to make the hundreds of phone calls necessary to churn a few good leads, then consider recruiting a telemarketing firm. These professionals in the art of telephone sales can generate a surprising number of good leads at a very nominal cost.

Don't keep your interest in buying a good business a secret!

A second effective way to reach prospective sellers directly is to advertise your interest in buying through newspaper and journal ads. Advertising, of course, is normally undertaken by sellers but can be far more effective for buyers because so few buyers do advertise. This allows you to stand out within the crowd of shy buyers who refuse to let sellers know of their interest.

Advertising also helps you reach the many prospects not easily contacted through direct-mail or telephone inquiry. Moreover, repetitive media advertising is more likely to reach owners at precisely the right time, should they decide to sell.

Where should you advertise? Newspapers of general circulation are best when advertising for common-type of businesses (retail, manufacturing, financially troubled, and so on). Trade journals, association publications, and other media targeted to the specific industry are best when you have a particular type of business in mind. Your local library can tell you where to obtain journal listings for your industry.

FIGURE 2-2

BUYER'S LETTER

TO PROSPECTIVE SELLERS


```
Apex Hardware
Main street
Anytown, USA
```

We are interested in acquiring a retail hardware store located within the greater Dallas area with sales in the $500,000 - $1 million range. Preference is for a business specializing in sales to contractors, however, we are flexible and will consider other opportunities.

We are principals and not business brokers. We have adequate capital and financing, and are prepared to close immediately on the right situation.

If you have an interest in selling, please call us at your earliest convenience. You have our assurance that all matters shall be held in the strictest confidence. We enclose our business card for future reference in the event you have no present interest in selling. Of course, we would greatly appreciate your directing this letter to any of your colleagues within the field whose business may be on the market.

Very truly yours,

John Smith

SUPPLIERS SUPPLY GREAT OPPORTUNITIES

Suppliers are another commonly overlooked key source of good leads because they can ferret businesses for sale well before they are listed on the open market.

Suppliers seem always to know who the likely sellers are within their industry. Credit managers, for example, know who may be having problems and wants to sell. Sales personnel develop strong relationships with their customers and therefore are often the first to hear when a business is about to be earmarked for sale.

How can you convince suppliers to bring you these valuable leads? First, you must realize suppliers will feel a strong obligation to offer their best leads to their other valued customers first. This not only builds goodwill, but the supplier benefits because he is assured of continued patronage after the sale. Unless you happen to be one of the supplier's better accounts, you're at a decided disadvantage. For that one reason, convince the supplier you will become a loyal and valued customer, should you acquire one of their leads.

Which suppliers sell to your target industry? Ask people within the trade. Don't overlook the smaller suppliers or local firms, as they are often closest to their customers and therefore most likely to know who is either for sale or planning to sell. Follow up! Out of sight is out of mind. Make it a point to call once a month to remind suppliers you're still anxious to become their valued customer.

A BUYER'S GUIDE TO BUSINESS BROKERS

Nearly 60% of all businesses are sold through business brokers; therefore, this valuable source of opportunities can hardly be ignored. But you must still think competitively, as the typical broker has 10 serious buyers for every good listing.

Considering the odds, how can you motivate a broker to work harder to find your right business? Follow 10 ironclad rules and you'll quickly gain the upper hand:

1. Convince brokers you're a serious and qualified buyer. This is the key. A broker cannot afford to waste time on dreamers, lookers, and the army of perennial "tire kickers."

2. Act successful. Call first for an appointment. Brokers are professionals and appreciate and prefer buyers who treat them as professionals. Dress and appearance also count. Impressions help convince a broker you are serious, qualified, and ready to buy.

3. Prepare a portfolio containing both your résumé and specifications about the business you are seeking. This quickly lets the broker know who you are and what you are looking for. Moreover, it shows the broker you have an intelligent, no-nonsense approach to buying.

4. Avoid revealing to the broker your limited cash or that you plan to negotiate creative or leveraged financing. Always allow the broker to believe you can raise the funds required for your deal. It's all part of becoming a "qualified buyer." You can always try to negotiate acceptable terms once introduced to the seller, but if a broker believes a business is beyond your reach, he or she may not willingly arrange that first meeting or waste time show-ing you other opportunities.

5. Create the impression that you rely upon that one broker exclusively. Brokers work considerably harder if they believe they have your undivided attention. Nevertheless, check avail-able opportunities with as many brokers as possible. You can't realistically afford to rely on one broker unless the broker, in turn, agrees to contact other brokers for access to their listings on a cobrokerage arrangement.

6. Candidly review your business objectives with the broker. Because the broker is the professional best qualified to market business opportunities, the broker is also best qualified to tell you if the business you are looking for can readily be found on the terms you anticipate or whether you should focus on another size or type of business.

7. Check every listing that could conceivably be of interest. Why bypass a listing simply because sales are too low, the price is too high, or other terms are out of line? Neither you nor the broker knows for certain (a) whether a business is right for you until the business is inspected or (b) whether terms are accept-able until they are negotiated.

8. Let the broker know why you decline a business. The broker will have a clearer idea of what you are looking for and be better able to hunt acceptable opportunities.

9. Stay in touch with the broker. A phone call every two or three weeks reminds the broker you are still an active buyer wait-ing for the right situation. New listings do come in every day, and you want to be first and foremost on the broker's mind.

10. Work only through the broker on any listing he or she presents. It is the broker's role to be the intermediary between buyer and seller, and brokers not only provide a valuable profes-sional service but rightfully expect their commission protected.

What brokers should you contact? When looking for a specific type of business, such as a restaurant or a motel, first try brokers specializing within that one industry. I prefer to work with specialty brokers because they offer the greatest number of list-ings within the industry. For the names of such specialty broker-age firms, check your local yellow pages.

Franchised brokerage offices such as VR Business Brokers with nearly 400 offices nationwide offer the advantage of listings in every geographic area. This national coverage is important if you are willing to relocate and want access to opportunities in other cities.

Many thriving independent brokerage firms also provide excellent services. For their listing, contact the International Business Brokers Association, Box 704, Concord, MA 01742. Their member firms offer excellent business opportunities for sale throughout the country.

WHO WANTS A TROUBLED COMPANY?

Apparently quite a few buyers have strong interest in companies with serious financial problems, since such firms can frequently be picked up at a bargain price, then turned around and successfully operated or quickly sold at a profit. If you want to try your skills nursing a near-bankrupt business back to health, the following search strategies will tell you who's on the current sick list:

1. Check public records for companies with recent tax liens. Creditors and professionals dealing with insolvent firms consider tax problems a surefire sign of financial crisis.

2. Contact commercial auctioneers. Since they are called upon to liquidate insolvent firms, perhaps you can arrange through them to buy such a business at private sale and thus bypass a public auction.

3. Court-appointed receivers and bankruptcy trustees are, of course, another obvious source of leads. Ask the local bankruptcy court for their list of attorneys who are routinely appointed trustees. Then contact the Commercial Law League, 222 West Adams Street, Chicago, IL 60606, for their free membership roster. Most bankruptcy specialists are members of this national organization.

4. Did you know Dun and Bradstreet, the national credit reporting service, will sell you a list of companies featuring the poorest credit rating? And all are conveniently categorized by size and type of business and their location. Contact your local Dun and Bradstreet office for further information.

5. At least one business brokerage firm handles only financially troubled companies. For their latest listings, buyers and sellers should write: Galahow & Company, 850 Boylston Street, Brookline, MA 02167, 617–277–4165.

6. Why overlook commercial banks and other small business lenders? Banks, for example, frequently have problem loans and will anxiously arrange a takeover, once they believe you can solve their loan problems by acquiring and successfully operating the business under a workout.

7. Turnaround management consultants are a small but growing breed of specialists. Since these corporate gunslingers work only with troubled companies, they can furnish excellent leads, particularly when looking for a failing medium- or large-sized business. Such consultants are located throughout the country, but you can obtain the names of the consultants within your area by contacting the American Turnaround Management Association, University of North Carolina, Chapel Hill, NC.

8. A new service to buyers of troubled companies is the *Business Bankruptcy Report*, which lists, on a biweekly basis, companies in the Northeast who filed for bankruptcy or reorganization. This timely resource provides a complete monograph about each company so you can easily spot interesting takeover prospects. For further information call 1–212–686–7412.

Observe carefully and closely listen and you will stumble across many more distressed companies than you can possibly handle on your own. Walk into a retail shop, for example, spot near-empty shelves and tired physical appearance, and you can correctly conclude the business is doing poorly. Listen and you will hear plenty of rumors about who in your neighborhood is in deep trouble. Circulate at trade conventions and you'll soon learn who is about to become their most recent casualty. Nearly 600,000 companies vanish each year, so there will never be a shortage of candidates for buyers with turnaround talent.

IS THERE A FRANCHISE IN YOUR FUTURE?

With over 2,000 franchise systems spanning virtually every field, plenty of franchise opportunities are available to choose from. Blessed with long lists of anxious buyers, McDonald's, Holiday Inn, and other highly successful franchisers have little need to advertise for prospects. However, many worthwhile and modestly priced franchise opportunities available through these sources are actively looking for hard-working people to join their rapidly growing ranks.

1. Write the International Franchise Association (IFA), 7315 Wisconsin Avenue, Washington, DC 20014, for a roster of member firms. Since the IFA imposes strict membership standards, you are somewhat assured of a quality franchise program when you deal with a member of their organization.

2. The federal government publishes an excellent guide, *The Franchising Opportunities Handbook*, compiled annually by the Department of Commerce. Write the U.S. Superintendent of Documents, Washington, DC for a copy.

3. *The Wall Street Journal* and Sunday *New York Times* are favored by national chains for advertising their franchise programs; however, you will most likely find regional and local systems advertised in your metropolitan newspaper.

4. Five magazines heavily feature franchise opportunities. *Inc., Venture,* and *Entrepreneur* are magazines available at any newsstand. *Entrepreneur* also publishes an excellent annual franchise directory well worth your review. Write for their most recent edition. *Income Opportunities* and *Spare-Time Business Opportunities,* also sold at newsstands, are recommended for their lower-cost or part-time dealerships and franchise opportunities.

5. Business/franchise opportunity shows are held once or twice a year in most major cities. Sponsored by different groups, these shows exhibit hundreds of distributorships, franchises, and small business opportunities. Check your local exhibition halls for upcoming show schedules.

Contact franchisor's directly for a listing of new or resale franchise units. But a word of caution: the better franchised businesses are in strong demand and are therefore either reacquired by the franchisor or quickly acquired by other franchisees within the system. Because there are few good franchise opportunities available on resale, your most practical option may be to open a new franchise outlet.

ARE GOOD BUSINESS OPPORTUNITIES ADVERTISED?

Contrary to popular belief, plenty of good business opportunities can be found every single day in your local newspaper classifieds.

A seller frequently tries to sell first through newspaper advertising before turning to business brokers for help. Very small businesses sporting low price tags can't justify the $5,000 to $7,500 minimum commission charged by most brokers; so newspaper ads provide a practical alternative for finding buyers. Of course, you'll notice business brokers themselves place many of the ads, and brokers rarely spend advertising dollars on losers. So plenty of winners indeed lurk in your daily newspaper if you know how to read between the lines.

Obtain back issues of your Sunday newspaper. Observe whether a particular business of interest repeatedly appears over several weeks and whether a decrease in price or other signs of desperation are noticeable. Look for "clue" words. "Owner must sell" or "Illness forces sale" are usually designed to attract buyer interest but don't necessarily signify either a bargain or a desperate seller. "Financing available," "Terms negotiable," or "Low cash down" are usually surer signs of a highly motivated seller. As with broker listings, ignore what an ad quotes as asking price and terms. If a business is of interest, *investigate!*

In your search, don't overlook either local or national newspapers. I know several buyers who spotted terrific opportunities in their own hometown tabloids. *The Wall Street Journal,* on the other hand, is a good place to shop for larger companies, particularly if you are willing to relocate. Other newspapers, such as *USA Today,* are also rapidly expanding their "business opportunity" sections and displaying more and more good businesses for sale.

MORE OPPORTUNITY SOURCES TO SEARCH

Six additional sources of leads may prove exceptionally useful:

1. *Trade or professional associations* oftentimes maintain buyer-seller rosters as a membership benefit. And their newsletters and journals can be an excellent place to plant ads expressing your interest in buying.

2. *Schools or colleges* who train people in your target industry frequently bring opportunities to the attention of their new graduates. Pharmacists, beauticians, barbers, and even physicians and dentists who buy or sell professional practices are prime examples of the types of businesses found through schools.

3. *Accountants and attorneys* usually know well in advance when a client plans to sell. Locate the professionals who specialize in representing companies within your field of interest and contact them by direct-mail inquiry much as you would those actually in the business.

4. The *Business Opportunities Journal,* published monthly, lists hundreds of interesting businesses for sale nationwide. If relocation is no problem, the journal is definitely worth scanning. Write them for a free review copy at: 1021 Rosecrans Street, San Diego, CA 92106.

5. The *Business Owners Multiple Listing Service* is a new and interesting concept for marketing business opportunities. For a very nominal fee, they advertise businesses for sale through their computerized listings. You can obtain a free copy of over 15,000 businesses for sale nationwide by phoning: 1–800–327–9630.

6. *"Search 6"* is another new and unique business finders service. For a nominal monthly fee, they search out opportunities to match your specific criteria from their computer bank of over 3,000 current listings. Contact them at 1–603–882–5150, if you have an interest in a New England–based business.

MARKETING THE BUSINESS FOR SALE

Marketing a business for sale closely parallels the process of finding a business to buy.

The initial question to be answered when marketing the business for sale is whether you can quickly and conveniently find a buyer on your own or whether a broker should be used.

Many business deals are made directly between buyer and seller with perhaps only their accountants and attorneys acting as intermediaries to resolve the more thorny issues. Frequently, the buyer and seller are previously known to one another, or they come in contact through word of mouth.

Should you decide to try your hand at selling the business on your own, you will necessarily rely on many of the same contact sources as are used by buyers. The earlier parts of this chapter show the proven media useful to promote the availability of your business.

Two obvious advantages may encourage you to market the business on your own. First, you save a hefty broker's commission, which on average is 10 percent of the selling price. A more important advantage is that you can control the marketing process and decide how your business will be promoted. You may also decide to sell the business on your own and turn to a broker for assistance only after your attempts to find a buyer are unsuccessful. However, by this time your business may be shopworn in the eyes of prospective buyers and more difficult for the broker to sell.

There is no one right answer as to whether you or a broker will more successfully sell your business. Many owners can sell their businesses far more efficiently and skillfully than a broker might. You must also consider the type of business. The highly specialized business may be more easily sold on your own because you have limited numbers of potential buyers and word quickly spreads within a small closely knit industry that your company is available. But before striking out on your own, consider the many ways the right broker can help you sell both faster and for a higher price.

FIVE WAYS A BUSINESS BROKER CAN HELP YOU

Despite the ever-present temptation to save a broker's commission, a qualified and skilled business broker offers a number of important services that may more than compensate for their fee.

Expertise

Good brokers do far more than simply find buyers. The broker, as a professional in the buy-sell process, should help guide you through each stage of the selling process. Expect valuable assistance pricing and packaging the business for sale and expect the broker by your side when you negotiate and close the deal.

Confidentiality

Since confidentiality is generally of great concern, a business broker can provide a greater degree of secrecy than if you attempt to sell the business yourself. Despite all precautions, prospective buyers may make embarrassing contact with employees, customers, or suppliers. However, the chances of such disclosure are far less with a broker as your intermediary.

Screening

Experienced business brokers effectively screen the qualified prospects from the "tire kickers" and save you both time and effort dealing with buyers. However, this does not eliminate the need for you to investigate a buyer thoroughly on your own, particularly when you provide financing and the creditworthiness of the buyer becomes important.

Negotiations

A broker provides an essential intermediary role for both buyer and seller, since brokers transmit the offers and counteroffers needed to cement the deal, avoiding the oftentimes antagonistic direct confrontation between the parties. Buyers and sellers generally agree this proves to be a broker's most valued function.

Availability of Buyers

Above all, a broker is retained to find that one ready, willing, and able buyer. It is on this performance alone that the broker is paid. Remember, brokers reach many more buyers than you can possibly reach on your own unless you have the time and talent to undertake an exceptionally aggressive marketing plan.

CHECKLIST FOR SELECTING A BROKER

Once you decide to use the services of a business broker, interview as many as possible. Discussing your plans with these professionals will be informative and will give you a sound basis for comparison and selection. Sometimes it's more helpful when evaluating brokers to listen closely to the questions they ask rather than the answers they give. Yet there are important questions to consider if you are to select the right broker.

Is the Broker Well Established?

You can't afford to commit your business to a broker who lacks a long and successful track record selling businesses similar to yours. Look for a broker who has been operating for at least three years and who has successfully built and maintained a brokerage practice.

Does the Broker Specialize in Your Type of Business?

This can be an important plus because a specialist will have a ready list of qualified buyers for your type of business and usually offers greater expertise marketing your business and valuable assistance helping you set price and arrange financing.

Will the Broker Aggressively Market Your Business?

Ask the broker in advance how the business will be marketed. Compare this approach with the marketing programs proposed by other brokers. Which broker has the more active plan? Which plan appears most logical? How actively does the broker advertise other listings?

What Additional Assistance Will the Broker Give You?

Will the broker help value the business? Prepare an offering brochure? Assist the buyer to obtain financing? Are there additional charges for these services?

What Type of Listing Does the Broker Insist Upon?

Most brokers ask for an "exclusive right to sell," which entitles them to a commission even if you find the buyer. Try to negotiate instead for an "exclusive agency" agreement, which allows you the right to sell the business to a buyer you found without paying a brokerage commission.

What Length Listing Does the Broker Expect?

Hesitate to give an exclusive broker a listing for beyond three months. If the broker does a good job, you can always renew the brokerage arrangement for an additional three months, but you can't afford to tie up the business longer with an inactive broker.

What Commissions Are Charged?

Brokerage commissions are not regulated by law and usually range between 7 and 12 percent of the selling price, with 10 percent the national average. Is the broker competitive? Does the broker require a minimum commission? Is the broker negotiable?

Did Your Attorney Approve the Brokerage Agreement?

A brokerage contract is an important document, so your agreement with the broker should be first approved by your attorney to avoid costly misunderstandings later.

HOW TO BOOST THE BROKER'S EFFORTS

Because selling a business requires a collaborative effort, there are many ways a seller can significantly help a broker achieve a faster, more profitable sale. But some tips are also needed to help protect yourself from a broker not doing his or her job adequately.

1. Work closely with the broker to package the business and devise a marketing strategy. Although the broker is the professional to sell a business, you know more about the peculiarities of the business and industry than does the broker.
2. Let the broker know about earlier prospects whose interests have waned. Oftentimes a broker can revive buyer interest.
3. Let the broker know about your confidentiality requirements and the degree of secrecy needed when marketing the business.
4. Work directly through the broker. Never circumvent the broker by dealing or negotiating directly with the buyer.
5. Stay in touch with the broker. A call for a progress report every two to three weeks will keep your listing more active and let the broker know you demand action and continuous attention.
6. Consult with the broker about the proposed price and terms of sale but use independent judgment when estab-

lishing price, as a broker may suggest too low a price to achieve an easier and faster sale.

7. Remain patient. It frequently takes many months to sell a business, and brokers, for all their diligence, aren't miracle workers.
8. Review results with the broker and periodically discuss reasons for the business not selling. It is the broker who hears the buyers' comments and can frequently pinpoint correctable problems and tell you about them.

There are, of course, plenty of other pitfalls to avoid in dealing with brokers. Perhaps the most important is never to disclose to the broker your lowest acceptable price. Similarly, other possible concessions, such as whether you will finance, are best reserved for the negotiating phase. Another mistake best avoided is the "net price" listing, which grants as a commission to the broker any excess over the net price. Should a broker accept such a listing, it may signal that the business is underpriced or that the broker will later demand a percentage commission to complete the sale. Few net price listings are equitable to both seller and broker; for this reason they should always be avoided.

SUMMING UP

1. Don't be hasty. You'll need to look at many businesses before you have sufficient knowledge of the market to buy.
2. Finding good opportunities requires you to be first in line when they are placed on the market. You must therefore think and act more aggressively than other buyers.
3. Actively solicit prospective buyers. Simply because a business isn't advertised for sale doesn't mean it's not for sale.
4. Suppliers are one of the best sources for leads and the one source most commonly overlooked.
5. Check every source of opportunities you can think of. You never know where you'll find your perfect deal.

CHAPTER 3

HOW TO SPOT THE WINNERS
FROM THE LOSERS

SCREEN OPPORTUNITIES QUICKLY

Exposed to a number of businesses for sale, you need a technique to screen each quickly and thus determine which justify further pursuit. Only a proper procedure to qualify a business for in-depth evaluation prevents premature rejection of a business that could become a very worthwhile acquisition. Conversely, good screening techniques help you avoid spending needless time and effort on a business that will later prove unacceptable.

A business should qualify for further investigation when four basic conditions are met:

- The business is located in an acceptable geographic area.
- The business can produce the required profits or income.
- The business can be easily turned into the operation needed to satisfy your goals.
- The business has an acceptable lease available.

The business should never be summarily rejected because existing sales or profits are too low. You may, for example, seek a business with sales of about $500,000. Should this eliminate the business with current sales of $300,000 but with potential to reach $500,000 or more? Does this lower-volume business generate the same large profits as a higher-volume business? To answer these questions demands more than a cursory look at the business.

Unrealistic initial demands of a seller often create the same artificial roadblocks to developing buyer interest. For instance, a seller may ask $100,000 for a business a buyer quickly estimates to be worth between $50,000 and $60,000. Discouraged by the high price, the less experienced buyer is apt to lose the business to the more experienced buyer who realizes that price and terms do not necessarily disqualify a deal but are ultimately matters of negotiation. You must essentially learn to distinguish fatal flaws from correctible problems when looking for a business—and in the process *modify* your criteria to match what a basically acceptable acquisition has to offer. Unfavorable asking price, down payment, and financing should therefore not discourage you from pursuing the business if the business otherwise qualifies, as these items are best left for negotiation.

To investigate the business adequately you need as much information about the business as possible. On the other hand, the seller may be reluctant to provide confidential information unless the seller is convinced you are a serious, qualified, and ready buyer. This means that you are not only serious about buying but have the financial capability to buy and present willingness to buy.

To enhance your credibility that you are that serious buyer, be prepared to provide a personal financial statement showing your financial capacity to handle the purchase, together with a personal résumé of your background and experience to display your capability to operate the business successfully.

The seller must independently verify the accuracy of the buyer's financial, credit, and personal representations. This may include obtaining bank and credit references, verifying educational and employment background, and checking on the prospective buyer through sources within the industry. Should the seller agree to provide financing, a more thorough credit check will be necessary, but at the early stage, a preliminary check on the buyer can separate the deadbeats, tire kickers, and time wasters from the serious buyer.

EIGHT OBJECTIVES OF THE BUSINESS EVALUATION

Because an enormous number of businesses touted for sale have serious problems, the importance of a thorough analysis cannot be overemphasized. A carefully planned, comprehensive and professionally assisted investigation of every aspect of the business will help you.

1. *Verify* the seller's representations about the business.
2. *Determine* the value of the business.
3. *Detect* serious problems and pitfalls with the business.
4. *Forecast* the true potential and future of the business.
5. *Negotiate* by pinpointing problems the seller may have with the business or reasons for the sale.
6. *Finance* the acquisition through closer analysis of the legal and financial structure.
7. *Protect* yourself by uncovering legal problems requiring special attention in the purchase agreement.
8. *Plan* the future business by highlighting areas of operational weakness, strength, and future opportunity.

Investigation procedures vary greatly depending on whether the business is manufacturing, wholesaling, retail, or a service enterprise. Other factors also influence the scope of the investigation. Age of the company, reputation, reason for sale or acquisition, investment required, and the buyer's own prior familiarity with the business are just a few.

Certain steps are fundamental to any well-executed analysis:

Obtain Assistance

Unless you have solid experience in the type of business you are about to buy, you definitely need help from someone who does. Never try to evaluate a type of business you know little about, as there are too many buried pitfalls easily overlooked. The solution? Hire a consultant who knows this type of business thoroughly. Your best bet is to look for an owner or manager of a successful similar business operating in a noncompetitive area.

Coordinate with Your Advisers

Map out a total investigation strategy with your accountant and attorney before you begin. Your accountant can pinpoint operational areas on which to focus based on the financial evaluation. Similarly, your attorney will require certain business information to help protect you on the purchase agreement. Make the investigation a closely coordinated team effort so no item is ignored.

Protect Confidentiality

Sellers are rightfully concerned about confidentiality, and sincere buyers respect this. The buyer and seller should determine in advance whether the buyer may approach outside sources such as suppliers, customers, and employees for further information about the business. The seller may also hesitate to allow the buyer access to trade secrets or other proprietary information unless the buyer first signs a nondisclosure or confidentiality agreement, ordinarily a reasonable request to which the buyer should happily comply.

Check Outside Sources

Evaluating a company can seldom be fully accomplished through analysis only of the seller's records or physical inspection alone. While internal sources of information are the foundation of the evaluation, the buyer must also contact outside sources to confirm facts. With the seller's permission, candidly talk to suppliers, customers, and employees. Inquire about the reputation of the company within the trade. Check credit with credit-reporting bureaus. What might you learn from neighboring businesses? How satisfied are customers? You see the idea: Ignore no source of valuable information.

Work the Business

The one best way to evaluate a business under consideration is actually to work within it. Checking financial and legal records never discloses the idiosyncrasies, the peculiarities, and the many hidden strengths and weaknesses of a business. Once at work in a business, you can see firsthand how loyal customers are, what employee morale is like, how efficient the operation is, and the countless other tricks and gambits that are part and parcel of every business. A seller may readily agree to your request to work within the business, once convinced that you are a sincere and serious buyer, that there is at least preliminary agreement on terms, and most important, that you agree to keep confidential your identity as a potential buyer.

Demand Complete Disclosure

One important word of caution: Do not proceed in your investigation unless the seller agrees to disclose fully *all* important information about the business. Should the seller refuse full disclosure, try to find ways to solve concerns but never agree to buy unless you are granted access to all the information you reasonably need to make an intelligent and informed decision as to whether this is the right business for you.

THE MASTER BUSINESS ANALYSIS CHECKLIST

Serious investigation of any business depends on sifting through masses of information. Checklists to investigate business operations vary greatly depending on whether the business is manufacturing, wholesaling, retail, or service firm. Owing to the many variables and characteristics of each type of business, no one checklist is ideal for all. Specific information to be obtained and questions to probe can be modified to your particular situation. However, from my experience, this 12-part checklist should enable you to review most opportunities thoroughly and intelligently:

Products

1. What is the description of each product line?
2. What is the relative importance of each product line?
3. What is the market share for each product line?
4. What are the growth trends for each product line?
5. What is the anticipated longevity or life cycle for each product line?
6. Who are the principal competitors for each product line?
7. What market share is held by each of the seller's competitors?

8. Is the product line complete, or are additional or "tie-in" products needed? Are any lines obsolete?
9. Are the seller's products licensed or subject to license rights? What are the terms?
10. What product planning has been done by seller? What new products will soon be released?
11. How stable is each product line?
12. Are any products threatened by new competition or governmental regulation?

Customers

1. Who are the major customers?
2. What sales are generated from each major customer?
3. What percentage of sales comes from each major customer?
4. How long has the seller sold to each major customer?
5. Do customer agreements exist? If so, what are the terms of contract?
6. Are customers likely to remain with a new buyer?
7. What percentage of sales is sold to foreign customers? Governmental or military customers? Low-profit customers?
8. How financially stable is each major customer?
9. Is repeat business increasing or decreasing?
10. Is repeat business comparable with industry averages?
11. Is there threatened loss of a major customer?
12. What pending or future orders exist? Are anticipated?

Sales

1. How are the seller's products marketed?
2. What percentage of total sales is produced by each sales or marketing method?
3. Is the outside sales organization well-organized?
4. Is the internal sales organization well-organized and sufficient in size to handle present business? Projected volume?
5. Are total sales and marketing costs comparable with industry averages?

6. Is the selling organization performing effectively in terms of cost in relation to sales?
7. Are sales personnel on salary or commission?
8. Does the sales compensation program provide sufficient incentive?
9. Are territorial allocations proper, or are new sales territories needed?
10. Is the sales staff adequately supported by advertising?
11. Are the sales produced by each salesperson acceptable? If not, why?
12. What changes in sales approach are needed to handle new products or prospective customers more effectively?

Advertising

1. Is there a formal advertising or promotional program?
2. Does the advertising program use institutional or product advertising, or both? Is the advertising mix appropriate?
3. How do advertising costs compare as a percentage of sales-to-industry averages?
4. What is the ratio of advertising costs to sales for each product line?
5. Is advertising handled internally or by an outside agency, or both?
6. Is the advertising agency under contract? If so, what are the terms?
7. How long has the advertising agency represented the company? How effective has the relationship been?
8. Are additional advertising expenses required to bring sales to an acceptable level?
9. Are extraordinary advertising expenses planned or necessary to launch new products?
10. What changes in advertising will be needed to improve sales and at what additional cost?

Management

1. Is there a formal organizational chart with clear delineation of management function?

2. Are lines of authority and responsibility adequately defined?
3. Is the organizational structure appropriate for the size and nature of the business?
4. Will the organizational structure require major revision under new management?
5. Are major administrative departments understaffed or overstaffed?
6. Are corporate executives rated or paid on performance?
7. Are key management personnel on employment contract? If so, on what terms?
8. What fringe benefits and perks are available to executive and management personnel?
9. Do the compensation and fringe benefit programs compare favorably with industry averages?
10. Is total management compensation favorable in relation to sales?
11. Will key management personnel remain with the organization after a sale?
12. Will increased compensation be required to retain management personnel should a sale occur?
13. How strong is morale among management personnel?
14. What reputation does management enjoy in the trade?
15. Is management centralized or decentralized? Does one person run the organization, or is decision making reasonably balanced?
16. Will additional or replacement management personnel be required? Are they readily available?
17. Can management personnel be terminated without legal difficulty or expense?
18. Are key management personnel bound by noncompetition agreements?

Employees

1. Is the company unionized or nonunionized?
2. Is there a threat of future unionization or a history of prior collective bargaining attempts?
3. Is the business or industry vulnerable to unionization?
4. Would a unionization effort be successful?

5. How is compensation presently structured?
6. Are wages competitive within the industry?
7. What percentage of employees are highly skilled? Unskilled? Professional?
8. Can personnel in each job category be readily obtained?
9. Can employees be hired or terminated to meet varying production or sales needs?
10. Do working conditions compare favorably with industry standards.
11. Is there an apprenticeship or training program?
12. What hiring policies and other personnel policies and procedures exist?
13. Does employee turnover compare favorably with industry standards?
14. What employee changes are required upon acquisition?

Research and Development

1. What research and engineering is planned?
2. What is the amount of research and engineering time devoted to each major product?
3. What are the short- and long-term objectives of the research and development program?
4. How much is spent on research and development? Do costs compare favorably with product revenues? Industry standards?
5. What projects are presently under way? What projects appear promising?
6. How many research personnel are employed? How are they allocated between supervisory, technical, and nontechnical personnel?
7. How productive has the research effort been in successfully developing new products?
8. What reputation for developing innovative new products does the department enjoy?

Market and Competition

1. What are the market demographics for the company's products or services?

2. Is the market growing? Stable? Declining?
3. Does the market exist, or is it emerging?
4. What market share does the company enjoy? Is market share growing or declining?
5. What internal factors will influence future market share?
6. What external factors will influence future market share?
7. Who are the major competitors? What are their strengths and weaknesses? (See Figure 3–1.)
8. What strengths and weaknesses does the company have compared with its competitors?
9. What future competitive changes are foreseeable?
10. Are there any pending or threatened legal matters to influence product demand?
11. What changes are required to maintain market share and competitive position?
12. What are the short-term and long-term growth prospects for the company?
13. What investments and expenditures are required to achieve potential growth? Required growth?

Facilities

1. Is the location stable?
2. Is the location adequately close to its market?
3. Are facilities adequate for present needs? (See Figure 3–2 on page 50.)
4. Can the facilities be expanded to accommodate future growth?
5. What renovations or improvements are required to improve efficiency?
6. Are facilities adequately served by public utilities? Transportation and shipping?

Lease

1. Are facilities leased or owned? If owned, is the property included under the proposed sale?
2. Is a sale and leaseback possible if the facilities are to be acquired?

FIGURE 3-1

COMPETITOR ANALYSIS

Major Competitors	Sales Volume ($000)	Growth Rate	Degree of Integration	Strengths	Weaknesses

3. Is the lease sufficiently long to justify the investment?
4. Are lease terms acceptable? Can the business be relocated at reasonable cost?
5. Are rents reasonable both on a square-footage basis and as a percentage of sales?

Material and Equipment

1. What equipment, machinery, furniture, and fixtures are owned and included in the sale?
2. What are the lease terms on equipment? Are leases in good standing? Assignable?
3. Is equipment in good working order?
4. Is equipment suitable for alternate uses?
5. What additional cost is necessary to upgrade equipment?
6. What is the value of the equipment and other capital assets included in the sale?

Inventory and Purchasing

1. Who are the present and past suppliers to the company?
2. Are inventories adequate, overstocked, or depleted?
3. What additional inventories are required to bring the business to its full potential?
4. What inventory is shopworn, obsolete, or unsalable?
5. Is inventory of appropriate mix?
6. Does the company buy on competitive terms?
7. Does the company have open credit or restricted credit?
8. Is the company obligated to purchase under vendor contracts?
9. How long have vendors sold to the company?
10. Are vendor relations satisfactory?
11. Are alternative sources of supply available on equally advantageous terms?
12. Does the company rely on any one supplier? If so, is continuity of supply assured?
13. Are suppliers related to the seller?
14. Do prices compare favorably with competitors' prices?
15. Are purchasing procedures well-organized and functioning properly?

FIGURE 3-2

FACILITY AND EQUIPMENT
EVALUATION

Facility Location	Use	Size (sq ft)	Capacity	Utilization (%)	Equipment	Age/ Capacity	Utilization (%)

BEWARE THE LEGAL BOOBY TRAPS

Legal problems, other than those of a routine, day-to-day nature, can have a devastating effect upon the reputation and financial stability of the business. Normally, the legal investigation will begin once preliminary approval of business issues is obtained. To gain a full and more objective analysis of pending legal matters, the buyer's counsel will necessarily need the cooperation of the lawyers who handle the various legal affairs of the business to be sold. Key points for discussion include the following.

1. Have there been any significant changes in legal services in recent years? If so, why and when were they made?
2. What are the major provisions of the firm's charter, registration, or license to be a business? Are any unduly restrictive?
3. In which jurisdictions (states, counties, and local areas) is the firm authorized to conduct its business?
4. What lawsuits, if any, have the firm initiated in recent years? Against whom and for what claims? Of those that have been settled, were the outcomes favorable or unfavorable to the interests of the business? Which, if any, are still active?
5. What lawsuits have been filed against the firm claiming damages and compensation for injuries resulting from accidents, negligence, or other causes related to operations? Of those that have been settled, what liability has the firm suffered? Are any cases current or pending? And what is the outlook for settlement?
6. Has the firm experienced any claims for product liability? Is the business covered by product liability insurance? If so, in what amounts and coverage? What is the status of any such claim?
7. Has the firm been denied any insurance coverage, or has any insurance been withheld?
8. Are any of the firm's operations seriously affected by federal, state, or local laws and regulations?
9. Is the firm subject to any lawsuits seeking compliance with such laws and regulations? Are any criminal charges involved? How seriously are these cases regarded?
10. What, if any, civil rights discrimination or violation cases have been, or are being, alleged on the part of the firm and any of its employees? What is their status?
11. Are there title disputes or mortgage provisions affecting any property that might complicate its sale?
12. Are there any liens outstanding against any property that might delay transfer of title?

13. Are there any contracts or formal agreements and "understandings" among those having interest in the firm that could be the basis for lawsuits seeking to block a sale? If such exist, what are they and what is the prospect that any action might be undertaken?

EVALUATING THE FRANCHISED BUSINESS

Because of the vast disclosures required, the investigation of the franchised business can be undertaken with greater precision than can the analysis of independent business. For example, accounting records are usually more detailed to comply with strict franchise requirements, and thus the opportunity to conceal sales or distort profits is greatly minimized by strict franchisor controls.

Nevertheless, the buyer of a franchised business should investigate both the business and the franchisor as thoroughly as he or she would an independent business, as the franchise industry hardly lacks its share of shaky franchise operations. And that's precisely why so many franchised units are resold. The franchisee, disenchanted with the franchisor or sensing the failure of the franchise system, shrewdly attempts to pass the problem on to an unwary buyer. Unless the franchise system is well-established, approach the acquisition with extreme caution because the more successful franchise businesses are usually reacquired by the franchisor or quickly snapped up by other franchisees within the network.

Start with the Disclosure Statement

Begin with a review of the disclosure statement that the franchisor is required to give to all prospective franchisees (including transferees of existing units) under Federal Trade Commission regulations. Many states impose equivalent or stricter disclosure requirements, and in these states, it is wise to review the state disclosure documents as well.

While the disclosure statement contains 20 required points covering the background of the franchise program and its prior performance, six points are of particular importance:

- Identification and experience of each of the franchisor's officers, directors, and key management personnel
- A description of lawsuits involving the franchisor
- Prior bankruptcies of the franchisor or its officers and directors
- Information as to the number of existing franchisees, projected franchisees, and terminated franchisees, including the number of franchises repurchased or not renewed
- A list of names and addresses of existing franchisees
- The franchisor's financial statements

Although disclosure of these and other items is mandatory, no governmental agency verifies accuracy. Therefore, it is left for the buyer to investigate the accuracy of the franchisor's disclosures independently. The nature of existing lawsuits is one important area to probe. While lawsuits against franchisors are common even within the most successful franchise systems, determine whether litigation appears excessive or is based on a common and serious complaint experienced by existing franchisees.

Study the growth of the franchise system and the number of franchises renewed or terminated. The attrition rate should not exceed industry averages for this type of franchise. This is an important point because many franchisors have experienced rapid initial growth only to fail several years thereafter.

Carefully review the franchisor's financial statements. Do the financial statements appear strong? If so, determine whether income comes primarily from the sale of new franchises or from royalty income, which is a sign of a much stronger franchise system because it is self-supported from current operations rather than expansion.

Check Outside Sources

Franchise experts agree that no investigative technique is more important than obtaining references from other franchisees who can objectively report the strengths and weaknesses of the franchise system and candidly answer 11 questions.

1. When and why did you buy the franchise?
2. Why did you select this franchise over others?
3. How effective was the training program?

4. Did the franchisor fulfill its obligations to launch the franchise?
5. What products or services are acquired from the franchisor? Are deliveries on time? Quality acceptable? Prices competitive?
6. How adequate is the supervision?
7. How effective is the training program?
8. Do sales and profits compare favorably with those projected? Are sales and profits increasing?
9. Has the franchisor honored the franchise agreement?
10. What specific problems do you have with the franchisor? Are they being resolved?
11. Are you generally satisfied with the franchise?

Poll at random a sufficient number of franchisees to obtain a fair assessment. The International Franchise Association encourages further inquiry to suppliers and franchisees who have terminated affiliation as well as the Better Business Bureau or regional office of the Federal Trade Commission, who may be aware of outstanding complaints under the franchise program.

Analyze the Franchise Agreement

Should the franchise appear a worthwhile business opportunity, next review the franchise agreement.

Franchise Fees
- What are the transfer fees and who must pay?
- Is a new franchise fee payable upon renewal?
- What are the continuing royalties?
- How often are royalties paid?

Controls
- Does the franchise allow absentee ownership?
- Are salary limitations imposed on the owner?
- Who controls the hours of operation?
- Who controls the product selection?
- Are sources of supply limited to those chosen by the franchisor?

- Is pricing policy controlled?
- Is there an operations manual? How closely must it be followed?

Support
- What training will be provided to the buyer?
- What training will a buyer receive?
- Will the buyer have franchisor assistance upon acquiring the business?
- What continuing supervision is provided?
- Are legal or accounting services provided? Are they mandatory? Are there additional charges for these services?
- Is inventory control provided?

Advertising and Promotion
- What are the local/national advertising plans?
- Must the franchisee participate in all promotional programs?
- Can the buyer undertake its own advertising? Is prior approval required?
- Is there a separate advertising charge?

Noncompetition
- Is the territory exclusive?
- Are competitive franchises planned within the area?
- Can the franchisor own and operate its own units?

Transfer
- Can the franchise be sold, mortgaged, or transferred?
- What are the transfer provisions upon death?
- What are the restrictions on transfer?
- Does the franchisor have a repurchase option? A right of first refusal?

Duration and Termination
- How long is the franchise term?
- Is the franchise renewable? On what terms?
- Is the new franchise fee payable upon renewal?
- What constitutes a default or breach? Is there a "cure" provision?

Financing
- Are there restrictions on the buyer's ability to finance the franchised acquisition?
- Does the franchisor offer financing assistance?

Guarantees
- Must obligations under the franchise agreement be personally guaranteed?
- What are the limitations and terms of the personal guarantee?

INTERPRETING THE RESULTS

The investigation of any business will invariably result in mixed findings. Every company features both strengths and weaknesses and advantages and disadvantages when compared against other businesses. Weigh the relative advantages and disadvantages against each other and against comparable businesses for sale. Your answers to the questions on the Business Analysis Chart (Figure 3–3) and the Business Screening Chart (Figure 3–4) can help you decide if this is the right business for you.

Logically, the business evaluation will precede the financial investigation, although to some extent they may overlap or proceed together. This is particularly so when there is strong initial interest in the acquisition, the business investigation merely validates prior representations, and the parties are anxious to close quickly.

While the business evaluation is primarily undertaken to establish the desirability of the acquisition from a business standpoint, many of the items investigated, and the problems encountered, will require attention in the final negotiation of the transaction and preparation of the sales agreement. This underscores again the importance of a closely coordinated approach among attorney, accountant, and client. Frequently, a buyer will not appreciate the legal or financial significance of an item he or she considers to be of only managerial importance.

Still, no matter how carefully the acquisition is screened, the final decision to buy rests more on entrepreneurial instinct than on any other one factor. As every businessperson can attest, an

FIGURE 3-3

BUSINESS ANALYSIS
CHART

COMPANY STRENGTHS AND WEAKNESSES

Functions	Strong +	Average 0	Weak -	Major Strengths and/or Weaknesses in Resources
General administration				
Marketing				
Finance				
Human resources				
Engineering				
Operations				
Production				
Purchasing				
Distribution				
International				
Other				
Other				

FIGURE 3-4

BUSINESS SCREENING CHART

	Yes	No	Uncertain
1. I have the background and experience necessary to own and operate this type of business.	_____	_____	_____
2. The business meets my investment requirements. I have enough money to do it right.	_____	_____	_____
3. This business meets my income requirements. I can make enough money and also pay any debt service.	_____	_____	_____
4. I feel comfortable with this type of business. The chemistry is right.	_____	_____	_____
5. It matches my "people orientation."	_____	_____	_____
6. There is good growth in this industry.	_____	_____	_____
7. The risk factor is acceptable.	_____	_____	_____
8. My family and spouse agree that this is the type of business to enter.	_____	_____	_____
9. This business provides the status that I need.	_____	_____	_____
10. This business fits in with my life-style requirements (location, hours, long- and short-term goals).	_____	_____	_____

---

analysis of the business by objective, quantitative standards alone is rarely sufficient. Invariably, the buyer must rely on a sixth sense, an intuition that the business can become an ideal opportunity.

SUMMING UP

1. Never reject a business before you check its profit potential. Consider what the business can become tomorrow—not what it is today.
2. Remain objective. Avoid allowing emotion to overcome a detached, professional analysis.

3. There are many ways to find out what you must know about a business.
4. Demand adequate disclosure of the information needed to evaluate the business intelligently. Don't let the seller keep you in the dark.
5. List the strengths and weaknesses of the business so that you can see how they compare.

CHAPTER 4

CRUNCHING THE NUMBERS: THE FINANCIAL INVESTIGATION

The worst business can become instantly attractive through even slight manipulation of the numbers. Therefore, a thorough financial investigation of the business to be acquired is needed to uncover the booby traps. Numerous cases abound where newly purchased businesses have failed with considerable loss to their owners only because they failed to uncover significant financial flaws easily detected by closer examination. In too many cases, the business never did or never could make economic sense, even when placed in the hands of the most capable manager.

Focus on two important objectives of the financial investigation: (1) to verify that the financial affairs of the business are completely as represented and (2) to project the financial viability of the business once it is acquired. Only when both findings are satisfactory does the acquisition pass the financial test. But in addition to these two broad objectives, a well-performed financial analysis can

- *Determine* areas of financial strength and weakness
- *Highlight* the best tax strategy for the takeover
- *Measure* future cash flow and financing that the business can safely support
- *Uncover* hidden liabilities and other adverse claims to be protected against under the sale
- *Provide* data to value the business objectively

PLANNING THE FINANCIAL REVIEW

The financial analysis should be closely coordinated with your accountant, whose service is vital at this point. Only your accountant is trained professionally to audit the seller's financial records for accuracy and best decide how the financial investigation should be conducted after considering the many factors that govern the scope of the examination.

Your accountant, for example, must know the changes you plan for the business, as this will be important to project new sources of income and expenses to plan its financial future more precisely. When the business will continue to operate under its new management without significant change, the future becomes only an extension of its past. Conversely, you may essentially buy location, customers lists, technology, or other specific assets that are then to be shaped into a very different business. In this instance, there may be less need to intensively evaluate the seller's profitability because it will bear very little relation to the buyer's future operation.

Similarly, how closely you investigate the balance sheet greatly depends on whether you plan to buy the assets or corporate shares. When acquiring assets, the hidden or undisclosed liabilities of the seller's corporation are of small importance to a buyer but rise to significant concern when acquiring the seller's corporation under a purchase of shares. There are, of course, many other examples of how the focus and scope of the financial investigation will be influenced and shaped by the objectives, structure, and future plans for the acquisition and underscores why the financial investigation thoroughly blends business and accounting considerations.

Rely upon your accountant to advise you best on the specific financial information needed to investigate and analyze the business properly. However, a comprehensive financial investigation usually requires a thorough professional review of the following financial records:

- Profit and loss statements (at least three years)
- Balance sheets or statement of financial condition
- Statement of change in financial position
- Federal and state tax returns (for the corresponding time periods)
- Secured and general indebtedness records
- Inventory records
- General ledgers, journals, and other standard books of account

- Financial control records such as budgets, cash flow statements, and cost systems
- Checkbooks, bank deposits, and/or cash receipts and disbursement journals
- Payroll records

Unfortunately, three nasty problems may rear their ugly heads when you attempt to obtain this information, and they commonly frustrate buyers. First is the possibility that the seller may have totally inadequate financial information. Small business owners are notoriously poor record keepers. Many are years delinquent in filing their tax returns. While lack of such basic records should certainly depress the price you are willing to pay, you and the seller may nevertheless agree to divide the cost to reconstruct basic financial statements if the business remains of sufficient interest and the financial history can be recreated with reasonable accuracy. Since a financial reconstruction involves largely the same work as would be undertaken by a buyer when auditing existing records, it can be cost-justified.

Inaccurate financial statements are a second and more common problem. Few small businesses report significant profit, as ample opportunity exists for an owner to hide income or pad expenses to reduce taxable profits. On the other hand, the seller may falsely inflate profits for purposes of obtaining a better price. Either deception can be counteracted only by a careful audit and reconstruction of financial statements.

The third common problem arises when the seller refuses access to financial information. This is usually the same seller who stubbornly withholds sensitive operational information. Faced with a hesitant seller, one solution is to convince the seller that you are a qualified buyer. The seller will also be more inclined to release his or her financial records if negotiations are reasonably close, although you should never enter into binding agreements without prior financial clearance by your accountant and approval of the agreements by your attorney. You can also alleviate the seller's concerns about disclosure if the financial records are left in the hands of the accountants rather than entrusted to the buyer. Should disagreement arise on obtaining financial information, it can usually be best resolved between the buyer's and seller's accountants, as these professionals have the experience to understand when it is appropriate to disclose financial documents and how the interests of both buyer and seller can be best satisfied.

A LOOK AT THE BOTTOM LINE

The income statement is by far the most important financial statement to review, for it serves as a basis to project future profitability. Its importance, therefore, is equally applicable whether a stock or asset transaction is contemplated.

For comparative purposes and to establish performance trends, study at least the prior three years. Request an interim statement for the current year (Figure 4–1). Closely examine the most recent months because the figures may reveal a marked decline in sales or other adverse trends prompting the sale of the business. Figure 4–2, the Chart of Monthly Sales, can be used for this purpose.

Since evaluation of the income statement requires some understanding of industry statistics, it is recommended that, for comparative purposes, industrywide statistics be obtained. The Bank of America, San Francisco, California, publishes representative financial statements for most industries, as do several other publishing groups and most national trade associations. Copies of publications that disclose industry operating ratios are also available for examination at most banks. A comprehensive income statement analysis answers these critical questions about income, gross profits, expenses, and net profit:

Income

1. Are sales increasing or decreasing?
2. Are sales increasing faster or slower than inflation?
3. Are sales increasing faster or slower than industry standards?
4. Are sales cyclical or steady?
5. Do sales depend upon one or more primary customers?
6. How are sales allocated among product lines, markets, and customers?

FIGURE 4-1

---

company name

CURRENT INCOME STATEMENT

For _____ (month) and year to date ended _____ , 19____
($000)

	Current Month		Year to Date	
	Amount	% of Sales	Amount	% of Sales
REVENUE				
Gross Sales	_____		_____	
Less sales returns and allowances	_____		_____	
Net Sales	_____	100	_____	100
Cost of Sales	_____	_____	_____	_____
Beginning inventory	_____	_____	_____	_____
Plus purchases (retailer) or	_____	_____	_____	_____
Plus cost of goods				
manufactured (manufacturer)	_____	_____	_____	_____
Total Goods Available	_____	_____	_____	_____
Less ending inventory	_____	_____	_____	_____
Total Cost of Goods Sold	_____	_____	_____	_____
Gross Profit (Gross Margin)	_____	_____	_____	_____
OPERATING EXPENSES				
Selling				
Salaries and wages	_____	_____	_____	_____
Commissions	_____	_____	_____	_____
Advertising	_____	_____	_____	_____
Depreciation (e.g., on delivery vans)	_____	_____	_____	_____
Others (detail)	_____	_____	_____	_____
Total Selling Expenses	_____	_____	_____	_____
General/Administrative				
Salaries and wages	_____	_____	_____	_____
Employee benefits	_____	_____	_____	_____
Insurance	_____	_____	_____	_____
Depreciation (e.g., on equipment)	_____	_____	_____	_____
Total General/Administrative Expenses	_____	_____	_____	_____
Total Operating Expenses	_____	_____	_____	_____
Other Operating Income	_____	_____	_____	_____
Other Revenue and Expenses	_____	_____	_____	_____
Net Income before Taxes	_____	_____	_____	_____
Taxes on Income	_____	_____	_____	_____
Net Income after Taxes	_____	_____	_____	_____
Extraordinary Gain or Loss	_____	_____	_____	_____
Income tax on extraordinary gain	_____	_____	_____	_____
NET INCOME (NET PROFIT)	_____	_____	_____	_____

FIGURE 4-2

CHART OF MONTHLY SALES

19 ____ to ____, 19 ____

	1st	2nd	3rd	4th	5th	6th	7th	8th	9th	10th	11th	12th

Month by month, 198____

7. Are there external factors that can adversely influence future sales?
8. What is the sales potential of the business?
9. What changes, investments, or expenditures are required to achieve the sales potential?
10. Do sales include extraordinary or nonreoccurring items?
11. Are sales reported on the cash or accrual method?

Gross Profits (Margins)

1. Are gross profits above or below industry averages?
2. What are the profit margins among the various product lines?
3. Has pricing undergone recent change?
4. Does the business purchase on unusually advantageous terms?
5. Do select customers, employees, and so on, buy at reduced prices?
6. Are profit margins based on actual or estimated inventory valuations?
7. Are accounts payable reconciled to project profit margins accurately?
8. What percentage of sales is lost to shrinkage or theft?
9. What inventory markdowns or discounts can adversely affect margins?
10. Can sales, margins, or profits be improved by price changes?
11. What are the past and future margin trends for the industry? For the business?

Expenses

1. Are total expenses above or below industry averages?
2. What individual expense items are above or below industry averages? Why? Can excess expenses be decreased?
3. Are expenses reported on the cash or accrual method?
4. How are expenses allocated among production, administrative, and selling functions?
5. What are the general and administrative expenses if the business is a division or subsidiary of a larger company?

6. Are payroll expenditures low, or are increases required?
7. Is the owner's salary overstated or understated?
8. Will rent increase as a percentage of sales over the lease term?
9. Are items expensed that should be capitalized?
10. What expenses would be higher or lower under new management?

Profitability

1. What are the profit trends for the industry? For the business?
2. What are the profits as a percentage of sales?
3. How do profits compare with industry averages?
4. What is the existing return on investment?
5. What is the projected return on investment to the buyer?
6. What factors tend to overstate or understate profits?
7. How do stated profits compare with operational profits after deducting extraordinary items?

EVALUATING THE BALANCE SHEET

The importance of the balance sheet evaluation depends mostly on whether assets or a purchase of shares is planned.

Should you decide to buy the seller's assets, the balance sheet evaluation will be less important. However, even then a balance sheet review is a useful exercise to detect financial problems and to underscore the need for greater legal protection from the seller's liabilities. On stock transfers, the balance sheet analysis must be particularly exhaustive, as you automatically inherit both disclosed and undisclosed liabilities when acquiring stock ownership in the seller's corporation.

In either instance, whether you buy assets or shares of stock, the balance sheet review can help you negotiate the transaction and refine tax and financing strategies. While these objectives are dealt with in later chapters, a general analysis includes a review of the seller's assets, liabilities, and net worth, using a format shown on the Actual Balance Sheet (Figure 4–3).

FIGURE 4-3

Company Name

ACTUAL BALANCE SHEET

Year Ending _____, 19_____

($000)

ASSETS
Current Assets
Cash _____
Accounts receivable_____
   less allowance for
   doubtful accounts _____
      Net realizable value _____
Inventory _____
Temporary investment _____
Prepaid expenses _____
   Total Current Assets _____

Long-Term Investments _____

Fixed Assets
Land _____
Buildings _____ at
   cost, less accumulated
   depreciation of _____
   Net book value _____
Equipment _____ at
   cost, less accumulated
   depreciation of _____
   Net book value _____
Furniture/Fixtures _____ at
   cost, less accumulated
   depreciation of _____
   Net book value _____

Total Net Fixed Assets _____

Other Assets _____

TOTAL ASSETS _____

LIABILITIES
Current Liabilities
Accounts payable _____
Short-term notes _____
Current portion
   of long-term notes _____
Interest payable _____
Taxes payable _____
Accrued payroll _____
Total Current Liabilities _____

Equity
   Total owner's equity _____
   (proprietorship)

or

(Name's) equity _____
(Name's) equity _____
   (partnership)
   Total Partner's equity _____
Shareholder's equity
   (corporation)
Capital stock _____
Capital paid in in
   excess of par _____
Retained earnings _____
   Total shareholder's
   equity _____
**TOTAL LIABILITIES
AND EQUITY** _____

Asset Analysis

Cash and Receivables

1. Is there sufficient working capital?
2. Have working capital reserves significantly changed? Why?
3. Is the business operating with a positive or a negative cash flow? Why?

4. What is the aging on accounts receivable?
5. Are credit policies overly lenient or strict by industry standards?
6. Who are the major customers owing the receivables?
7. Is any one significant receivable owed by any one customer?
8. What is the credit rating on receivable customers?
9. What guarantee or security exists for nonrated accounts?
10. Is the bad-debt allowance reasonable for this business?
11. Are any receivables in collection? What is their status?
12. Are the receivables pledged or factored?

Inventories
1. How are inventory values allocated between finished goods, work in process, and raw materials?
2. How are inventories allocated among departments or product lines?
3. What method is used to value inventory?
4. Is any inventory on consignment?
5. How is obsolete inventory handled? Slow-moving inventory?
6. How does the inventory turnover compare with industry averages?
7. Is inventory excessive or depleted? Why?

Plant, Property, and Equipment
1. What is the acquisition price for each major asset?
2. What are the current fair market values?
3. What is the current book value?
4. How are these items depreciated?
5. What remaining depreciation exists?
6. Is the capital equipment list current?
7. Are all capital assets fully paid for and clear of encumbrances?

Liabilities

1. What is the allocation between current and long-term liabilities?
2. What is aging on payables?
3. Are trade debts being paid within due dates?

4. Are any payables in collection? In suit?
5. Are there any contingent or disputed liabilities?
6. What is the credit rating of the company?
7. Is the debt capacity fully used?
8. Are all tax obligations current?
9. Are there any debts owing to or from officers or stockholders?
10. Are long-term debts secured or unsecured?
11. Are notes and other long-term debts current and in good standing?
12. Do notes or loan agreements impose operating restrictions?
13. Does the company have the present and future ability to discharge debt?

Capital

1. What is the total stockholder net worth or equity?
2. What are the retained earnings? How has this figure changed in recent years?
3. Do retained earnings correspond to accrued profits or have dividends been declared?
4. Have there been recent contributions to capital or new stock issues?
5. How is the capital stock distributed?

INTERPRETING THE RESULTS

While ratio analysis is most frequently used to evaluate managerial performance, these same ratios are equally useful when evaluating the business for acquisition purposes. The chief difference in purpose is one of priority or emphasis. Under an acquisition, you are most interested in the ratios that pinpoint operational weaknesses and strengths that will continue after the acquisition and thus influence your profits. The Financial Performance Analysis chart (Figure 4–4) can be useful for this purpose, whereas Key Performance Trends (Figure 4–5) can quickly show the relative change in performance over prior years.

Ratios point out relationships between the various components of the financial statements, and the acceptability of any

FIGURE 4-4

FINANCIAL PERFORMANCE
ANALYSIS

Key Indicators	19 ____	19 ____	19 ____	19 ____
Income data				
Net sales				
Cost of goods sold				
Gross profit				
Net profit before taxes				
Net profit after taxes				
Asset/liability data				
Accounts receivable				
Inventory				
Total assets				
Accounts payable				
Short-term debt				
Long-term debt				
Total liabilities				
Net worth				
Ratios (see Industry Analysis section for definitions)				
Current				
Total debt to total assets				
Collection period				
Net sales to inventory				
Net profit margin after taxes				
Return on net worth				

particular ratio will depend largely on how it compares with industry standards. Industrywide comparisons (see Figure 4–6), however, do have significant limitations. The first is that industry averages remain only averages and certainly do not reflect the individual characteristics of each business within the industry. Comparative analysis, then, should only serve as an approximate guide rather than as a rigid standard. The important objectives in undertaking comparative analysis are (1) to understand why the target business has ratios that differ from industry norms, (2) to consider the causes and cures of poor ratios and their

FIGURE 4-5

KEY PERFORMANCE TRENDS

(Six-Year Analysis)

	19___	19___	19___	19___	19___	19___
Revenues ($000)						
Net income after taxes ($000)						
Return on sales (%)						
Return on net assets (%)						
Number of employees (count)						

relationship to other ratios, and (3) to decide what areas of operation require improvement and how changes might best be obtained.

Three types of ratios require review: (1) solvency ratios, (2) operating ratios, and (3) profitability ratios.

Solvency Ratios

The solvency analysis is necessary to determine whether the business is so heavily indebted that a sale cannot be readily accomplished without some form of an insolvency proceeding to reduce indebtedness. Similarly, the evaluation may disclose whether cash proceeds available to the seller under the transaction will be sufficient to pay creditors in full or whether remaining debt will exist that will require legal safeguards.

From an operational viewpoint, the solvency ratio becomes important only if you plan a stock purchase and will therefore take over an indebted business with a weak financial structure. You must approach such a troubled-company takeover with a plan to achieve a fiscal turnaround either through investment of additional capital, a plan to reduce or restructure excess debt, or a combination of both. Similarly, you must anticipate and plan

FIGURE 4-6

FINANCIAL COMPARISON
ANALYSIS

	Industry			Company	
	19 ____	19 ____	19 ____	19 ____	19 ____	19 ____
Assets:						
Accts & notes receivable						
Inventory						
Total current						
Fixed assets (net)						
TOTAL ASSETS						
Liabilities						
Accts & notes payable						
Total current						
Long-term debt						
Net worth						
TOTAL LIABILITIES						
& NET WORTH						
Income Data						
Net sales						
Cost of goods sold						
Gross profit						
Operating expenses						
Operating profit						
All other expenses (net)						
PROFIT BEFORE TAXES						
Ratios						
Current						
Total debt/total Assets						
Total debt/tangible net worth						
Collection period days						
Net sales/inventory						
Total assets turnover						
Gross profit margin						
Operating profit margin						
Return on net worth						

for immediate cash flow problems and the need to stabilize the business financially until a successful turnaround can be achieved.

The primary ratios to determine solvency include:

- *Current ratio* (current assets − current liabilities)
- *Acid-test ratio* (liquid assets ÷ current liabilities)
- *Debt-to-equity ratio*
- Cash or current asset coverage of interest and debt amortization

Operating Ratios

Operating ratios pinpoint managerial efficiency in deploying the various assets for maximum return. The importance of operating ratios depends on whether the buyer plans significant operational change in the company. Under an asset transfer, and a totally new operational approach, historical inefficiencies are of no particular importance to the buyer except to highlight the true potential of the business in the hands of more capable management. Nevertheless, even in these cases, profit evaluations will depend somewhat on operating ratios to determine whether poor profit results are due to internal (managerial) deficiencies or are externally caused and thus not readily correctable by a buyer.

There are numerous ratios employed to measure operating efficiency, the relative importance of each largely dictated by the particular industry. These ratios include:

- *Net sales to receivables* (used to determine the percentage of charge sales to cash sales)
- *Inventory turnover* (used to measure whether there is excessive or slow-moving inventory)
- *Fixed asset turnover*
- *Cost of sales per sales dollar*
- *Returns to total sale* (used for quality control analysis)
- *Sales discounts to net sales*
- *Purchase discounts to purchases*
- *Indirect labor expense to direct labor expense*
- *Maintenance expense to fixed expense* (used to determine the condition of equipment)

- *Net sales to current assets* (used to determine current asset turnover)
- *Net sales to working capital* (used to find working capital turnover)
- *Net sales to plant investment* (used to determine what percentage of plant capacity is utilized)
- *Net sales to total assets* (used to determine the utilization of asset capacity)
- *Net income to net worth* (used to find the rate of return on capital employed)
- *Operating expenses to sales* (used as an itemized approach to determine excessive line items)

Profitability Ratios

Profitability ratios are generally most important to a buyer because the acquisition, when based on past profits, must accurately forecast future profitability.

Profits must be viewed from several perspectives. The first is to measure the amount of profit on a comparative basis to determine whether profits compare favorably with similar businesses within the industry. Where profits are low, the evaluation must probe the cause and the likelihood of improvement under a new owner. Determine whether poor profits are primarily internally caused through inefficient management or whether they are due to external factors such as market, industry, or competitive problems. Obviously, the poorly performing business should only be acquired if you can confidently bring to the business a feasible plan to generate acceptable profits.

Look beyond present profitability and see how profits evolved over recent years. As with other operating and financial trends, profit trends are vitally important. Since profits reflect overall business performance, the profit trend over a five-year period will disclose either improving or deteriorating operations. Severely fluctuating profits also require in-depth investigation. Significant profit changes may be easily explained when the business is in a cyclical industry. However, rapid fluctuations within stable industries almost always result from either internal operational change or inconsistencies in accounting. No matter what the cause, unexplained changes must be carefully investigated.

A reasonable approach to project future profits is to average the prior five years' accrued profits, assuming a relatively stable profit trend exists. Where profits are declining, a conservative approach assumes no future profitability other than profits created through the buyer's own initiative.

Various ratios measure the profitability index and the adequacy of earnings. The debate continues as to whether the profit-to-sales ratio or the profit-to-net-worth ratio (return on investment) is the more meaningful indicator of managerial efficiency. From a strict investment viewpoint, the latter ratio is the more significant, but you must nevertheless consider the two ratios in context to each other. Many successful companies operate with lower-than-industry profits perfectly justified by the exceptionally high return on investment these profits produce.

PROFIT PLANNING

All that has been said about the evaluation and analysis of the seller's financial statements is meaningless unless you can translate the profitability of the past into a reasonably accurate projection of profits under your management. The entire financial investigation centers on this one primary objective.

How can you accurately project the future profits of the business?

Expect Change

Don't simply project the profit trends based on how the business currently operates. You will introduce many operational changes to the business, each having an important impact on sales, margins, expenses, and of course, profitability.

Plan Your Business

Then plan your profits. You must first know precisely how you will operate the business and what changes you will make before you can make meaningful financial projections.

Prove Your Numbers

Don't work on assumptions as to costs, expenses, and the like. Do your homework to verify the numbers with the greatest possible accuracy.

Be Conservative

A classic error is to be overly optimistic projecting profits. Projection error helps to explain why so many acquired businesses fail. As a good rule of thumb, cut projected profits by 30 percent and *never* rely on profits that exceed industry averages.

Involve Your Accountant

Your accountant can provide valuable objectivity, challenging your projections, encouraging you to take a more realistic look at your numbers, and guiding you to a more intelligently reasoned forecast of what your profit picture will look like.

Prepare a Pro Forma Income Statement

As the final step in the financial analysis, prepare pro forma or projected financial statements as a guide to plan how profitable your business will be over the next four years (Figure 4–7 and Figure 4–8).

To forecast accurately, carefully conceive the various income and expense items:

Sales
What is the most accurate estimate of present sales? Are sales likely to increase or decrease, considering present trends? What new sales will be generated? How? When? What assumptions are sales increases based on? What expenditures are required to produce those sales?

Cost of Goods
Your margin of profit, both as a percentage of sales and in absolute dollars, will differ from the seller's. New product lines may be

FIGURE 4-7

PRO FORMA INCOME STATEMENTS

(Four-Year Projections)

Item				
Revenues				
Sales allowances				
Net Revenues				
Cost of goods sold				
Gross Margin				
Expenses				
Selling				
Salaries				
Advertising				
Other				
General/Administrative				
Salaries				
Employee benefits				
Professional services				
Rent				
Insurance				
Depreciation				
Amortization				
Office supplies				
Interest				
Utilities				
Bad debt/doubtful accounts				
Other				
TOTAL EXPENSES				
Net Income before Taxes				
Provision for taxes				
Net Income after Taxes				
Prior period adjustments				
Net Increase/(Decrease) to Retained Earnings				

FIGURE 4-8

PRO FORMA BALANCE SHEET

(Four-Year Projections)

Item	19 ___	19 ___	19 ___	19 ___
Current Assets				
Cash				
Accounts receivable less allowance for doubtful accounts				
Net accounts receivable				
Notes receivable				
Inventory				
Prepaid expenses				
Other				
Total Current Assets				
Fixed Assets				
Land				
Buildings				
Equipment				
Total Net Fixed Assets				
Other assets				
Total Assets				
Current Liabilities				
Accounts payable				
Notes payable				
Accrued payroll				
Taxes payable				
Other				
Total Current Liabilities				
Long-term liabilities				
Equity				
Withdrawals				
Net equity				
Total Liability & Equity				

added or deleted, change of merchandise mix planned, price changes contemplated, or buying patterns altered. How will each of these factors influence your profit margins?

Owner's Salary

Disregard what the seller declares as a salary. Use a salary that represents the fair value for the owner's managerial effort. An inflated figure only diminishes actual profit, and a reduced salary artificially distorts profit on the high side. How much salary will *you* require?

Payroll

As the major expense item, payroll, after sales, remains the second most speculative item to forecast accurately. The seller's financial statements may have the payroll padded with family members; or understated if they work for exceptionally low wages. Therefore, payroll must be reconstructed to show what it will cost to staff the organization efficiently, considering how *you* plan to operate the business.

Rent

The seller's rent may be far lower than what you will be required to pay. In all probability, a new lease will be required—and typically at a higher rent. For this reason, you cannot accurately forecast rent until the approximate rent under a new lease has been determined by preliminary negotiations with the landlord.

Utilities

While utilities can be easily verified as to their present cost, new equipment or major renovations can materially increase utility costs. For energy-intensive businesses, cost estimates by electricians should be obtained.

Depreciation

When planning the acquisition, your accountant will normally attempt to allocate as much of the purchase price as possible to capital assets, thereby providing the maximum possible depreciation for tax purposes. But for forecasting purposes, depreciation should be adjusted to reflect the actual decrease in equipment and capital asset values each year.

Interest

The existing business may have little or no long-term debt and therefore little or no interest expense to contend with. Conversely, you will probably require financing, underscoring the need to estimate accurately both the amount and sources of planned financing and the interest required to carry the debt.

Advertising

As a new owner, you will ordinarily want to increase advertising, particularly if increased sales are your goal. On the other hand, a seller contemplating a sale may decrease advertising and show minimal expenditures for promotion that must be substantially increased to sustain sales.

Insurance

With additional inventory, new fixtures, and rigid financing requirements, both levels of insurance coverage and insurance costs may dramatically increase over what the seller incurs as an insurance expense. Obtain an estimate from your insurance broker, based on the insurance you're likely to need.

This synopsis of a changing income statement is certainly not all-inclusive. Other costs and expenses, according to the nature of the business and the changes planned, must be similarly thought through. But these few examples do show how to forecast whether your financial statement will take on a rosier hue.

Properly prepared, the pro forma income statement will not only highlight the true profit potential of the business but can be equally useful as an operating budget for your new business. More important, a properly planned pro forma statement will help you decide (1) the desirability of the acquisition, (2) the price to be paid, (3) the financing the acquisition can support, (4) operating problems to anticipate and correct upon acquisition, and (5) how to maximize profits once you own the business.

Profit planning must also include precise cash flow planning. Your business may be profitable and still operate with a deadly negative cash flow, particularly if the business is to be heavily financed. Once the projected income statement and balance sheet are prepared, undertake a similar exercise with cash flow (Figure 4-9). This can be the most important step of all because if the bus-

FIGURE 4-9

PROJECTED CASH FLOW

(Quarterly)

Item	19___			
	1st Qtr	2nd Qtr	3rd Qtr	4th Qtr
Receipts				
Cash sales				
Loans				
Other				
Total Receipts				
Disbursements				
Direct materials				
Direct labor				
Equipment				
Salaries				
Rent				
Insurance				
Advertising				
Taxes				
Loan payments				
Other				
Total Disbursements				
Total Cash Flow				
Beginning Balance				
Ending Balance				

iness cannot operate with a surplus cash flow, the profitability will be of little consequence.

SUMMING UP

1. A well-designed financial analysis can help you achieve several key objectives in buying the business.
2. Your accountant is vital to a thorough analysis.
3. What are the financial trends of the business? This is a key indicator.
4. Objectively evaluate how profitable the business will become under *your* management.
5. Don't forget that good cash flow planning is an essential part of the financial analysis.

CHAPTER 5

A LOOK AT THE LOCATION AND LEASE

The value of a small business is often nothing more than the value of its location. This is particularly true in a retail venture where the economics of the business are directly tied to the location.

From the seller's viewpoint, the salability of such a business depends on the availability of a suitable lease for the buyer. Further, the price obtainable for the business will greatly depend on the terms of the lease, as a favorable lease will of course allow the enterprise to become more profitable.

For this reason, a seller cannot intelligently offer the business for sale until certain a suitable lease is available for the buyer. Unfortunately, many small businesses cannot be sold because the seller cannot offer the buyer a reasonable lease, and many more are sold at low or distressed prices because the business offers poor lease terms. This problem is increasingly common in today's rapidly escalating commercial space market, where prime locations are renting at premium rates—not always affordable by the small independent business.

The opposite possibility may also be true. A seller may hold a very favorable lease assignable to the buyer, but these sellers may still fail to benefit from the value of their lease. A long-term assignable lease with a rent well below market price may yield the seller a far greater sales price once he or she approaches the transaction emphasizing to the buyer the economic value of the favorable lease. In fact, many shrewd owners have capitalized on their highly advantageous leases by liquidating their assets and subleasing their space, for even greater rental profits than the profits obtainable from a sale of the business.

While most businesses are sold with the expectation that the business will remain at the present location, buyers do frequently consider relocation. This is far more common with service and manufacturing businesses where buyers consider the location of little or no importance and may prefer instead to relocate the business to a more suitable location or perhaps merge it into their existing plant. Although a buyer's plans can seldom be anticipated in advance by a seller, the relative importance of the location cannot be overlooked.

The buyer interested in operating at the seller's present location broadens his or her investigation and looks closely at both the location and the available lease. This inevitably includes a careful four-part evaluation of the market area, the site, the premises, and the lease.

LOCATION, LOCATION, LOCATION

Location analysis remains critical for a location-dependent business because the commercial real estate scene is changing so rapidly. For example, few retail areas remain unthreatened by rapid shifts as shopping malls continue to displace strip centers, which in turn have blighted the downtown or main street locations, considered prime properties only a decade ago. It is particularly true today that success in retailing (which accounts for nearly 50 percent of all businesses) requires a strong real estate orientation and the ability to land in prime locations. This perhaps best explains the growing strength of the retail chains. Their consistent ability to capture space in the newest shopping malls, leaving weaker independents behind in secondary locations, has made retailing the chain-dominated industry it is today.

A real estate professional can make a valuable contribution to the location evaluation process. With knowledge of local market conditions, competitive influences, prevailing rents, and planned changes and the intuition for what is essentially a good real estate transaction, a leasing specialist can be an important member of the buyer's professional team. The corporate chains well understand the importance of a professional approach to commercial site evaluation and leasing. For that reason, the best retailers characteristically have aggressive, knowledgeable real estate departments. As an independent buyer, you can do as well by retaining the services of an independent consultant, easily found through local real estate associations or real estate licensing boards. More sizable transactions certainly justify their assistance.

Market (Trading Area) Evaluation

When evaluating the primary trading area, a professional leasing specialist will seek answers to these important questions:

- Is the population growing, stable, or decreasing?
- If population growth is required to sustain the business, is the growth rate sufficiently rapid?
- Is the ratio of population to competitive businesses favorable by industry standards?
- Are the population demographics (age, income, and the like) suitable for the planned business?
- Who are the primary competitors? What has their effect been upon the business? What future competitive impact is foreseeable?
- Are additional competitors planning to enter the area? Are locations available or planned that are likely to attract competitive businesses?
- Is the business located within an area that draws customers from other areas, or does the reverse situation exist?

Site Evaluation

Location experts tend to place more emphasis on site evaluation as opposed to focusing on the general trading area. Trading areas are usually reasonably stable except perhaps for deteriorating inner-city areas and fast-growth communities. But a particular site is never stable and is always vulnerable to new and better situated competitive locations within the market area. As location specialists suggest, businesses themselves are becoming less competitive, whereas shopping centers are becoming the true competitors.

This hardly suggests that secondary locations cannot sustain a profitable business. The true test is whether a *particular* location can create profitable sales. While historical sales can provide the immediate answer, the more important question is whether the location will continue to generate adequate sales or whether it will fail to newer, more competitive locations.

Adverse changes are not always foreseeable or easy to predict. For example, how can you foresee whether a new shopping mall will suddenly spring up nearby, or whether the town will unexpectedly restrict parking near the business? These are among the few unforeseeable factors that account for the demise of so many small businesses. Frequently, the seller alone knows of such adverse plans, thus motivating him or her to sell quickly to the unwary buyer. It is for the buyer to detect these crippling location problems *before* buying. To a large extent, the future of a location is foreseeable if you ask these questions:

- Is the customer traffic count acceptable by industry averages?
- Is the customer traffic count (shopping center, and so on) increasing or decreasing?
- Are the customers who frequent the site (or the passing traffic) customers who are inclined to patronize this type of business?
- Are there any planned traffic or parking changes that would adversely affect customer access?
- Is the tenant mix within the site suitable for this type of business?
- Is the business protected by noncompeting businesses within the site? Will the business have protection from future tenants featuring competitive lines?
- Are the major tenants or "anchors" within the site financially stable? Do they hold long-term leases?
- Are there plans for competitive shopping sites within the immediate area?
- What is the rate of tenant turnover within the site?
- What is the vacancy rate within the site? What are the reasons for a high turnover or vacancy rate?

Premises Evaluation

Evaluating the physical facilities will reveal many subtle points commonly overlooked by business buyers. The importance of a thorough premises evaluation increases with the physical changes contemplated or required by the type of business. A good working checklist suitable for all but the most specialized businesses includes these questions:

- Are the premises of sufficient size for present needs? Future needs? Is it possible to add (or relinquish) space as future needs require?
- Is the layout or floor plan suitable for the type of business?
- Is parking adequate?
- Is visibility to passing traffic adequate?
- Is there adequate space for signs? Will signs be sufficiently visible?
- Do the premises have adequate utilities to handle special equipment needed by the business?
- Are there any structural problems that may prevent or interfere with the installation of equipment or renovations?
- Do the facilities provide adequate storage or warehousing space?
- Do the facilities provide for reasonable efficiency of operation?
- Is there adequate access for receiving and shipping goods?
- Do the facilities comply with Environmental Protection, Occupational Safety and Health Administration (OSHA), and other regulatory requirements?
- Is the facility properly zoned for its intended use?
- Have all improvements and renovations needed to bring the facility to specification been defined and estimates obtained? Are costs justifiable and affordable?
- Will the premises comply with standards required for licenses or permits?

NEGOTIATING A FAVORABLE LEASE

Available lease terms should be determined early when considering the acquisition. It obviously makes no sense to investigate and negotiate the acquisition only to discover later that a suitable lease cannot be obtained. Preliminarily, the buyer needs to know five essential terms: proposed rent, rent escalations, ancillary occupancy charges, length of lease, and the options available. Other points useful to the buyer may be negotiated during this early stage. However, less important issues are usually left for formal lease negotiations, once the acquisition process is well underway and sales terms are agreed upon in principal.

Planning for Lease Negotiations

Planning begins with a thorough analysis of market conditions to determine the prevailing rates for similar rental properties within the area. Confine the investigation to locations comparable in terms of traffic count, tenant mix, and the ability to generate equivalent sales per square foot. Although properties are never equivalent in all respects, a comparative analysis will provide a reasonable rental range for the location under consideration.

Next determine prevailing rents and terms granted by the landlord to other tenants within the site. Verify what similar tenants are paying for rent and the concessions routinely extended. It is important to inquire about the most recent leases, as older leases, of course, may not accurately reflect current rental rates, and concessions made to earlier tenants when the complex or shopping center was first developed may be withdrawn once the complex is established and proven successful.

The seller's existing lease often provides a basis for projecting new lease terms. Don't assume that a new lease will automatically result in a higher rent. While this generally occurs, there are too many situations where rents have actually decreased with new leases offered at substantially reduced rents and other concessions willingly granted because the location is in less demand.

Check the demand for space within the site. Equally important, assess the landlord's bargaining position. Vacancy rates, tenant turnover, and the duration of vacancies are clear signals. Review whether weaker tenants are replacing strong tenants and whether renewal options are being exercised. Of course, a deteriorating location should cause concern over the long-term suitability of the location and desirability of the business as an acquisition.

The reputation of the landlord must also be explored. Some are notorious for granting only short-term leases, only to demand excessive rents upon renewal. Others are financially weak, with their properties in disrepair or in jeopardy of foreclosure. Many more disregard their own responsibilities under the lease or unreasonably interfere with their tenant's rights. Such landlords often have a history of poor tenant relationships, and you therefore must enter negotiations well-armed to protect yourself.

The Lease-Negotiating Checklist

Before negotiating, you and your attorney should prepare a detailed and comprehensive lease-negotiating itinerary on these points:

Premises to Be Leased
1. Are the premises adequately identified and defined?
2. Does the description include reference to the use of parking and other common areas?

Lease Term
1. When will the initial term commence?
2. Will the commencement date be deferred if renovations are required?
3. If the commencement date is deferred, will the initial term have a corresponding extension?
4. What is the length of the initial term?
5. Is the lease term (including renewal options) of sufficient length to justify the acquisition price?

Rent
1. What is the base rent?
2. What are the increases in base rent over the lease term?
3. Does rent include a percentage of sales? If so, is the percentage expressed as a percentage "override" on sales over a stated minimum? What sales are included in the percentage rent calculation? What sales are excluded? How are sales reported and percentage rent override paid? What are the landlord's rights to an accounting? Are sales reported on a cash or accrual method of accounting?
4. Does the rent include a cost-of-living or Consumer Price Index (CPI) increase? If so, what CPI is used? What base year is used? When are CPI increases assessed and paid?

Taxes
1. Does the tenant pay for real estate tax increases?
2. What percentage of the tax increases are charged to the tenant? Is the percentile proportional to the share paid by other tenants?
3. What is the base year for determining tax increases?
4. How will the tax apportionment change if further construction is added to the present real estate?
5. Do tenants have the right to seek abatement on real estate taxes?
6. How are tax increases billed? Paid? Are deposits toward anticipated tax increases required?
7. Is the property under review for a new tax assessment?

Additional Occupancy Costs
What is the tenant's responsibility for

1. Common area maintenance
2. Building insurance
3. Building repairs
4. Maintenance of premises
5. Rubbish removal
6. Common sign maintenance
7. Common area utilities
8. Security guard services
9. Snow removal

If applicable, how are each of the foregoing apportioned between tenants? Adjusted for vacancy? Billed? Paid?

Use
1. What are the defined or permitted uses for the lease premises?
2. What are the prohibited uses?
3. What merchandising lines are restricted or subject to noncompetition for the protection of other tenants?

Noncompetition
1. What merchandising lines can be offered exclusively?
2. Do the noncompete provisions restrict present cotenants or only future tenants?

3. Are the noncompete restrictions enforceable by the landlord? Tenant? Either?

Utilities

1. Does the landlord provide heat and/or air conditioning to the leased premises? If so, are there additional charges? How are these costs measured? Paid? What minimum heating and cooling requirements? Who maintains or repairs heating or air-conditioning equipment?
2. Does the tenant pay for its own electricity? Water? If provided by landlord, are there additional charges? How are they measured? Paid?

Renovations by Landlord

1. What renovations will the landlord provide?
2. What landlord renovations may be undertaken by the tenant? What allowances are made for such tenant renovations?
3. Will landlord renovations conform to tenant's specifications?
4. Will landlord renovations be completed within specified time? If not so completed, will tenant be entitled to rent abatement? Self-completion and charge-back? Extension of lease?
5. Are landlord renovations included in rent or subject to charge-back to tenant? If a charge-back item, how is it paid? Can tenant take leasehold improvements as a depreciable item?

Renovations by Tenant

1. Are tenant renovations subject to landlord's prior approval? If so, are specifications approved?
2. Are renovations by tenant required as a condition of the lease?

Maintenance and Repairs

Who is responsible for repairs and maintenance of

1. Interior walls, ceilings, and floors
2. Plate glass

3. Plumbing
4. Electrical
5. Heating and air conditioning
6. Exterior premises

Insurance
1. What public liability insurance must the tenant carry?
2. What casualty insurance and plate glass insurance are required?
3. Must landlord approve insurance underwriter?
4. Must landlord be a named insured?

Signs
1. What signs may the tenant place on the premises?
2. What are the tenant's rights to display on common area signs?
3. What additional signs are allowed within the common area?

Trade Fixtures
1. Can tenant remove trade fixtures upon the termination of the lease? How are *trade fixtures* defined?
2. What are the conditions for removal?

Fire or Casualty
1. What are tenant's rights to abate rent during casualty period?
2. What are landlord's/tenant's obligations to repair premises after casualty?
3. What are tenant's rights if premises are not restored following casualty?

Assignment and Subletting
1. Can tenant assign the lease or sublet the premises?
2. If the lease is assignable, is the landlord's consent required? Does the landlord agree not to withhold consent unreasonably?
3. What is the tenant's remaining liability if landlord consents to an assignment of lease?

Nondisturbance
1. Will the lease be subordinated to future mortgages? If so, what are the conditions for subordination?
2. Will subordination be subject to the tenant's obtaining a nondisturbance (*attornment*) agreement from the mortgagee?
3. Is the lease conditional upon the tenant's obtaining a nondisturbance agreement from the prior mortgagees?
4. Will the landlord grant a "quiet enjoyment" provision and suitable indemnification for the landlord's breach?

Options to Expand
1. Does the tenant have the option to expand into adjoining or other space, if available?
2. If an option to obtain additional space is allowed, what rent and other terms will apply to the expanded space?
3. Does the tenant have the right of first refusal to obtain additional space?

Option to Extend or Renew Lease
1. For what additional terms may the tenant extend the lease?
2. What rent is payable during the option period(s)?
3. How is the option exercised?
4. What additional conditions, if any, exist to exercise option?

Option to Purchase Property
1. Will the tenant have an option to purchase the property? If so, on what price, terms, or conditions?
2. What is the option period?
3. How is the option exercised?
4. If an option to purchase is unacceptable to the landlord, will the landlord grant a right of first refusal in the event the property is to be sold?

Default
1. What constitutes a default under the lease?
2. What are the notice requirements under a default?
3. What are the tenant's rights to cure a default?

Security Deposits
  1. What security deposits are required under the lease?
  2. Can security deposits be applied to the final rent?
  3. Are security deposits to be held in escrow? Deposited to an interest-bearing account? Is the tenant entitled to interest? Can the tenant draw interest?

Guarantors
  1. Does the landlord require personal guarantees as a condition of granting the lease?
  2. Are the guarantees absolute or limited in amount?

Rent and Lease Term Considerations

From a business viewpoint, the rent and term of lease are the two principal items for negotiation. While the other lease terms have legal significance, the willingness to consumate an acquisition will usually depend on the acceptability of these two issues. Rent and lease term must be considered together because they are closely interrelated. The buyer–tenant must consider not only the length of the lease but how the rent will evolve over its term.

There are, of course, several widely used methods for assessing rent. Most commercial leases impose a fixed or base rent coupled with a method to increase rent periodically to keep pace with inflation. For this reason, all but the shortest-term leases will either feature a cost-of-living (CPI) index increase or impose as additional rent a percentile of the tenant's sales over a defined sales base. Whether one approach is preferred to the other depends on whether sales are likely to increase faster or slower than inflationary increases. Some landlords shrewdly combine the two, or apply them alternatively, with the objective of thus earning the highest rent possible. Regardless of formula used, evaluate the reasonableness of the total rent. Avoid prohibitive rents that erode profits. The best approach is to translate rent to a percentage of sales based on varying sales. The percentage of rent should then approximate industry averages.

Every industry has permissible rent ranges. For example, supermarkets hesitate to pay over 0.5 percent of sales for rent, whereas jewelry stores may safely pay up to 8 percent. Independent pharmacies routinely pay 3 to 4 percent of sales, yet most pharmacy chains refuse to pay in excess of 2.5 percent. Strict industry averages, however, fail to account for many variables. For example, a location may allow for higher margins or advantageous operating efficiencies, each with its own positive impact on profits. Further, the lease may provide valuable concessions, such as extensive landlord renovations, that justify a higher rent.

The most common problem in assessing whether rents will prove reasonable is the dependency of the calculation on accurate sales projections. When base rents are low, a poorly performing business can survive; however, a high rent will require a substantial increase in sales. Therefore, more speculative enterprises may prefer to negotiate a lower base rent, being more flexible on variable rent escalators tied to actual sales performance.

Determining fair rents beyond the first five years is extremely difficult. Neither a CPI increase or percentage-of-sales formula may accurately reflect the then-current rental value of the property. For this reason, terms beyond the first five years are best left as options allowing the tenant either to abandon the premises or to agree to a new fixed rate based upon then-prevailing rental levels using third-party arbitration.

How long a lease is acceptable? As a tenant, you would ideally prefer a 20- or 30-year lease divided into many short-term options. However, in a rapidly changing and competitive real estate market, such a favorable lease is seldom attainable. The question then narrows to the minimal term acceptable. The answer? The lease must be of sufficient duration to allow you to recoup your investment in the acquisition. As a practical matter, most buyers of a retail business would not consider an acquisition unless assured of a 10-year tenancy. However, small service businesses are readily sold with two- to three-year leases because such businesses command far lower prices and can be easily relocated without destroying goodwill.

Oftentimes, a seller will operate for a number of years with a series of short-term leases. While a short-term lease should be unacceptable to the buyer, the seller may attempt to convince the buyer to accept the risk, pointing to his or her own history of obtaining new leases. This clearly is an unacceptable risk for the buyer to assume. Offered only an unacceptable short-term lease, a portion of the purchase price should be escrowed and released to the seller as a contingent payment only upon renewal of the lease on predefined terms.

WHEN YOU ASSUME THE SELLER'S LEASE

With many acquisitions, the decision must be made as to whether it is preferable to assume the seller's existing lease or negotiate a new lease instead. Frequently, it is better to assume the present lease, provided (1) the present lease has more favorable rents than anticipated under a new lease and (2) the present lease has a sufficient term remaining. In fact, the benefits of assuming a very favorable lease may justify increasing the price of the business.

For the seller, the assumed lease offers the same opportunity to share in this economic benefit. However, it also imposes upon the seller a potential risk of liability, should the buyer default under the assumed lease. The buyer and seller must therefore each quantify the benefits and the risks of transferring the present lease. The buyer needs to measure the anticipated rent savings accurately and to consider further both the burdensome and beneficial features of the present lease against any new proposed lease.

While the benefit to the seller of allowing a lease takeover may be translated into a higher price for the business (or other negotiating concession), the risk of remaining liability may be unacceptable unless the buyer is financially strong or the seller stands ready to reoccupy the premises, should the buyer default as a subtenant. This risk, however, may be reduced through indemnifications granted to the seller by the principals of the buyer corporation or its parent corporations where the buyer is a corporate subsidiary.

For a buyer to consider a lease assumption, the present lease must offer a remaining term (including options) comparable with that required under a new lease. Oftentimes, the remaining term is not of sufficient length and yet offers very favorable terms for the few years remaining. Faced with this situation, try to negotiate a new lease to commence upon the expiration of the present lease.

The one major roadblock to a lease assumption is generally the nonassignability of the lease. Few leases allow the tenant to assign their lease without prior landlord approval. Many leases incorporate the language, however, that "the landlord shall not unreasonably withhold consent." The law is unclear as to when a landlord may withhold consent. Nevertheless, the threat of legal challenge may be sufficient to negotiate more favorable terms on a new lease than would otherwise be obtainable.

Where the seller is a corporation, the problem of a nonassumable lease may be best resolved through an acquisition of corporate shares. Many small businesses are transferred through stock acquisitions for precisely the reason that the buyer automatically acquires a favorable existing lease held by a seller's corporation.

When the lease can be assigned without need for landlord consent, the buyer should verify that the lease is in good standing and is on the represented terms without subsequent modification. Although the seller would normally provide these warranties under the contract, independent verification should always be requested from the landlord before the acquisition is finalized.

ACQUIRING REAL ESTATE WITH THE BUSINESS

Special considerations exist when the real estate is sold with the business. Where the real estate and business are sold at a combined price, the two should be independently appraised and their values segregated. The contract should provide for the allocation of the purchase price between the real estate and business both for financing and for tax purposes. If the real estate is owned by an affiliated entity or party other than the seller of the business, the title owners to the real estate must join as parties to the agreement. The agreement must also provide that the obligations to sell—or buy—the real estate and business are mutually dependent and are not to be construed as separate agreements. The buyer should have the right to accept title to the real estate in an entity other than the company acquiring the business for purposes of protecting the real estate, should the business fail. If the seller is financing either the real estate, the business, or both, decide whether the financing will be collateralized by both the real estate and the business in one combined financing package. If the seller does not presently plan to sell the real estate, will the seller instead grant an option to purchase at a later date or a right of first refusal?

SUMMING UP

1. Many businesses have only their location to sell. Location must then become the focus of the investigation.
2. Inquire about new changes in the neighborhood. Oftentimes, there are plans that would adversely affect the business and explain precisely why the business is for sale.
3. Involve a local real estate expert. It can be a very wise investment.
4. Demand a sufficiently long-term lease to enable you to safely recapture your investment.
5. Watch rents! A business has no value if all the profits are earmarked for the landlord.

CHAPTER 6

WHAT IS THE BUSINESS REALLY WORTH?

Many questions accompany the sale of a business, but few are as important or as difficult to answer as the question of determining what the business is worth.

A buyer and seller share the same problem as each asks: How can the value of the business be determined? What are the various methods for evaluating the business, and how does each differ? When should each be used? Is the business being sold or acquired at too high or too low a price?

Small business valuations can be complex. Unfortunately, it is far from a precise science, as no one equation can resolve the many factors that must be considered. Valuation is ultimately a blend of many subjective and objective considerations reduced to a perceived value. In turn, this perceived value must be closely shared between buyer and seller for a sale to result.

The basic concept of business valuation is to establish value — or perhaps even more realistically, a range of value — upon which the seller can establish a standard upon which to set a sale price.

For those companies whose securities are traded in a public market, their value can literally be determined on a daily basis. Even in these circumstances, there are emotional influences as well as external conditions that can impact on the price of the securities that may not have any financial or other logical basis. These same influences and conditions come into play frequently in the case of small, closely held businesses before a final selling price is determined.

There are several dangers with a faulty valuation process. If the seller places too high a price on the business, the business will remain unsold and become "stale" and less attractive to buyers even if the price is eventually lowered. If the business is priced too low, the seller is needlessly forfeiting a considerable sum of money that may represent a significant share of what he or she has worked many years to build. Conversely, the buyer faces the danger of paying too high a price for the business; and with inadequate earnings in relation to price, the business either yields its new owner a very poor return on investment or the inability to satisfy the excessive loans needed to fund the acquisition. Whether you are a buyer or a seller, proper pricing is essential for a successful deal.

THREE VALUATION PROBLEMS

Unlike the publicly owned company whose value can readily be determined by the trading value of its shares, the small business can be difficult to value for several reasons. First, small businesses typically suffer from lack of records to portray the true performance of the enterprise accurately. The seller—perhaps the only person who really knows the value of the business as an income producer—will value the business on the earnings, including the many hidden benefits he or she realizes from the business. Yet, unable to prove profitability to the buyer, a successful deal remains unlikely because the buyer places a far lower value on the business based on its lower reported earnings.

Next, small businesses are oftentimes extensions of their owners. The seller has an emotional as well as a financial relationship with the business. This is particularly true when the seller owned the business for many years. The seller may have started the business, nurtured it to maturity, and seen it through numerous problems; and it is thus difficult for such a seller to use objective standards when measuring business value in strict economic terms. This explains why so many small businesses are overpriced and remain unsold. The subjectivity of the emotional factor does not, of course, change the business valuation, but to the extent the seller refuses to sell at a reasonable price, it presents a stubborn obstacle to resolving the price issue.

Finally, since the value of the business is based on how much the business can earn under the buyer's management, accurate forecasting becomes speculative. Small businesses as income producers are exceptionally volatile. A small business is typically built around one or two owners, and the success of the business is never more than the contribution of its owners. A successful operation in the hands of the seller may or may not be duplicated by the buyer. The small business field has numerous examples of businesses whose sales and earnings quickly doubled or trebled under new management. Others with a successful past failed owing to rapidly diminished sales. Valuation, then, when viewed in terms of anticipated future earnings, may look entirely different to the buyer and seller.

FIVE COMMON VALUATION MISTAKES

Since valuation procedures remain something less than a science, small businesses are commonly valued by unreliable "rule-of-thumb" formulas. These conventional yardsticks are conveniently used because of their simplicity, yet each fails as an accurate valuation method because each ignores valuation in terms of future earnings.

Sales Multiplier Valuations

Every industry suggests rough formulas to translate sales into an approximate valuation. Supermarkets, for example, are supposedly worth inventory plus one month's sales. Luncheonettes and small restaurants are popularly priced at three to four months' sales. Drugstores, according to industry averages, should sell for 100 days' sales. Obviously, sales multipliers cannot logically establish business value because this standard measures only sales with curious disregard for profits.

Sales are an important factor when valuing the business—but only when expenses fall into line to produce proportionate profits. Without such projection, the sales multiplier remains a faulty valuation technique.

Comparison Valuations

The comparison valuation technique is often a misguided attempt to compare a business against prices asked for comparable businesses. This approach is not entirely wrong because the value of any commodity is based largely on what comparable items sell for. Since market conditions can influence value, both the buyer and seller should have a clear idea of prices for competitive businesses.

The major difficulty with comparison valuations, however, is that unlike most other commodities, businesses cannot be compared accurately. As an economic entity, too many variables exist. Since earnings are dependent on the unique characteristics of the business (volume, expenses, loan terms, competition, potential, and the like), few businesses have sufficient points of economic similarity for credible comparisons even when within the same industry.

When comparisons are made, the comparison is likely to focus on sales, making this approach similar to sales multiplier valuations. Buyers who have had the opportunity to investigate the total financial picture of other ventures, unlike sellers who know only a competitor's sales and selling price, can, however, use comparison valuations with far greater accuracy.

Sales multiplier valuations would make sense if business profits were always proportionate to sales, which seldom occurs. Examine a number of small businesses, and you will see little correlation between size and profit. Some businesses show substantial sales and losses, whereas small-volume enterprises often have solid histories as profit producers.

The franchised business is one exception to the rule. Franchising is based on a high degree of uniformity. Therefore, franchised operations featuring near-equivalent sales should show equivalent profits, since profit margins, expenses, and other operating features should conform to chain standards.

Asking Price Valuations

A third common but costly approach is a buyer's belief that "value" relates to the seller's "asking price." It certainly may from the seller's viewpoint—but seldom from the buyer's.

Unwary buyers often use asking price as an arbitrary threshold from which to negotiate. Many buyers erroneously believe that if the asking price is reduced 15 to 25 percent, "value" has suddenly been found. Never assume that the seller's asking price has any rational relationship to value. A seller is least qualified to determine value from a buyer's perspective. Burdened by years of emotional attachment to the business, together with the obvious financial benefits of a high price, the reality remains that 90 percent of all businesses on the market are over-priced. After the overpriced business sits unsold for a year or two, sellers gradually drop their price until it finally enters the reality zone.

Rather than start at the top with the seller's asking price, assume the business has *no* value, qualifying every dollar you are prepared to offer against the profit potential of the business.

Asset Valuations

Another equally faulty method used to value the small business is to value each of the various assets being sold. This approach is particularly commonplace with retail stores. A seller, for exam-ple, may believe the business to be worth $100,000 based on a $50,000 inventory at wholesale cost, $25,000 as the replacement or fair market value of fixtures and equipment, and $25,000 for the goodwill. Of course, if other assets were also to be sold, these assets would also be valued and added to the price.

Valuing a business by the sum of its assets has its own obvious limitations. Tangible assets can be accurately appraised. Inven-tory can be precisely tabulated at its cost price, and the approxi-mate replacement value for fixtures and equipment can be determined by appraisal. The problem arises when placing a value on goodwill, the intangible asset that may be the most valu-able asset of all.

Frequently, goodwill has greater value than all tangible assets combined. The total value of the business, then, is depen-dent on an accurate appraisal of goodwill. Since goodwill repre-sents nothing more than anticipated profitability, the buyer must nevertheless develop a profit orientation to achieve accurate valuation.

Nor does the business selling for the value of its tangible assets alone represent an easier situation. A seller, for instance, may bargain to sell a retail business for the value of inventory and fixtures alone. But what are those same assets really worth if they cannot produce future profits? Without the profit poten-tial, these assets are worth nothing more than their liquidation value.

Book Valuations

Book value is an accounting term that reflects the owner's equity in the business. If total liabilities are deducted from total tangible assets (excluding goodwill), the difference is what the business is worth on the books, or its book value. Larger companies are frequently sold through a transfer of corporate shares for their book value.

There are, however, several problems that arise when using book value to determine the value of the smaller business. First, it fails to consider the profitability, earnings potential, or goodwill of the business. Second, fixed assets (real estate, equipment, and the like) are shown at their depreciated value rather than at their fair market value. Since there can be a considerable difference between the two, value can be greatly distorted, which perhaps explains why so few smaller businesses utilize this method.

BUSINESS VALUATION TECHNIQUES

So there are many varied and often incorrect ways to value a small business. In most situations, the so-called formulas are applied against limited data. Also, there is usually only one formula applied, which sets up a likely possibility of a faulty conclusion being reached as a result of a single flaw in the computation. Instead, the use of several well-recognized valuation methodologies, adjusted and reconciled to produce a value range, largely eliminates the possibility of gross error.

All the approaches to valuation simply attempt to establish a reasonable basis upon which a business value can be established, be it for a corporation, partnership, or sole proprietor. In the case of a closely held business, this can be the value of a single share of stock, the value of assets, or its value as an "enterprise" or "going concern."

The price that is ultimately established must bear a relationship to the benefits or investment return that is generated for an owner or stockholder or both. It has been well-established that the economic benefits of small business ownership can take many different forms, particularly in the case of the owner-operated business, who has so many perks available.

Ultimately, where a business is being sold, a value perceived fair to both seller and buyer must be achieved. That price is generally defined as that fair market value that a buyer might be expected to pay a seller on the open market, with all pertinent facts known to both parties and neither party being unduly compelled to consummate the transaction.

The valuation process will principally consider the business's balance sheet and income/expense statements. The following methodologies usually applied rely on both. Of course, the non-financial aspects also play an important part, particularly as they impact on the financial statements.

While every business is truly unique, whether large or small, the valuation process has been somewhat standardized. There are recognized methodologies that are generally applied. There are certain adjustments that are made to recognize individual business differences. One fundamental principle in the establishment of value is its relationship to the income or cash flow that is generated by the business and the assets that compose the substance of that value. Without that income or cash flow being generated, there is no investment value, as the business lacks a future as a going concern.

While time has proved over and over again that these standards have validity, the determination of value is not based on mathematical formulas alone. They are applied by individuals whose background and experience come into play in the selection and analysis of available information, as well as the application of appropriate investment analysis ratios, formulas, and the like. Thus, we see that the process truly is a combination of art and science. It is work that can only be accomplished by an experienced business valuation professional.

For best results, the actual valuation process should utilize several methodologies. This simply avoids dependence on just one method wherein an error in one computation could drastically alter the result. Also, the use of several methodologies provides a more balanced conclusion.

The variety of methodologies used are applicable regardless of the type of business (Figure 6–1). When each separate method is completed, a final result is achieved through a reconciliation that adjusts to the particular circumstances and conditions surrounding the business being valued.

FIGURE 6-1

BUSINESS VALUATION
WORKSHEET

Business Name   Year End

I. Capitalization Value

Company Profits Before Taxes _____
Depreciation _____
Interest Expense _____
Owner's Wage _____
Reconstructed Expenses: _____   Reason for Expense Change _____
   1. excess T/E _____
   2. excess payroll _____
   3. expenses that should be cap'd _____
   4. non-bus. ventures _____
   5. one time charge-offs _____
   6. owner's personal items _____
      a. _____
      b. _____
      c. _____
   7. Other _____
      a. _____
      b. _____
Total Available Income _____
Less: Owner's Fair Wage _____
Reconstructed Cash Flow _____
25% Capitalization Value (Multiply RCF by 4)
20% Capitalization Value (Multiply RCF by 5)
Ending Inventory Level

II. Fair Market Value of the Assets

Cash (if applicable) _____
Accounts Receivable (if appl) _____
Inventory _____
Furniture and Fixtures _____
Equipment _____
Franchise or License _____
Other _____
    Total Fair Market Value of Assets
If Asset Sale: add total FMV Assets
to Reconstructed Cash Flow for Bus. Selling price

III. Capital Stock Value

Accounts Payable _____
Notes Payable _____
Notes Payable-Owner _____
Accrued Expenses _____
Withheld items & income taxes _____
Other Liabilities _____
    Total Liabilities
Subtract Total Liabilities From
Asset Sale Price For Capital Stock Value

Internal Revenue Service Ruling 59–60 set forth the general standards and specific criteria that should be covered, where applicable, in every business valuation. An outline of these follows:

1. Nature and history of the business
2. General economic outlook and specific industry conditions
3. Book value and financial condition of the company
4. Earnings record
5. Tangible and intangible asset values, including goodwill
6. Dividend-paying capacity
7. Other sales of the company stock and the size of the block to be sold
8. Market price of comparable companies traded in the open market

In the usual process of valuation of a small, closely held business, all the above, with the exception of items 6 and 7, will be developed, analyzed, and applied through several standard methods and the accompanying procedures of implementation. Therefore, the process of establishing business value involves many different factors, financial and otherwise. Analysis and investment in a publicly traded company is a passive act relative to investing in and taking control of a business and all its assets. The value of the assets will not necessarily reflect the value of the business. A company's net worth is not the value of the business. Even though value tends to be in the eyes of the beholder, a value established by a buyer, in itself, would not reflect the value, certainly as the seller would see it.

Owning a small business is inherently a risk investment. Ownership can bring substantial financial reward and personal satisfaction. The risk-reward scale must indeed be carefully balanced. Both have an interest in that balance. A properly constructed valuation provides the scale.

Approaches to valuation tend to follow two broad patterns: those based on the balance sheet (net assets) and those based on the income statement (net earnings). Examples of asset-based techniques include not only the book value method previously discussed but also (1) the liquidation value of the business and (2) replacement of reproduction costs (the costs of starting a similar business and gaining entry into the industry).

While asset-based techniques focus on the economic value of the firm's properties, they are seldom applied to companies with any presently demonstrable earning capacity because such valuations do not contemplate profits in the valuation process. For this reason, the preferred valuation procedures are those based, at least in part, on the *earning capacity* of the company.

EARNING POWER VALUATIONS

Professionals recognize that earning power is the most logical indicator of value. Under this technique, commonly called the "capitalized earnings valuation," you begin to look at the return on investment the business will produce.

There are three basic steps involved:

Step 1. Calculate Present Profits

Reconstruct the seller's income statement to determine the true pretax operating profits (Figure 6–2). Key items to adjust are owner's salary, which may be inflated to hide profits, and other perks buried in other expense categories. Depreciation should also be adjusted to the actual annualized decrease in asset values. Review each line item until *present* earnings have been established with reasonable accuracy.

I underscore *present earnings* because many buyers use projected profits under their management as the basis for determining value. The error with this approach is that value is what the business is *currently* worth, not what it will be worth after you invest time and money building the business. Potential, to some degree, can and should influence value, but it should never control value. Pay the seller only for the profits the seller delivers and not the profits your hard work and talent will produce.

Step 2. Set an Acceptable Return on Investment

Once present profits are established with the greatest possible accuracy, the task is then to translate those earnings into a value for the business. This step also requires consideration of several points.

FIGURE 6-2

**TRUE NET PROFIT
ANALYSIS**

Net profit (seller's books - 12 months)		$_____
Add back:		
Depreciation	$_____	
Amortization	$_____	
Debt service (loan interest)	$_____	
Income Tax	$_____	
Owner's salary	$_____	
Manager's salary	$_____	
Personal expenses		
Promotion	$_____	
Insurance	$_____	
Travel and entertainment	$_____	
Auto	$_____	
Other (specify)	$_____	
Expenses buyers may eliminate		
Equipment rental	$_____	
Discounts and refunds	$_____	
Bad Debt	$_____	
Donations	$_____	
Extra employees	$_____	
Other (specify)	$_____	
Add: total adjustment		$_____
Total annual "True Net Profit"		$_____
Less buyer's debts:		
Debt service payments	$_____	
Equipment rental payments	$_____	
New loan payment	$_____	
Other (specify)	$_____	
Less total adjustment		$_____
"Net Spendable Cash" to new buyers		$_____

The first is to determine the minimal return on investment acceptable to you. For example, if the business shows current profits of $20,000 and you demand a 25 percent return on investment, the business justifies a price of $80,000. This leads to the question: What return on investment should you realistically expect from a small business? Considering that businesses are neither a safe or liquid investment, you may rightfully expect a return on investment of 25 to 40 percent. But you must understand and establish your own investment objectives. For example, if you are planning to buy with the objective of building the business for quick resale at a sizable profit, you will demand a far higher return but expect to obtain that return on profits from the sale of the business rather than through operating profits.

Earnings multiples are most appropriate for companies large enough to bear some of the characteristics of their comparable publicly traded counterparts in the same or a similar line of business. Mergers, acquisitions, and sale prices of other similar companies can provide a careful researcher with clues to implied rates of return and premiums paid for corporate control. Capitalization rates or yields often are used to value firms with steady but modest growth prospects. Discontinuing future projected earnings, whether in the form of net income or cash flow net of funds reinvested in the business to support growth, is particularly useful for rapidly growing firms that have yet to reach their full potential. It may be useful to use several of these techniques in order to cross-check the results of each approach. The technique that most closely reflects all the relevant influences on a value should receive the most weight in arriving at a final recommended value.

Step 3. Establish a Range

The capitalized valuation approach can only provide a broad valuation range. Obviously, asset values must be factored into the equation. A service business with virtually no assets and a retail store with $100,000 in assets may each generate a $20,000 profit, yet you would obviously expect to pay more for the retail store because of its asset values.

Leverage in financing the business is another consideration and even points out the problem in defining "investment" against which the profits should be measured. With some logic, many acquisition consultants argue that you should consider only the down payment as the true investment and then measure available profits remaining after financing costs (net cash flow). Others suggest that the total price is the best yardstick against which to measure profitability, as this is what the buyer will have invested after debt financing used to buy the business is paid.

FACTORS THAT INFLUENCE VALUE

In strict quantitative terms, return on investment *controls* value. Many other factors influence it.

So far we have been speaking of value as the appraisal of what the business is worth. *Value*, of course, is not synonymous with *price*, as the latter simply reflects what the seller and buyer are willing to buy and sell for. Therefore, value remains a function of appraised worth using rational economic measures, whereas price remains a function of negotiation and external factors. The only relationship between value and price is that value becomes the reference point or threshold from which price is negotiated. Nevertheless, value and hence price are both affected by many factors, the most common of which are:

Supply and Demand

This first law of economics plays an important role when arriving at a price. The value of a business is largely influenced by the number of buyers available compared with the number of similar businesses for sale. This shift between a buyer's market and a seller's market may alter price by 20 percent or more. For example, businesses experience rapid price increases in periods of high unemployment when large numbers of unemployed turn to small business ownerships as a welcome alternative. Values, of course, are never created in a vacuum but are always a function of competitive pressures.

Nature of the Business

Similar to supply and demand is the influence imposed by the type of business involved. Many categories of small business are on the decline, forcing a general decline in the number of interested buyers and thus the obtainable price. Brokers report that fading industries such as independent clothing, hardware, and drugstores are selling at very low prices in relation to their earnings, whereas independent convenience food stores have again become popular and now sell at premium prices. Businesses that do not require specialized training and thus allow easy entry have historically sold for more than those requiring specialized skills and hence have a limited buyer market.

Risk

For many buyers the lack of risk or "downside" of the transaction justifies a higher price. A higher price is more than a reasonable concession for reduced risk. When the buyer has little to lose either in down payment or personal liability from financing the business, a more generous price is in order. Consider, for example, the buyer who acquires the shares of a corporation for $15,000, with the balance of a $150,000 price paid by assuming existing debts of $135,000 on which the buyer has no personal liability. This buyer will normally be less likely to resist the $150,000 price than will one with the entire $150,000 at risk through down payment and/or personal guarantees on financing obligations.

Down Payment

Financing leverage has been earlier mentioned for purposes of calculating return on investment. However, reducing the down payment and providing the buyer opportunity for a leveraged buyout can have a dramatic influence on price. Buyers focus more on down payment than they do on price. Therefore, price resistance decreases as down payment requirements decrease. Many sellers report that they had little difficulty selling their business at a premium price, often 30 to 40 percent more than their original asking price, once creatively financed to cut entry capital. Reducing the down payment required, of course, expands the potential buyer market and offers lower risk, which in either case supports a higher price. Conversely, a seller demanding a cash sale may be forced to discount the price of the business by 30 to 40 percent.

Financing

Advantageous financing can eclipse price in importance. Astute buyers always consider price in relation to financing, because the two together determine the total price paid for the business.

High interest rates depress business values the same way they soften demand for real estate, automobiles, and other high-priced consumer items. Consider the economic impact of 22 percent interest on a 10-year, $100,000 loan versus the same loan at 15 percent. The interest saved is about $35,000, encouraging a higher price if the seller provides lower-than-market financing. Some buyers astutely adopt the view that if financing requires interest in excess of the prime rate, the excess should be charged against appraised value. Should the seller, however, offer financing at lower than prime rate, then interest savings are rightfully added to the value.

Interest is but one financing factor to influence value, yet in the minds of many buyers, cash flow can be an even more important factor. Long-term loans ensure additional surplus cash flow for expansion or modernization. The loan period also sets a lid on price, as astute buyers limit price to what the business can afford to pay from its own cash flow and thus demand a self-liquidating proposition without need to add further capital to keep the business afloat.

Potential

Although valuation is largely based on the present profitability of the business, price will be influenced by the long-term profit potential of the firm. As stated earlier, there is considerable difference between a seller selling an enterprise with profits in place and a seller relying upon the buyer to produce profits.

Sellers frequently attempt to sell marginal or losing operations on the basis of potential in the hands of the right buyer. While the buyer is essentially buying potential, the obvious question is: Why should the buyer pay the seller for what the buyer will himself produce? The clear answer is that the buyer shouldn't. At best, the seller may be entitled to a nominal payment of one year's anticipated profit to reflect the fact that the business offers the prospects of additional profits.

Nor is it an easier situation when the business is already at its top earnings potential with no realistic way to improve upon its performance. At best, the buyer can hope to stabilize sales and profits at their present levels. While the seller has the right to demand a price reflecting current income, the buyer should use a more conservative valuation approach because the business not only lacks potential for further growth or profitability, but profits may in fact decline under new management.

Most experienced buyers agree that the best acquisition is one operating at a fraction of true potential and yet one that can be (1) acquired at a low price consistent with present earnings and (2) rapidly and easily turned around. Fortunate buyers finding such rare opportunities typically pay slightly more than what the business is worth by strict valuation standards; however, such acquisitions ultimately prove to be a bargain based on their later performance.

Motivation

How anxious is the seller to sell? How anxious is the owner to buy? Personal pressures ranging from illness and death to unemployment can have a dramatic effect on the price a business will be sold for.

Personal Goals

As a seller may develop an emotional attachment to his or her business, a buyer will also expect the business to satisfy certain nonfinancial objectives. Therefore, the buyer may be willing to pay a premium for the "right" business that will offer considerable enjoyment and self-satisfaction.

Once the various valuation methods have been applied and valuations derived, the process of reconciliation must be completed. As previously mentioned, this process mitigates against a valuation result dependent on a single method wherein one miscalculation could drastically alter the result. The reconciliation process also allows for further adjustments of the individual valuation methods to accommodate the differences inherent in each business being valued. The result is a broader, more balanced result, presenting a range of business value from which a so-called target price can be suggested for the purpose of positioning the business for sale. This target price will always fall within the range. It will represent the valuation specialist's blending of the particular facts and information about the business made known, as well as the general marketplace factors, into a conclusion. The application of these reconciliation-weighing considerations, as with other factors, must combine the various formal valuation techniques with the practical aspects appropriate in a "real world" environment.

SPECIAL VALUATION SITUATIONS

The diversity of valuation approaches is as varied as the type of transactions. No one method proves suitable for every type of acquisition. Special situations each require their own unique approach.

Valuing the Insolvent Company

More than a few insolvent businesses are acquired under bankruptcy, receivership, or foreclosure and then rehabilitated for continued profitable operation or resale.

Although buyers of such businesses view profits or turnaround potential as motivation for the acquisition, future profitability is seldom the criterion for determining value. Instead, the buyer should approach valuations from the seller's unfortunate alternative, which is to liquidate the assets at auction instead. If other buyers are bidding for the business, the competition may influence price upward. However, each buyer will use liquidation value as the starting point for negotiations.

Buyers are frequently offered insolvent businesses not yet under formal insolvency proceedings. As frequently, sellers arbitrarily set their price to match the proceeds necessary to liquidate their debts fully. Such arbitrary pricing will, of course, bear no relationship to the actual value of the business.

The shrewd buyer approach in this situation is to encourage the seller to discharge the debts through formal insolvency proceedings, with the buyer acquiring the business at liquidation price. As an incentive to the seller, the buyer may offer the seller personal compensation in the form of a "covenant not to compete," a contingent earnings agreement based upon future profits, or perhaps only the opportunity for employment.

Valuing the Service Business

Service businesses, aside from selling nominal fixed assets, rely on existing accounts and customers' lists as their primary asset on which to base a price.

The difficulty in establishing a value on businesses such as professional practices, brokerage firms, and service trades is that sales and goodwill are closely tied to the existing relationship between the seller as an individual and the customer. Once the business or practice is sold, many of these same customers will discontinue patronage. The traditional approach in valuing the service business is to set a price equivalent to a certain percentage of future sales generated by the acquired customers list. Tangible assets may be valued separately.

The percentage of sales reserved as price will depend on prevailing industry custom, but generally it is between 15 and 35 percent of annual income over three to five years on the premise that patronage continued beyond that time is due to the new goodwill created by the buyer. There are, of course, instances where the buyer will acquire the accounts' and customers' lists for a set price. However, even in this situation, the price should mirror anticipated future sales.

Should the seller agree to a contingent price arrangement based on future sales, the seller's concern will be the ability of the buyer to retain goodwill and build sales on which the contingent price is based. An additional concern will be the safeguards necessary to define earnings and to ensure the payment of the contingent price.

Valuing the Merged Business

If the acquired business is to be dismantled and merged into the buyer's existing business, the buyer cannot base value on the profitability of the business as an independent entity. The more appropriate approach is for the buyer to weigh the economic benefit of the merger by measuring the increased profits on his or her own income statement and then apply an acceptable capitalization rate to determine the value of those profits. This requires a careful analysis of each of the operational changes resulting from the merger and careful reconstruction of the buyer's profit and loss statement showing the financial impact of the acquisition.

The functional merger may produce a synergistic effect on the buyer's profits since the combined operations usually produce greater profits than the profits of the two separate entities, each with its own overhead. Less frequently, greater profits are achieved by operating the two firms separately. The functional merger may justify a higher value than could be justified operating the acquired company separately. However, this subtle benefit to the buyer rarely enters into the negotiation.

Valuing the Business with Real Estate

Motels, hotels, nursing homes, and similar businesses that include real estate as the primary asset should nevertheless be valued as a business operation rather than as a passive real estate investment.

Sellers often offer commercial property together with the business for one package price. In this situation, appraise the real estate and business separately. The starting point is to determine the fair rental value of the premises occupied by the business and from this and other rentals determine the appraised value of the real estate. A licensed real estate appraiser can help set a value on the real estate, whereas the business should be separately valued using the procedures found in this chapter.

CHOOSING A BUSINESS APPRAISER

Considering the complexity of business appraisal and the massive investment needed to buy a good business, many more buyers and sellers are turning to professional appraisers.

Finding a qualified business appraiser is not a difficult task if you know what you need and where to look. Two leading professional societies, the American Society of Appraisers (ASA) and the Institute of Business Appraisers (IBA), offer lists of members in each state. The ASA, which demands background checks, evidence of experience, and passage of a rigorous exam before admitting members, has a toll-free number (1–800–ASA–VALU) for persons wishing to obtain a free directory of certified business valuation members. The IBA, located in Boynton Beach, Florida, trains and credentials specialists in business appraisals. The institute will send you a list of their members if you call (407)–732–3202.

When hiring an appraiser, be sure to find one with experience in valuing companies in your particular industry. Always ask for specific details about the appraiser's background and related experience. Often, industry associations can help in locating qualified appraisers. Another excellent source for locating a valuation professional is local law firms that have used business appraisers as expert witnesses—a particularly demanding specialty that requires extensive knowledge of valuation techniques. In addition, appraisers can be found through financial institutions, investment banking companies, accounting firms, business brokerage firms, and independent consulting firms.

Professional appraisers should willingly present a written estimate, provide references, and sign a service contract that sets forth the fee terms, the time necessary to complete the work, and the type of report needed to document the conclusions. Fees vary in direct proportion to the hours necessary to complete the due diligence work of gathering information, preparing an analysis, and writing the report. The cost of the appraisal is also affected by the size and level of complexity of the company and the professional reputation an appraiser puts behind the efforts. Fees typically range from $5,000 to over $250,000 for a thorough, fully documented appraisal. Typical fees for small business valuations usually range between $5,000 and $40,000, depending on the scope of the valuation. If documentation is not a priority for your business, shorter forms of valuation reports such as opinion letters and outline memorandums can help you to minimize fees. Remember that a conflict of interest may arise should the appraiser's fees be partly or completely contingent on a subsequent successful sale of the business.

An appraisal not requiring a short deadline usually takes between 30 and 90 days. The time you are required to spend with a valuation specialist who is conducting a business appraisal may range between several hours and several days. During that time, the appraiser will interview key management, gather data, and thoroughly inspect the company premises.

Over the past few years, an increasing number of business valuation computer programs have been marketed at prices ranging between $95 and $10,000. However, most of the software available still requires that the operator input all critical assumptions, thus demanding more objectivity and specialized knowledge than most business owners have or would care to develop.

SUMMING UP

1. There are many approaches to business valuation and many factors to consider, but earning power is the most important factor.
2. Pay the seller for what the business *presently* earns, not what it will earn under your management.
3. Remain conservative when projecting profits. Most buyers are too optimistic and therefore tend to overpay.
4. Financing terms can and should influence the price you are willing to pay for the business.
5. A well-qualified business appraiser can help you objectively determine a fair price.

CHAPTER 7

NEGOTIATE THE DEAL YOU WANT

Whether buying or selling a business, to win the terms you want you must first sharpen your negotiating skills to a fine edge. Lack of an effective negotiating strategy can greatly influence both price and terms and even jeopardize your chances of a successful deal.

The final objective of the negotiation process is a written agreement covering the details of the proposed buy-sell transaction. Some of the details—price, terms of payment, price allocation, form of the transaction, liabilities, warranties—are matters over which the interests and motivations of the buyer and seller may be in sharp conflict.

The seller is interested in

- The best possible price
- Getting his or her money
- Favorable tax treatment of gains from the sale
- Severing liability ties, past and future
- Avoiding contract terms and conditions that he or she may not be able to carry out

In contrast, the buyer is interested in

- A good title at the lowest possible price
- Favorable payment terms
- A favorable tax basis for resale and depreciation purposes
- Warranty protection against false statements of the seller, inaccurate financial data, and undisclosed or potential liabilities

The agreement reached by the parties, if they succeed in reaching one, will be the result of bargaining. Depending on the relative bargaining position of the buyer and seller, the buy-sell contract may reflect either compromise or capitulation.

The central bargaining issue in the transaction is price. The process of price determination is sometimes described as "horse trading." This element is important. But granted that tactics and compromise play a part in price determination, other explanations often account for the relative success or failure in the bargaining process.

The price paid often reflects the bargaining position of one of the parties. Is the seller's desire to sell stronger than the buyer's desire to buy, or vice versa? The reason behind the decision to buy or sell is important. This would be true of a seller who must sell because of age, health, or personal financial reasons. If the buyer knows that sale of the business is urgent, the seller is less likely to get a reasonable price for his or her business, although the reasons bear no relation to the value of the business or the ability of the buyer to pay cash.

The seller's willingness to finance part of the price, or perhaps all of it, will also depend on the urgency of his or her need to sell. Sometimes a purchase price is agreed upon but later raised because the buyer is unable to get outside financing. The price may also be adjusted in order to get favorable tax treatment or in exchange for more favorable terms in other aspects of the contract.

Another important factor affecting bargaining position is the time element—when to sell, when to buy. Economic conditions cannot be overlooked. The seller is more likely to gain his or her bargaining objectives when business conditions are good, particularly if the business is sharing the prosperity. During periods of recession—either general, local, or in a particular industry or activity—the pessimistic outlook of both buyers and sellers tends to depress prices.

There are countless other reasons why you—or your opponent —may hold the upper hand in the negotiation process, but the trick is to keep the upper hand until you have the very best terms you can possibly obtain.

CREATE THE RIGHT NEGOTIATING CLIMATE

Despite the fact that buyers and sellers have opposing interests, negotiations move forward more easily once a positive and trusting climate is developed.

There are several practical ways to establish this favorable negotiating climate. First, build an atmosphere of trust. This generally takes time, and serious negotiations should be deferred until the buyer knows enough about the business to feel comfortable making an offer. If seller financing is anticipated, the seller must feel equally confident about the buyer, and this confidence also takes time to develop.

The second way to build trust is to make both open and honest disclosures. A seller's unwillingness to provide the buyer reasonable access to financial information, for example, will force the buyer to adopt an overly cautious and hesitant attitude. Similarly, a seller may speak only in positive ways about the business, whereas greater trust would be established if the seller balanced the conversation, revealing several problems with the business.

Finally, be candid when discussing problems with your opponent. Although a good negotiator guards certain information, he or she also brings out into the open perceived problems and concerns that may be easily resolved once your opponent understands what bothers you.

SET FIRM OBJECTIVES

Before you can start serious negotiations, you must clearly and objectively define your goals. To start, review the major points to be negotiated. Initially, you should focus on

- Price
- Assets to be sold
- Financing terms (down payment, term, and interest)
- Security for financing
- Liabilities to be assumed
- Tax aspects of the sale

Minor negotiating points can be attended to, once these issues are resolved. While you can add or delete items to fit your situation, don't get bogged down on less important details without first resolving these central issues. Develop a clear perspective on each negotiating point. Set limits. What is the best you can reasonably expect on each negotiating point? Where will you draw the line on each? With a range established, you can detect whether you are ahead or behind in achieving your objectives as negotiations progress.

Negotiation, of course, is a process of give and take. To come out ahead on one point, you inevitably have to concede another. Therefore, you need to prioritize each point so that you know its relative importance. Define those terms that are non-negotiable, but proceed carefully before adopting fixed positions. Flexibility is the key for putting successful deals together.

Before you negotiate seriously, you must first determine two numbers. The first is what I call the *buy price*. This is what you'll offer the seller, although you'll expect to bid higher once negotiations are under way. The more important number is what I refer to as the *bye-bye price*, which is literally the figure above which you walk away from the deal. Why is this important? With an upper price limit established, you'll avoid the later temptation to pay a price above what you determined the business to be worth before negotiations and when you were less emotionally involved in the deal. Spending weeks or months on a deal can blur your objectivity, so it's best to set limits when you can think most clearly.

PREPARING YOUR INITIAL OFFER

The buyer's decision to submit an offer signals the beginning of formal negotiations. As a buyer, you must decide upon the terms of your initial offer, how to communicate best those terms to the seller, and how to interpret properly the seller's response as a basis for further negotiation.

The most common question asked by a buyer is, How much should I initially offer? There are many factors to consider and some rules of thumb to follow. If the business has strong buyer competition, offer 25 percent below estimated value. Offer 40 to 50 percent below value if there is little buyer competition or you propose an all-cash purchase. Note that the offer is based on your idea of what the business is worth and not necessarily on the seller's asking price, if higher. You must frame your offer based on what the business is worth to you even if substantially below the asking price. Don't be intimidated by the seller's asking price. If you consider your offer realistic, put it forward and stick with it.

I have seen sellers accept offers that were a small fraction of their asking price, and you never know what a seller will accept until you try. Never forget: Sellers tend to overprice their business, as they often have no idea of what their business is worth. Brokers may also discourage a low offer, suggesting higher offers have already been refused. That, too, is unimportant. Such tactics may be a bluff to spur you to raise your offer. Then again, the broker may be unaware of what the seller will actually accept until an offer is presented. Keep in mind that the broker works for the seller, and the broker has an obligation to present *all* offers to the seller.

The danger with too low an offer is that the seller won't consider you a serious buyer. However, experienced sellers do expect offers 25 to 40 percent below the asking price. Within that range, a realistic seller will consider your offer worthy of a counteroffer and begin the ritual of more serious negotiations.

Preparing Your Offer

The well-prepared offer will

- Set forth the proposed terms in detail
- Require a timely decision by the seller
- Bind the seller if accepted
- Provide conditions or "escape" clauses to the buyer

The well-prepared offer in Figure 7–1 serves as your model. Notice how terms are adequately detailed so the seller understands the offer precisely. Commit the seller to a specific date for acceptance. Ten days is sufficient time for a seller to consider your offer without using it as a hedge to shop for a better deal. Don't overlook the conditions or escape clauses. Is your offer conditional upon financing? An acceptable lease? Verification of the books by your accountant? If your attorney did not review the offer, it should be subject to his or her approval. Enclose a binder–$1,000 or even less is an acceptable binder for a small business with a further deposit upon acceptance and signing formal agreements. Allow yourself the flexibility to walk away from the deal by insisting upon a small deposit and numerous conditions that must be satisfied.

FIGURE 7-1

MEYERS, GOLDSTEIN, CHYTEN & KOSBERG
A PROFESSIONAL ASSOCIATION
ATTORNEYS AT LAW

IRVING S. MEYERS
ARNOLD S. GOLDSTEIN, P.C.
EDWIN R. CHYTEN
BARRY R. LEVINE
JAMES A. RICE
JAMES J. LARKIN

OF COUNSEL:
LOUIS K. NATHANSON

850 BOYLSTON STREET
CHESTNUT HILL, MASSACHUSETTS 02167
(617) 277-4100

CABLE: MEYGOLD

President
Board of Directors
Apex Mill Manufacturing Company, Inc.
Apex Mill Road
Maintown, MA

Gentlemen:

Please be advised that this firm represents Francis J. Jones relative to his interest in acquiring the business of Apex Mill Manufacturing Company, Inc. This is a fourth offer, which supercedes the prior offer, dated May 19, 1986, June 18, 1986, and July 1, 1986.

Mr. Jones (Buyer) is interested in acquiring Apex Mill on the following terms:

1. The transfer to Jones or corporate nominee shall be through a sale of assets and not by a conveyance of shares of the corporation. The sale shall include the following items that comprise the assets of Apex Mill:

    a) All machinery, equipment, fixtures, tools, dyes, office machines and furniture, computers, computer programs and software, shop and office supplies, spare and replacement parts, and all other tangible assets of the business of Apex Mill wherever located, excluding inventory

    b) All motor vehicles, owned outright by Apex Mill and not leased

    c) All leases, contract rights, leasehold improvements, and prepaid insurance, including (i) computer software lease with █████ Credit Corporation, Account No. █████████; (ii) 1986 Saab motor vehicle lease with ███ Vehicle Leasing, Inc., Account No. █████; (iii) ██████ Phone System financed with ████ Commercial Corp., Account No. ███████████; (iv) 1986 Toyota Cargo Van financed with █████ Community Bank, Account No. ████████████

(continued)

FIGURE 7-1
Continued

---

d)   All trademarks, trade names, patents, proprietary
     processes and designs, all advertising, sales
     literature, customer lists, proprietary sales and
     marketing information, pricing lists and formulas,
     and any other items relating to manufacturing
     processes and marketing

e)   Originals or copies of all books and records of
     the business, including, after inspection by Mr.
     Jones, all materials deemed necessary to maintain
     the continuity of the business (Copies or
     originals will be available to the Seller.)

2.   Excepted from this sale shall be the following items:

a)   All cash on hand or deposits in banks

b)   All accounts receivable

c)   All inventory, works in progress, and finished
     goods except as provided in Section 3a below

3. a)   <u>Inventory</u>. At the time of passing, Buyer shall
         inspect the inventory and shall select those items
         that he wants to purchase at Seller's cost or
         current market value, whichever is less. The
         selected inventory shall be valued at the time the
         selection is made. Buyer shall pay for this
         inventory in three (3) equal monthly installments
         commencing three (3) months after the passing.

b)   <u>Work in Progress</u>. At the day of passing, Buyer
     and Seller shall evaluate and determine the value
     of all work in progress. The value of the work in
     progress shall be determined by (1) price paid for
     the raw materials, (2) the cost of direct labor
     calculated at the standard rate of labor on that
     date, and (3) the cost, if any, of any outside
     labor utilized in the manufacture of the product.
     Payment of the foregoing shall be made only when
     same is paid by the customer, provided, however,
     Buyer shall first deduct any material and labor
     costs incurred by him from the payment before
     remitting the balance up to the above formula to
     Seller.

c)   <u>Finished Goods</u>. Buyer shall remit seventy (70%)
     percent of the actual net selling price (less
     shipping costs, if any) to Seller, if and when the
     product is sold and same is paid by the customer.

4.   Mr. Jones hereby offers the full purchase price of
     Five Hundred Fifteen Thousand ($515,000.00) Dollars
     for all the above plus the items set forth in Article
     10b below. The specific allocation of the purchase
     price to the particular assets to be acquired shall be
     agreed upon by the parties and shall be set forth in
     the purchase agreement.

(continued)

FIGURE 7-1
Continued

---

5. The above purchase price shall be paid in the following
    manner:

    a)   Cash tender (deposit) with this offer $ 2,000.00
    b)   Cash at time of passing   338,000.00
    c)   Note to be held by Seller   175,000.00
                                      Total $515,000.00

6. The note contemplated in 6(c) above shall be a secured
    seven- (7) year obligation with no accrual of interest
    or payment of principal in the first year.   Thereafter,
    the note shall be paid in Seventy-two (72) equal
    monthly installments of principal and interest at a
    rate of eight (8%) percent simple interest per annum.
    Seller shall agree to subordinate its security interest
    in the business assets to a security interest(s) of
    lenders advancing fund for this acquisition and for
    working capital.

7. If there are any adjustments in the above purchase
    price (according to the terms of a comprehensive
    purchase agreement as provided for herein), all
    adjustments shall be made to the cash portion of the
    purchase price.

8. Except for any liabilities expressly assumed hereunder
    or as a condition of the comprehensive purchase
    agreement, all assets shall be sold free and clear of
    all liens, claims, encumbrances, and other liabilities,
    with Buyer receiving good and marketable title.

9. This offer is expressly conditioned upon the following
    terms and conditions that are deemed material aspects
    by the Buyer:

    a)   The execution within ten (10) days of acceptance
         hereof by the parties of a comprehensive purchase
         agreement (encompassing the terms of this offer)
         and ancilliary documents in a form acceptable to
         both parties on or before the proposed date of
         passing

    b)   The execution at the time of passing of covenants
         not to compete by the following officers and
         shareholders of the Seller:

         1.   Edward J. Taggart

         2.   Robert Johanson

         3.   Alan Goodfellow

These covenants shall pertain for a period of two (2) years
and cover a geographical area encompassed by the six states that
compose the New England region.

(continued)

FIGURE 7-1
Continued

---

c)   The execution of a standard form "triple net"
commercial lease of the Buyer with the landlord of
the premises where the property is located, for a
five- (5) year lease with five (5) one- (1) year
options, at a rent of $3,000 per month for the
four (4) months following the passing, $4,500 per
month for the next eight (8) months, and $5,000.00
per month for the remaining forty-nine (49) months
of the original term. During the first year of
the lease, landlord shall share equally with Buyer
in the cost of insurance and real estate taxes.

Buyer shall be required to pay a one-month
security deposit to the landlord for said lease.
Rent during the option period shall be negotiated
by the parties ninety (90) days prior to the
expiration of the original lease terms, provided
that (1) the operative terms of the lease shall
remain essentially the same during the option
period and (2) the base rent during the option
period shall be generally reflective of the market
rent for similar property in the ███████████
Middlesex County area.

Further, Seller (as landlord) may reduce the area
occupied by the Buyer on the second floor attic in
order to rent same to other tenants, provided (1)
that Buyer's rent is reduced proportionally and
(2) that Buyer reasonably approves of the
reduction of space so same does not interfere with
its operation of the business.

Seller may also after a period of twelve (12)
months cancel this lease, provided (1) Buyer shall
have found suitable facilities to move his
operation to, (2) Buyer and Seller shall cooperate
in finding such facility, and (3) Seller shall pay
Buyer in advance an amount equal to the costs of
breaking down the existing operation, moving the
equipment, and completely setting up at a new
location, including the new fixtures and wiring.

d)   A complete review shall be conducted by the Buyer
of the Seller's business operation and books and
records to determine if the business generally
conforms to the representations made by the
Seller's broker, United ████████ Financial
Corporation, and by the officers and
representatives of the Seller. The Seller shall
make available to the Buyer all the records of the
business, including but not limited to:

1.   Financial records
2.   All contracts and leases
3.   All insurance policies, records, and claims
4.   All existing loan documentation

(continued)

FIGURE 7-1
Continued

---

5. All records concerning orders, order backlog, and work in progress
6. Records, formulas, programs, and other items relating to job pricing and quotes
7. Customer records, quote histories
8. All personnel files
9. All records of compensation paid to employees and officers
10. All records pertaining to manufacturing processes, quality control, defective goods adjustments, and credits
11. All bank statements

Buyer shall complete its review of items 1-11 within ten (10) days after execution of this offer to purchase.

e) The maintenance of the business operation and the preservation of the assets by the Seller in generally the same condition as presently constituted, until the day of passing; if any substantial portion of the assets shall be destroyed or rendered unusable before passing, Buyer shall not be obligated to acquire the business.

f) The obtaining of a firm financing commitment from a recognized financial institution for funds of not less than $340,000.00 within thirty (30) days from the execution of the comprehensive sale documents contemplated herein.

g) The obtaining of an appraisal within fifteen (15) days of acceptance of this offer by a recognized equipment appraiser, which indicates the value of the equipment to be at least $515,000.00 at quick sale.

h) The existence of customer orders of at least $75,000.00 at the time of passing, provided that Seller shall reasonably bid on contract leads provided by Buyer before the passing.

10. a) If the Buyer, having used all due diligence, fails to obtain a written commitment for the loan as set forth in Subsection 9f) within thirty (30) days from the execution of the comprehensive sale documents, then at Buyer's option all payments made hereunder by the Buyer shall be forthwith refunded and all other obligations to the parties hereto shall cease, and this agreement shall be void without recourse to the parties hereto. The Buyer shall be deemed to have waived its rights under this paragraph if the Seller has not been notified in writing within thirty (30) days after execution of this offer to purchase that the Buyer desires to terminate this agreement.

(continued)

FIGURE 7-1
Continued

---

b)   If the Buyer is not satisfied with his review of
the records of the Seller Corporation as set forth
in Subsection [d], 1-11], then, at Buyer's option,
all payments made hereunder by the Buyer shall be
forthwith refunded and all other obligations of
the parties hereto shall cease, and this agreement
shall be void without recourse to the parties
hereto.   Buyer shall be deemed to have waived its
right under this paragraph if the Seller has not
been notified in writing within ten (10) days
after execution of this offer to purchase that the
Buyer desires to terminate this offer to purchase
because of an unsatisfactory review of said
records.

11.   The Buyer states that he was introduced to this
business by United ████████ Financial Corporation; Seller
shall be solely responsible for any commissions payable
to United ████████ Financial Corporation, and Seller
shall hold Buyer harmless and indemnify him against any
commission claims for United ████████ Financial
Corporation or any other party.

12.   The Seller shall, as part of the comprehensive purchase
agreement, warrant the veracity (within general
accounting principles) of all financial statements.

13.   The Seller to the best of its knowledge shall warrant
to the Buyer that its operation as of the date of
closing is in conformance with all applicable
provisions of the various state and federal
environmental agencies in force and effect at the time
of closing and shall agree to indemnify and hold the
Buyer harmless from any claims for such violations
occurring prior to the date of closing.   This provision
shall survive the passing.

14.   If Seller determines it is beneficial to sell any
equipment before the closing, it shall obtain the
consent of the Buyer prior to doing so, and if the item
is sold, the price of same shall be deduced from the
cash portion of the purchase price.

15.   The Seller shall comply with the Bulk Sales Law (so-
called) as enacted in the Commonwealth of
Massachusetts.

We have previously tended the buyer's check for $2,000.00 to
be held in escrow by your counsel, pending the closing and
transfer.

(continued)

FIGURE 7-1
Continued

    If this offer is acceptable, please signify by signing where
indicated and return a signed copy to our office within ten (10)
days of above date. If this offer is not accepted within the
ten- (10) day period, you should consider the offer withdrawn.
Upon acceptance, we propose to immediately enter into a formal
purchase and sales agreement on these terms.

    An acceptable date of passing would be July 15, 1986.

                    Very truly yours,

                    Francis J. Jones

                    By his attorney,

                    Arnold S. Goldstein

ASG/dm

The foregoing offer is accepted on its terms:

                    Apex Mill Manufacturing
                    Company, Inc.

                    By: _____
                            President

There are many pitfalls to avoid. The first is not to make a premature offer. Brokers urge you to submit an offer once you show interest in the business, but you cannot intelligently submit an offer on any business until you have definite interest in acquiring it and have had sufficient opportunity to investigate the business.

A second vitally important point to remember is that an offer *is* a contract. You can incur considerable liability if you do not perform once an offer is accepted. Therefore, never sign an offer prepared by a broker. Although brokers are professionals, they are neither qualified nor licensed to prepare binding offers and, of course, do not represent your interests as a buyer. The best advice is to have an offer prepared by your attorney.

What will happen once the seller receives your offer?

There are only three possible responses a seller can make. The seller can accept, refuse your offer (or not reply), or submit a counteroffer. Should the seller accept your terms, which is a most unlikely event, it means you submitted too high an original offer.

However, it may still be possible to negotiate tactfully downward by threatening to withdraw from the deal because one or more of the conditions under the offer have not been fulfilled.

Will the seller ignore or flatly reject your offer? The seller may if he or she is holding a better offer, had no serious interest in selling, or views you as a less-than-serious buyer. Chances are, however, that you will receive a counteroffer. What does the counter offer say? You want more than an invitation to submit a higher bid because you are then forced to bid against yourself. Insist on a specific counterproposal stating the seller's position on each of the terms raised in your original offer.

Read between the lines of the counteroffer. How low did the price drop? Does the seller seem more resistant on price or financing? What terms does the seller appear flexible on? What seems non-negotiable? Don't react too quickly to the seller's counteroffer. Draw the seller out. Allow the seller to do the chasing, because you want to test the seller's motivation or anxiety level. With patience, you obtain greater concessions than you give up.

RULES FOR SUCCESSFUL NEGOTIATIONS

Negotiating a business acquisition follows the same time-proven basic strategies used when negotiating any other transaction except the stakes are usually far greater. How can you improve your negotiating techniques?

Investigate the Seller's Position

How motivated is this seller? Why does he or she really want to sell? What are his or her problems and pressure points? Remember that you always bargain from your opponent's position – never your own. Do your homework and investigate the seller as thoroughly as you do the business and never accept at face value a seller's reasons for selling.

Listen – Don't Talk

When you listen, you pick up valuable clues, when you talk, you tip your hand. Encourage your opponent to disclose as much as possible. Ask questions. Draw your opponent out. You'll not only receive information useful to negotiate a better deal: By being a good listener, you help improve your relationship as well.

Divide and Conquer–Address Multiple Issues One at a Time

Where multiple issues exist, multiple problems exist. Separate issues and discuss each individually. Larger problems become more manageable when divided into smaller parts, and each part is tackled separately. But remember that you cannot commit yourself on any one point unless in agreement on other points, as an acceptable deal requires favorable resolution on all points.

Address Easy Issues First–Put Problem Issues Off Until Last

Avoid becoming stalled on one particular issue or on one aspect of the deal that is difficult to resolve. Set areas of disagreement aside and address more easily resolved issues. When you and your opponent return to the original problem issue, you will have resolved most issues and will have invested considerable time and effort to bring negotiations that far along. At that point in the negotiating process, an earlier obstacle will take on a different perspective and be more easily resolved.

Work with Your Opponent to Create a Joint Solution

Encourage your opponent to participate actively in creating a proposed solution. Draw him or her into the process. Work collectively to identify the problem, seek advice, and share opinions and suggestions. Literally work together so that both parties can claim ownership in the solution.

Put Yourself in Your Opponent's Position

Consider your opponent's point of view. Does the deal satisfy his or her needs, goals, and objectives? Where does it fall short? What are the alternatives to satisfy those needs and still produce an acceptable deal?

Develop Multiple Solutions

Once you have identified the issues to be resolved, determine how you can solve those problems at the least possible cost. Walk into negotiations with all possible alternatives and solutions in mind. But don't rely on your solutions alone. Ask your opponent for his ideas on resolving issues. However, neither you nor your opponent should be limited to your own solutions. Brainstorm with advisers and associates until all possible solutions are on the negotiating table and fully explored.

Deal with the Decision Maker

Beware of two-step negotiations where your opponent must clear every point with a partner, attorney, spouse, or some mysterious third party. Find out in advance whether your opponent shares your authority to make a deal and, if not, insist that all decision makers be present at negotiations so a binding agreement can be simultaneously reached.

Be Patient

Negotiating a business acquisition can take many months and cannot be rushed along without paying a steep price for your impatience. Conversely, patience to extend negotiations can create a much more favorable deal.

Be Prepared to Take a Walk

Never become emotionally committed to a prospective acquisition. You objectively defined your limits before you started negotiation to control emotions, so if an acceptable deal cannot be reached, be prepared to walk away. Until you are handed the keys, the business isn't yours and may never become yours.

Other Strategies

Becoming a successful negotiator doesn't require the persuasive powers of Dale Carnegie. Even if it did, you wouldn't negotiate more effectively because you must rely on your own unique personality to be a sincere negotiator, and sincerity is the key to successful negotiations. Remember: The primary objective of a well-negotiated deal is to have each party leave the negotiating table well-satisfied that he or she won the points he or she wanted and to achieve this, you need some empathy toward your opponent's objectives as well as your own.

Yet while negotiating to buy a business follows most of the principles for negotiating any other deal, there are a few mistakes rookie business buyers are more likely to make. The first is that you may let your emotions and enthusiasm for the business get the best of you. Many buyers are far too anxious, and their anxiety clearly shows, much to their detriment. Those afflicted by the "eager-beaver" syndrome ignore reality and can't be bothered by hard numbers or dismal facts. Their blind desire to buy the business transcends their objectivity in deciding whether it's the business to buy. Even when the business is worthwhile, their ability to negotiate the best deal possible fares poorly because they lack the patience to set realistic negotiating terms objectively or to remain sufficiently aloof so those terms can be won.

Negotiations can take considerable patience, and it can be difficult to keep your anxiety level under control. Seldom do buyers and sellers move at the same pace. Some sellers make decisions at a snail's speed, whereas others push for sudden resolution. But beware of the hard sell. If a seller is too pushy, step back and take whatever time you need to evaluate matters objectively. The seller, indeed, may have something to be pushy about.

Negotiating a small business acquisition can easily take three to six months from the day the initial offer is made to the day final agreements are signed. Part of the delay is because the typical deal involves more than just you and the seller. For a deal to come together, other interests need to be satisfied. A landlord may stubbornly refuse terms you need, a bank may drag its feet on preliminary financing, or a partner may resist or be indecisive. There's no end to what can delay a deal in the making.

There are other common mistakes to avoid. Another deadly error is to knock the seller's business for purposes of depressing the price. Although problems with the business should be tactfully pointed out, style becomes all important, as a tactless approach will achieve nothing more than to alienate the seller, destroy the negotiating climate, and make future negotiations either more difficult or impossible. I have yet to see a seller bludgeoned into submission. Much more can be gained with small doses of flattery.

The point is that if the seller has trouble relating to you personally, your job will be twice as difficult. You must handle the seller properly to build the confidence and trust vital to most business deals—and particularly those deals where the seller must extend substantial financing. "Chemistry" between buyer and seller can make or break a deal, so you must learn to adapt your unique personality to the seller's, as sellers are only people with the same likes, dislikes, prejudices, and concerns as you.

Harvey can show you how *not* to win friends. He thought he was a skillful negotiator, but it turned out that he didn't know the first thing about handling people.

Harvey's goal was to buy a typical gas station from a nice enough fellow to whom the business represented years of hard work. Harvey knew he could make the business far more profitable, but he didn't have the down payment the seller was looking for. In walked Harvey to negotiate a deal. The seller and his wife greeted him with customary cordialities, but Harvey decided it was time to impress everyone with his managerial brilliance. Turning to the seller, he mumbled, "The first thing I'm going to do is paint that dump of yours. And how did you survive without opening on Sundays?" On and on Harvey stormed, trying to prove what a shrewd operator he was by knocking the seller's ability. After listening to Harvey's many insults, the seller quietly walked out, leaving Harvey to his old job sorting mail at the post office. The world is full of people like Harvey. They seldom learn diplomacy. Those who understand human nature needn't take lessons from a book. Those who do not cannot learn it from all the books in the world.

Contrast Harvey's approach with Mark's. Mark understands people. He never discusses or negotiates a deal until he has formed the closest possible relationship with the seller. Once the bond exists, he finds everything else falls into place.

For several years Mark owned a small but prosperous Cape Cod restaurant. Although relatively new to the business, Mark had already enjoyed modest success, and his business still had tremendous potential. Before long, Mark discovered a larger and more prosperous restaurant for sale for which the seller wanted

$300,000 with a $100,000 down payment. Mark first met the seller at the seller's restaurant, engaging him in constructive and pleasant conversation concerning their mutual business interests. To their mutual advantage they compared menus, costs, customers, and suppliers. Mark disclosed to the seller the recipe for his best-selling dessert. That made his restaurant a local landmark. A week later, at Mark's invitation the seller toured Mark's business. Never once did they discuss a business deal. Instead, Mark sought the seller's advice on several problems, which, in turn, flattered the seller by allowing him to demonstrate his broad knowledge. Soon Mark and the seller became fast friends. When Mark finally presented his offer, the seller instantly agreed to the favorable terms requested, and Mark soon owned his second restaurant. Mark's story proves this important point: When two people like and trust each other, they can work out the most beneficial and creative terms.

Business deals are much like romances, and the best have as their foundation a "courting" period. It's people getting to know each other, building a friendship or, at the very least, an understanding of each other's needs. In this book, I refer to the negotiating table, which is, of course, only a figure of speech, for a lawyer's or accountant's conference table is absolutely the worst place to negotiate. Smart buyers avoid austere negotiating environments and instead try to build relationships slowly and gradually in an atmosphere more conducive to favorable negotiation.

So sell yourself before you try to sell the deal. Once the seller sees you as more than just another buyer, you will be well on your way to winning your ideal terms.

PLAYING GAMES

None of what I have said before suggests that you should naively walk into negotiations believing your adversary is always noble and righteous. The fact is that you are bound to meet up with some scoundrels whether you are a buyer or a seller.

Sellers come in all shapes and sizes, and they all play predictable games. Camouflaged by their own smokescreen, you're bound to meet:

Mr. I Don't Really Want to Sell

This classic character languishes behind his big desk with his hands folded behind his head. He smiles broadly and utters, "My business isn't really for sale, but I'll entertain an interesting offer." This master intimidator wants you on the defensive while he maintains the upper hand throughout the game. But this same seller has frantically beaten the bushes for five years looking for a buyer. He has run so many ads that he's on a first-name basis with the local newspaper editor. Every night he kneels down beside his bed and adds to his prayers, "Please find me a buyer." If you naively accept his pitch, you may begin your own begging and whimpering for a chance to shovel his gold mine.

There's only one way to pierce the smokescreen of Mr. I Don't Really Want to Sell: Let him know early in the game that you don't really want to buy. Expect a humbling phone call.

Mr. Just Testing

Some sellers are the counterparts of the buyers who spend their lives looking but never buy. These sellers happily advertise, and love to negotiate, but they never close a deal.

Why do such sellers persist in wasting your time and money? For several reasons. Some only want to reassure themselves that their businesses are valuable. Others enjoy dickering with buyers. Finally, there's the seller who figures he'll put his business on the market at a ridiculously high price to see if one poor sucker might take the bait.

The only seller in this category worth dealing with is the one who sincerely wants to sell but can't quite tear himself away from his lifetime investment. Why not offer a job? This works especially well with the seller facing retirement.

How can you smoke out the testers? Predictably, they never call in their accountants or lawyers because accountants and lawyers cost money and make his hobby annoyingly expensive. Whenever you suspect you're up against a tester, ask him to have his accountant work with your accountant to go over the books or request that his lawyer prepare an agreement. That's when you can say "good-bye" to Mr. Just Testing.

Mr. Desperate

This cunning creature peeks out from behind his smokescreen to entice you to take advantage of his desperation. "I've got to sell—and fast," he tells you, recounting his problems with his impetigo that demands his immediate relocation to Arizona. Maybe it's the broker handing you this yarn, but you see the message. Snap it up before it gets away—today's your lucky day.

Mr. Desperate is seldom desperate. He, of course, just wants a fast offer to get the ball rolling so he can spend the next four months negotiating you up to his price when he's not busy nursing his imagined impetigo.

Mr. In Demand

His strategy is to get you crazily bidding against yourself by believing every buyer in town is banging down his doors for a chance at his gold mine. Last week he had three offers that he's still considering and tomorrow he expects two more. Mr. In Demand is a very busy man sifting through all his wonderful offers. But since he's the benevolent type, he'll gladly add yours to the growing pile.

What's your next move? First, tell him you don't care about other buyers or what they offer. Your only concern is what the business is worth to you. Period. Next, let him know you won't be rushed because you have too many other businesses to consider. Don't worry about competition. Mr. In Demand has been running his ads longer than Mr. I Don't Really Want to Sell.

Mr. Who's in Trouble?

Now here's where you'll find the *real* Mr. Desperate. Bill collectors are closing in, the landlord's about to throw him out, and the sheriff's hanging auction signs outside his door, but there he sits and smiles, pretending he's on top of the world.

Faced with the seller who must sell to bail himself out, but will never admit it, you can only use one strategy. In fact, this strategy can work wonders in bringing any of these game players out from behind their smokescreen: Simply walk away!

SALVAGING COLLAPSED NEGOTIATIONS

Even when dealing with a sincere seller or buyer, negotiations frequently collapse when the parties remain too far apart to reach agreement. How can you revive negotiations without weakening your bargaining position? First, always break off negotiations on a friendly note. The fact that you can't easily reach agreement shouldn't create a hostile relationship. Leave ajar the door to reopen negotiations at a later date. You may, for instance, agree to reconsider certain points. The business may have had some favorable developments of possible interest to the buyer. A buyer may conceive a new approach to the problem of interest to the seller. Bargaining positions do change. Why not involve your attorney or accountant? Direct negotiations may not have been successful, but your advisers negotiating directly with your opponent's advisers may find ways to break a stalemate or simply see solutions you and your opponent could not see. Don't stand on principal. If you have to give in on one or two small points to make the deal, don't let your ego stand in your way. If the business is basically good and the deal is reasonably sound and equitable, a few extra dollars becomes a meaningless concession when you are to own a prosperous business for many years.

CEMENTING THE DEAL

Congratulations! You just bought or sold a business . . . or so you thought.

There is a considerable difference between reaching a "handshake" agreement and concluding a legally binding agreement. Between the two events, the deal can easily fall apart. The buyer, for example, may find a more attractive opportunity, be unable to receive financing, discover problems with the business, or simply lack sufficient confidence to complete the acquisition.

The seller, for numerous reasons, may also withdraw from the deal. The seller may have been approached by another buyer with a more generous offer or may develop his or her own anxieties about selling. Predictably, both the buyer and seller will receive well-intentioned advice from friends and relatives on why they shouldn't buy or sell. Considering Murphy's Law that all that can go wrong usually does, it takes a determined buyer and seller, and several essential strategies, to keep the hard-fought deal together. To begin with, insist on binding agreements within 10 days of reaching verbal agreement. The longer you wait for a formal agreement, the less chance you have to cement the deal. So don't allow your attorney to delay. Keep the escape clauses or postagreement conditions to a minimum and, of course, bind the buyer by requiring a sufficient deposit to compensate you adequately, should the buyer walk away.

Neither a buyer nor a seller should spread word that the business has been sold (or acquired) until binding agreements have been signed. As a buyer, you don't want to invite last-minute bids from competitive buyers. As a seller, you don't want to reveal to your employees, suppliers, and customers that the business is for sale or actually sold until certain the sale will go through or actually be transferred. A seller would be wise not to disclose to the buyer information about the business not previously provided. New information invites the buyer to find new problems and to withdraw his or her offer. Until closing, the seller should only reinforce the merits of the business.

No matter how hard you and the seller may have negotiated, it is important that you each leave the negotiating table with the same mutual trust and confidence you began with. This advice is particularly vital if you are to maintain a continued relationship such as when the seller finances the deal or perhaps remains as the landlord under the lease. All too often you will need the seller's cooperation, and small battles unfairly fought can prove enormously costly later. The real key to a successfully negotiated deal is that both parties emerge victorious!

SUMMING UP

1. Negotiation begins with a good relationship and negotiating climate between buyer and seller.
2. Carefully define all the terms you want before you begin to negotiate.

3. Investigate your opponent's bargaining position. His or her weakness can be your negotiating strength.
4. Don't rush the negotiating process. It takes time and patience to put together the right deal.
5. Remember: You never really have a deal until you're handed the keys.

CHAPTER 8

FINANCING THE DEAL

Formulating a sound approach to financing the acquisition is critical to both the seller and buyer for several reasons.

While financing may be viewed by the seller merely as a means to facilitate the sale, for the buyer it must mean considerably more than the ability to buy the business. Statistically, more businesses fail because of improperly structured financing than any other factor. Improper financing can also restrict growth, create adverse tax consequences, and needlessly increase personal liability. In a large sense, the future of the business is influenced, if not controlled, by the initial financing.

As you approach the complicated field of financing, you will face a maze of questions answered in this chapter:

- How much capital is needed?
- How should the capital requirements be divided between borrowed funds and invested funds?
- What are the best financing sources for acquisition?
- How do you successfully apply for business loans?
- What financing terms should be negotiated?
- How should the loan be structured?

MEASURE YOUR FINANCING NEEDS

Determining your financing needs goes beyond calculating the amount required to buy the business. You must also forecast the capital needed to operate properly and build the newly acquired enterprise.

Many buyers make the error of approaching financing as a

two-step process. They first exhaust their capital or borrowing power to finance the acquisition and later attempt to find additional financing necessary to operate the business properly. Such buyers are typically unsuccessful in their two-step approach to financing because their collateral has been previously pledged, and it's usually not feasible to restructure the original financing arrangements to accommodate additional financing. Therefore, it is wise to anticipate and incorporate working capital requirements into the initial financing package (Figure 8–1). When projecting your financing requirements, consider the capital needed

- To build sufficient inventory to achieve sales projected under the business forecast
- To renovate and modernize the physical plant
- To add or replace fixtures and equipment
- To finance accounts receivable
- To finance planned advertising or promotional programs
- To maintain adequate working capital

FIGURE 8-1

CAPITAL REQUIREMENTS
ANALYSIS

Down Payment (price financing) plus (if applicable):	$_____
Inventory to be added	$_____
Renovation costs	$_____
New fixtures and equipment	$_____
Utility deposits	$_____
Licenses, permits and fees	$_____
Legal and accounting fees	$_____
Adjustments due at closing	$_____
Advertising launch	$_____
Working capital requirements	$_____
Other: _____	$_____
_____	$_____
_____	$_____
Total Capital Requirements	$_____

Be guided by your own operational plans and financial forecasts for the business. It obviously makes little sense to acquire the business on the premise of required changes without the matching resources necessary to achieve it.

Don't forget to check each item that can affect cash flow and working capital needs. Examine the balance sheet, for oftentimes redeploying assets and liabilities can release cash, thereby reducing the need for financing. Inventory, for example, may be excessive and partially liquidated to raise cash. If you do not assume the seller's debts, cash flow projections should reflect the cash equivalency of available short-term credit. The purchase of the seller's receivables will certainly impact greatly upon financing. Purchasing receivables provides an immediate income stream. On the other hand, if you must first generate your own receivables, it significantly reduces cash flow during the initial collection period. What fixed assets can be disposed of for cash? Each of these cash-raising possibilities should be carefully considered by you and your accountant, not only to reduce capitalization needs but also to serve as a basis for negotiating those points necessary to create the most favorable postacquisition cash flow

FINDING THE MONEY

Financing for the small business acquisition usually comes from three primary sources: internal financing, external financing, and equity. Internal financing is the portion of the sales price financed through seller financing, or the assumption of debt or similar financing opportunities existing within the business and made available to the buyer. External financing includes funds borrowed from external sources, such as banks, Small Business Investment Companies (SBICs), and other third-party lenders. And equity is the amount invested by the buyer from his or her own funds and thus not scheduled for repayment.

Hunt financing from all three sources, but look first to the internal financing available, for only then can you determine the additional capital that must be obtained from external sources or personal funds. Consider, for example, the business sold for $100,000. To the buyer overlooking internal financing sources, financing the business becomes a $100,000 problem. Should the buyer, however, negotiate a $70,000 loan from the seller and also assume $10,000 in trade debts, financing is suddenly whittled to a $20,000 problem and becomes very manageable.

A GUIDE TO SELLER FINANCING

From their separate perspectives, both the seller and buyer should consider what portion of the price the seller will finance. Seller financing is exceptionally common in business acquisitions. The majority of small business acquisitions involve some form of seller financing to bridge the difference between the agreed price, the buyer's down payment, and the other sources of external financing available to the buyer. Nor is it unusual to find sellers financing 80 percent or more of the price.

Buyers strongly negotiate for seller financing for several important reasons.

Reduced Down Payment

Buyers can usually finance 50 to 60 percent of the purchase price from external sources such as banks. However, even when such financing can be found, the opportunity for additional seller financing can substantially reduce the needed down payment. This is, of course, particularly important (1) to buyers who are unable to raise the required down payment or (2) to the increasing number of buyers interested in a leveraged buyout either to conserve their capital or to obtain higher returns on their smaller investments.

Reduced Interest Rates

Seller financing is ordinarily the least expensive financing available to a buyer. Interest rates charged by the average seller are about 4 to 5 percent below banks' rates. The reason is that sellers provide financing primarily to sell their business rather than to make money on their loan. Most sellers are therefore content to accept interest rates equal to or slightly higher than could be earned by investing cash proceeds from a sale in a money market account, certificate of deposit, or other safe investment. As a matter of compromise, buyers and sellers often "split the difference" between what a bank would charge the buyer for a loan, if available, and the interest the seller would earn from certificates of deposit if the seller had sold the business for cash.

Extended Terms

Banks and other asset-based lenders limit their loans to three to five years and thus impose a cash flow strain on the newly acquired business. Sellers, on the other hand, must usually offer considerably lengthier loans extending from 7 to 10 years if the business is to have a reasonable chance to succeed. Even when a seller refuses extended loan terms, he or she may alternatively agree to other flexible financing arrangements. For example, a seller may accept a balloon note to satisfy the buyer's short-term cash flow needs with lower payments in the early years or may offer other creative loan arrangements unavailable through more rigid institutional lenders.

Recourse

One major advantage of seller financing is that the buyer has a practical way to obtain recourse against the seller in the event he or she discovers any misrepresentation or subsequent contractual breach. Many buyers wisely hesitate to pay cash for a business when continuing obligations by the seller remain and instead bargain for seller financing for no other reason than to ensure the seller performance on his or her obligations. Owing the seller money is, of course, rather quite convenient, should it later surface that the seller made false representations or is otherwise not in compliance with the terms of his or her agreement.

Reduced Collateral

Although a negotiable point, sellers are less inclined to demand personal collateral to secure their financing than are banks, the SBA, and other external financing sources. Sellers are generally satisfied to accept the business alone as collateral, because upon default the business represents a higher collateral value to a seller who can reclaim the business than it would to a bank with only the alternative of liquidation.

WAYS TO OBTAIN SELLER FINANCING

There are numerous reasons why sellers resist financing a buyer. The seller may need all the sale proceeds for personal use or for a new business venture. Others can afford to finance but prefer to break clean with the business. Perhaps the most common reason is because financing suggests potential risk of loss, should the buyer default, a risk unacceptable to all but sellers with a high degree of confidence in the buyer or willingness to reclaim the business if the buyer defaults.

Despite the seller's predictable resistance to financing, there may be no other alternative but to finance a sale. While sellers may prefer the cash buyer, the essential questions are whether the seller can readily find a cash buyer and whether the cash buyer would pay an equivalent price.

Seller financing must be objectively analyzed by the seller from a strict risk-benefit viewpoint. The primary benefit to a seller offering attractive financing is the prospect for not only a faster sale but a higher price as well. Buyers place considerably more importance on down payment requirements than price, and when the two are negotiated together, a seller may find that the increased price more than compensates for a small amount of secondary financing granted to reduce a buyer's down payment. Consider, for example, a business selling for $100,000. A buyer may be able to obtain $60,000 in bank financing but only be able to raise $20,000 cash for the down payment. The final negotiations may lead the buyer to pay an increased price of $110,000 if the seller provides secondary financing for $30,000. From the seller's perspective, the question becomes whether the $10,000 added to the price is sufficient benefit to risk financing $20,000.

While the possible benefits can be accurately measured, whether in terms of a faster sale, higher price, or other negotiable buyer concession, it is difficult to measure the risk. Ultimately, it is a question of whether the remaining balance can be collected, should the buyer fail or default. Essentially, the seller must look at it from a worst-case scenario; assess his or her options, alternatives, and recourse, assuming an immediate default; and make a reasoned decision whether the risk of financing is justified.

Seller financing can impose less risk through three strategies: reduce the financed amount, accelerate payback, and obtain adequate security.

Lowering the Amount Financed

While seller financing may be necessary to sell the business, it is frequently possible to reduce the amount of seller financing substantially and still meet the buyer's down payment objectives. The seller should insist that the buyer first exhaust other sources of possible financing. For example, on the sale of the $100,000 business to a buyer with $20,000 cash, financing may come together with a $60,000 bank loan and perhaps the assumption by the buyer of $10,000 in trade debts owed by the seller. Clearly, all that would be then required of the seller is $10,000 in secondary financing.

The most common technique to reduce seller financing is the possibility of a buyer's assuming part, or all, of the seller's indebtedness as a credit against the price (and the remaining balance requiring financing). It makes little sense for a seller to agree, for example, to a $10,000 down payment and a note for $40,000 when the seller must liquidate $20,000 in debts at the time of sale. A more logical approach for the seller would be to shift the $20,000 indebtedness to the buyer and reciprocally reduce the financed amount to $20,000.

When a sale of corporate shares occurs, the existing liabilities would normally remain with the corporation and be reflected in a reduced purchase price for the shares. The only concern of the seller in this situation would be those debts on which the seller would remain liable if unpaid by the buyer. Here, the seller would normally be protected by the buyer's indemnity.

Faster Payback

Short-term seller financing poses considerably less risk than does long-term financing because accelerated payments leaves a smaller unpaid balance in later years (three to five years after the sale) when the business is most likely to fail. However, the seller must bear in mind that rapid payback demands can itself create the insolvency and the inability to pay a loan otherwise manageable if extended over a longer term.

Absent other factors, the loan term should correspond to the projected cash flow available to retire the seller's note. Frequently, balloon notes can resolve both the buyer's immediate cash flow limitations and the objective of the seller to be paid within a reasonably short time. For example, the seller may negotiate a loan carrying a 10-year amortization schedule for 3 years but fully payable at the end of the third year. The premise is that the business will then be sufficiently positioned to refinance and pay the seller fully.

Obtain Adequate Collateral

There is no substitute for adequate collateral to reduce risk and protect a seller. Even a financially strong buyer may become insolvent, and it is then that the seller must look to pledged assets to recover his or her loan (Figure 8–2).

Drafting the financing documents are necessarily left to the attorneys for the buyer and seller, but as a negotiating point, the seller should bargain for a pledge of sufficient business assets

FIGURE 8-2

**BUSINESS LOAN
COLLATERAL VALUE ANALYSIS**

Business Assets Pledged	Fair Market Value	Auction or Liquidation Value
Accounts receivable	$	$
Inventory		
Fixtures and equipment		
Motor vehicles		
Real estate		
Other:		
Subtotals:	$_____	$_____
Personal Assets Pledged		
Real estate (less prior mortgages) Securities and stocks Others:		
Subtotals	$_____	$_____
Total:		

with a liquidation value at least equivalent to the loan amount. The value of the collateral may be increased by an assignment of lease, pledge of shares of stock, or other terms allowing the seller to reacquire and operate the business easily upon default.

When the buyer is a corporation, the seller should, of course, require personal guarantees from its principals, as well as guarantees from corporate affiliates. Frequently, a buyer will also pledge personal assets such as real estate or securities. These stricter terms should be insisted upon by the seller where the buyer is negotiating for a leveraged acquisition, where the business assets are inadequate collateral for the financing, or where the buyer has an unproven track record in the successful management of a business.

THE FINANCING CHECKLIST

The financing checklist is essential to both buyer and seller as an aid to negotiate the financing terms:

A. The amount to be financed:
   1. Adjustments to amount
   2. Additional charges or credits
B. The term
   1. Rights to accelerate payments
   2. Application of prepayments
   3. Balloon provisions
C. Payment schedule
   1. Deferred payments
   2. Frequency of payments
   3. Interim lump-sum payments toward principal
D. Interest rates
   1. Tied to prime
   2. Other structured interest
E. Default provisions
   1. Nonpayment and cure periods
   2. Death of guarantors
   3. Insolvency
   4. Material change in financial condition

    5. Breach of security agreement or other collateral agreements
    6. Breach to senior lenders
F. Security agreement on business assets
    1. Subordination to primary lenders
    2. Collateral covered
    3. Obligations covered
    4. Asset maintenance
    5. Insurance requirements
    6. Other default provisions
    7. Lease assignments as security
G. Guarantors
    1. Identification
    2. Credit investigation
H. Guarantor collateral
    1. Personal assets to be pledged
    2. Stock pledges
 I. Insurance on principals
    1. Amount

EXTERNAL SOURCES OF FINANCING

Finance books are replete with the many diverse sources of small business financing. As a practical matter, the buyer for the small business has few sources to choose from, and each of these lenders are asset-based, relying primarily on tangible collateral to make the loan. The scarcity of loan sources in the small business field explains in part the popularity of seller financing. It is not that it is always desirable but rather that it is all that may be obtainable. And as many small business buyers have discovered, the only other likely lenders may be relatives or friends.

    If we are, for our purposes, to define a small business as one grossing under $1 million or $2 million annually or perhaps requiring an acquisition loan under $200,000, then commercial banks and SBA guaranteed loans remain two other prime candidates. A study of over 500 small business acquisitions reveals that these two sources account for 85 percent of all external debt funding. Nevertheless, other sources do exist, and the buyer should understand the lending characteristics of each.

Banks

Commercial banks are by far the most common external source of small business acquisition loans.

As asset-based lenders, banks generally set loan limits proportional to the liquidation value of the pledged assets. However, some banks will lend above liquidation values when the acquired business has a strong earnings record and the buyer has a good track record. For this reason, the bank's primary consideration will be verification of the assets and their value, should a forced sale become necessary. For more speculative loans, the bank may require a pledge of personal assets such as a home or securities as additional collateral. Once personal collateral is pledged, the bank may increase the line of credit to reflect the added value of these personal assets; however, other banks prefer to limit the loan to the value of personal assets, placing little value on business assets. This latter type of loan is, of course, really in the nature of a personal loan, although the loan may still be structured as a business loan.

The selection of the right bank can be an important consideration. The seller's bank is the logical starting point because it is familiar with the business. Local banks are preferred to distant banks since local banks are community-oriented and knowledgeable of local market conditions. Proximity is also important because the bank will also expect to be used as the depository bank.

Most small business buyers prefer smaller banks to their larger metropolitan counterparts because their size creates a more logical match. While the size of the bank probably is not decisive on whether a loan will be granted, it may be true that a smaller bank is capable of developing a closer relationship with the account and greater flexibility, should later problems arise.

SBA Business Loans

The SBA offers several types of loans to start, acquire, or expand a business. Buyers unsuccessful with direct bank borrowing usually consider SBA financing as their next alternative.

There is one practical reason why SBA loans are not widely used in business acquisitions: It can take the SBA anywhere from two to six months to approve a loan, and few sellers will allow the buyer the extended time to satisfy their financing needs. This is perhaps the most important point for a seller to bear in mind if the sale is conditional upon SBA financing.

Most SBA loans are participatory through local banks rather than loans made directly by the SBA. The prerequisite for an SBA guaranteed loan is that two banks must first refuse the loan. The SBA then agrees to guarantee the bank loan, adding 0.5 percent interest as payment to the SBA for the guarantee. The SBA guarantee is limited to 90 percent of the loan, thereby splitting the risk 90:10 between itself and the participating bank who actually loans the funds and administers the loan.

Under exceptional circumstances, the SBA will make direct, rather than participatory, loans. However, these are usually reserved for businesses in more depressed locations and thus cannot qualify for even a participatory loan. Direct SBA loans represent such a small percentage of the SBA portfolio that few business transfers rely on this type of loan.

The SBA loan does offer at least one important advantage over bank financing. The SBA routinely allows for a 7-to-10-year payback period, whereas bank loans typically have a 5-year maturity. This extended term can be important for easing cash flow for the newly acquired business.

Aside from the slightly higher interest and inevitable delays in obtaining SBA financing approval, the SBA loan signals one other problem: The SBA, as its very purpose, deals in the more speculative and risky loan that banks refuse. The very fact that the business cannot qualify for bank financing signifies a perceived risk justifying a careful reconsideration of the acquisition or the financing requested.

Commercial Loan Companies

Larger acquisitions in the $300,000 to $2 million range may look to commercial loan companies for borrowing. Walter E. Heller & Co., James Tolcott Business Finance, Aetna Business Credit, ITT, Commercial Credit Business Loans, and other firms have offices throughout the country, and smaller counterparts exist locally, all of whom actively pursue acquisition loans for the purchase of midsized companies.

Because commercial loan companies deal in larger loans, they are generally more flexible than banks in their lending arrangements and are often better able to design a loan package more responsive to the buyer's needs. Their flexibility allows these firms to consider leveraged buyouts or the more creative financing arrangements unacceptable to more conservative banks.

In exchange for the higher risk, loan companies may charge 3 to 8 percent higher interest than banks, demand closer control over the business, and even bargain for an equity interest in the business as a condition for the loan. This feature of equity participation does not put them on par with SBIC and venture capital groups, as commercial loan companies view themselves primarily as lenders, whereas venture capitalists are equity-oriented, although both use a mix of "loan" and "equity" in their financing arrangements.

Factors

Consider factoring as a form of financing when receivables are the primary asset. Firms such as New York's Meinhard-Commercial Corporation will lend up to 85 percent against current receivables. Banks, on the other hand, may limit loans to 50 to 60 percent of receivable values. Oftentimes, the buyer can achieve greater borrowing leverage by pledging tangible assets to a bank on an installment loan basis while factoring receivables. A factoring arrangement, even when necessary to fund the acquisition, may be essential to sustain cash flow after acquisition and therefore actively considered in the buyer's total financial planning.

Leasing Firms

Financing the equipment-intensive business? Investigate the services of one of a burgeoning number of leasing firms. Commercial leasing firms may loan up to 80 percent of the fair market value of equipment, or they may agree to acquire the equipment and lease it back to the buyer under a sale-leaseback arrangement.

PREPARE A WINNING LOAN PROPOSAL

Whether you seek financing from a bank, the SBA, or a finance company, you will need a well-designed loan proposal to be successful.

Most loan applications are declined for no other reason than because the applicant failed to provide the lender sufficient documentation to justify the loan. While large corporations understand the need for a well-presented loan proposal, less experienced buyers seeking capital to acquire a smaller firm often approach a lender much as they would if they were seeking a car loan or home mortgage.

Preparing a well-documented loan proposal need not be too burdensome a task. Most of the information and documentation has already been gathered during your evaluation of the business and only requires compilation in a logical manner to be turned into a winning loan proposal that should feature these items:

Credit and Personal History

1. Name and address
2. Marital status
3. Employment history
4. Education
5. Personal assets and liabilities
6. Military status
7. Bank references
8. Credit references
9. Outstanding debts and obligations

Business History

1. Name and address of business
2. Narrative description of business
3. History and age of business
4. Financial statements for prior three years
5. Tax returns for prior three years
6. Summary of proposed business changes
7. Capital improvements required

    8. Pro forma balance sheet
    9. Pro forma income statement
  10. Pro forma cash flow statement
  11. Lease or proposed lease terms

Terms of Sale

1. Sales price
2. Method of transfer (shares of stock or assets)
3. Buyer's investment
4. Other financing
5. Date of proposed purchase
6. Copies of letter of intent or agreement

Collateral for Loan

1. Description of business assets
2. List of major assets
3. Acquisition or replacement cost of principal assets
4. Liquidation value of assets
5. Insurability of collateral
6. Financial statements of guarantors

Proposed Loan

1. Amount of loan
2. Loan period
3. Interest
4. Guarantors to loan
5. Collateral to be pledged
6. Other loan terms
7. Date for loan approval

Beyond the Three C's of Credit

Approval of the loan depends on the lender's assessment of the traditional three C's of credit. The lender must first be satisfied that the applicant is *creditworthy*, that the business has adequate *cash flow* to perform on the loan, and that there is sufficient *collateral* pledged to secure the loan. But lenders do look deeper and may shift their emphasis among the various considerations. Some lenders, for example, place priority on the quality of management; others are more concerned with the stability of earnings; and other asset-based lenders rely largely on the collateral as the essential ingredient for lending, with all other factors of secondary importance. Therefore, it is important to match your deal to the right lender, and this means knowing what each will look for.

Borrowing should not be considered an adversarial relationship. Lenders share your concern for the success of the venture, for that is the only way the loan can be repaid. In many cases, lenders will turn down a loan because they see fundamental flaws in the acquisition. The contribution of a prospective lender in evaluating an acquisition is indeed valuable. The opinion of the lender essentially makes him or her part of the acquisition team and one who may be most experienced and objective in spotting potential pitfalls.

NEGOTIATING LOAN TERMS

Buyers anxious for an acquisition loan often overlook the need to negotiate the loan as thoroughly as they do the purchase of the business itself. Take your time. It may be necessary to shop several prospective lenders before you will find the best available loan. Aside from testing the loan market, you will benefit from talking to as many lenders as possible, as you will see the wide range of terms available only by shopping. What terms should you negotiate?

Amount Financed

1. Will the borrowed amount equal your total financing needs?
2. Will you be allowed an additional line of credit above the initial amount borrowed? How much? On what terms?
3. Will additional lines of credit be secured or unsecured? Will it be at the same or a different interest rate?

4. Can you refinance back to the original amount once the loan balance decreases?

Interest

1. Is the interest adjustable or fixed?
2. If the interest is adjustable, does it have a "cap" and a "floor," defining the upper and lower range?
3. How is the prime rate determined?
4. How often is the interest rate subject to adjustment?
5. Will interest be reduced as the loan balance decreases?
6. Is the interest competitive with rates charged by other lenders?
7. Will the loan require the payment of "points," loan fees, or origination fees?

Term of Loan

1. Is the term of sufficient length to be amortized from projected cash flow?
2. If a shorter-term loan, is the loan automatically renewable? What are the terms for renewal?

Payment Schedule

1. Are payments made monthly or quarterly?
2. Is the loan on a direct reduction basis as to principal payments?
3. If a renewable loan, what amortization schedule will apply to principal during the original term? What amortization on the extended term?
4. Can the loan be prepaid without penalty?

Collateral

1. What collateral must be pledged for the loan?
2. Will the lender release the collateral or subordinate its security on the collateral upon reduction of the loan? What are the terms and conditions for release or subordination?
3. Are you required to maintain collateral at defined levels?

4. If accounts receivable are to be financed, which receivables qualify?
5. What guarantors are required for the loan? Will the guarantees be absolute or limited?
6. Are the guarantors obligated to pledge personal assets? Will these assets be released upon reduction of the loan balance?

HOW TO STRUCTURE THE ACQUISITION LOAN PROPERLY

The loan should be made by the lender directly to the acquiring entity. The principals of the acquiring entity will ordinarily be required to guarantee the obligation and may additionally be required to pledge personal assets to support the loan. Nevertheless, you should not accept the loan in your name for purposes of reinvesting into the acquiring entity.

There are several advantages for this recommendation. With the acquiring corporation as the borrower, the lender can obtain a direct mortgage on business assets. This helps shield you as a guarantor from a deficiency on the loan, should the business fail, because under a bankruptcy the lender would be the first paid from the liquidation of business assets, leaving either less or no balance on the loan. From a tax aspect, the corporation as the obligor on the loan would be allowed the interest deduction with no taxable consequence to you as the owner.

The structure becomes equally important when funds are invested personally by the principal. The buyer must initially decide how to apportion investment between debt and equity.

As a minimum requirement, limit not less than 10 percent of your initial capitalization to equity in the business. A more leveraged capitalization will result in disqualification of the allocation as creating a "thinly capitalized corporation" under the Internal Revenue Code. Certain states have their own strict capitalization requirements. The buyer conservatively desiring to allocate as much investment as possible as debt should follow a 20:80 or perhaps 30:70 ratio, with the larger amount representing loans to the corporation and the lesser payment the price paid for the corporate shares.

Your attorney should carefully document loans between your-self and your corporation. For the loans to withstand scrutiny by the Internal Revenue Service, loans should be reduced to a promissory note, bear a competitive interest (in excess of 10 per-cent), and require repayment on a fixed schedule within a reasonable time. The principal may also consider a "split" approach to capitalization, providing the equity one or two months before the loan. This time differential can be important in sustaining the validity of a subsequent loan.

The safest way to loan to your own corporation is to pledge your personal assets to the lender, who will then loan an equiva-lent amount to your corporation. Structured in this manner, your loan is protected by the same business collateral securing the lender's original loan. You cannot achieve this same protection by lending directly to your own corporation on a secured basis, as stockholder or "insider" loans are usually set aside and subordi-nated to the claims of nonaffiliated creditors, should a business failure result.

DO THE NUMBERS WORK?

It is only after the total financing for the venture reaches the for-mative stage that you can measure the capabilities of the busi-ness to pay the proposed financing (Figure 8–3). Within this entire area of financing, the one vital role of your accountant is to ascertain that the "numbers work" and that the business can indeed pay committed debt with a reasonable margin of safety.

Many acquisitions are doomed to fail at the outset because no effort was made to assess realistically the ability of the business to retire debt through future cash flow. It is axiomatic that too many buyers and their accountants are too concerned about profit projections rather than cash flow projections. While the business may attain its profit goals, it's of little consequence without adequate cash flow to meet its obligations.

Cash flow projection needed to validate future loan perform-ance must necessarily extend to three years or profile at least the earlier years when loan balances are highest. Although financ-ing may extend five years or more, a cash flow over that same extended period becomes too speculative to be meaningful.

FIGURE 8-3

CASH FLOW/DEBT SERVICE
ANALYSIS

	19 ____	19 ____	19 ____	19 ____
Total receipts	____	____	____	____
Disbursements	____	____	____	____
Cost of sales	____	____	____	____
Total expenses (minus depreciation and interest on loans)	____	____	____	____
Capital expenditures	____	____	____	____
Other	____	____	____	____
Total disbursements	____	____	____	____
Total cash flow before debt service	____	____	____	____
Annual payments on debt service	____	____	____	____
Net cash flow after debt service	____	____	____	____

The feasibility of financing should be based on the most cautious or conservative projections possible. Buyers, for their part, have the optimistic tendency to work their calculations backward and thus inflate projected sales to cover debt service. When projections prove less than accurate, the buyer is left with the alternatives of collapsing the business, modifying the debt through voluntary agreement with its lenders, achieving forced restructuring through reorganization proceedings, or adding further equity capital via the owners. No matter which remedy is employed, it nevertheless points to poor initial financial planning.

The trend in small business acquisitions is toward increased leverage, with buyers preferring to invest as little of their own money as possible. This same trend can be seen even in large acquisitions, with an estimated half of all such buyouts made with an equity investment of 5 percent or less. Leveraged buyouts

(LBOs), as they are conventionally called, have become a sign of the times.

A convincing case can be made for leverage as a financing strategy. First, a reduced investment means reduced risk. Second, a small down payment allows you to retain reserve capital for growth or unanticipated contingencies. Finally, you may be able to acquire a far larger business with the same limited capital. The downside, of course, is that excessive leverage may leave the business undercapitalized and unable to pay obligations as they fall due. For the acquisition to work, the business will require additional investment and reduced debt.

Will the financing for your acquisition work?

SUMMING UP

1. Consider the total capital you need to buy and operate the business effectively.
2. Seller financing can be the best financing you can obtain.
3. Understand what a bank and other lenders look for before you apply for a loan.
4. Don't be afraid to negotiate loan terms. It can save you a considerable amount of money.
5. Do the numbers work? Financing has no value if you cannot repay the loan.

CHAPTER 9

POINTERS FOR AN IRONCLAD PURCHASE AGREEMENT

STRUCTURING THE DEAL

Before reaching final agreement, the parties must decide how the business will be legally transferred, as the structure of the transaction involves important legal, financial, and tax issues.

For the smaller business, a sale can occur through one of two methods: transfer of assets or sale of corporate shares.

Transfer of Assets

If the seller operates as a sole proprietorship or as a partnership, the sale must be handled as a sale of assets, as there is no corporation in existence, and therefore, you cannot acquire its shares. Under a transfer of assets, the seller conveys to the buyer title to specified business assets. The buyer ordinarily sets up his or her own corporation to accept title; enters into new leases and contracts with employees, customers, and suppliers; and begins as a new business entity.

Sale of Corporate Shares

Should the business be incorporated, the transfer can still be through a sale of assets, but it can also be through sale of all or part of the corporate shares. Essentially, ownership and management of the existing corporation change. The new stockholders as the buyers then elect new officers and directors and continue operating through the existing corporation.

There can be a modified approach to a direct sale of shares. The selling stockholders may sell their shares to the corporation, who redeems or acquires the shares for a stated price. The buyer simultaneously acquires new shares in the corporation and thus assumes ownership and control of the existing corporation. The redemption sale, as it is called, is commonly used when the selling stockholder wants to secure his or her financing with a mortgage on business assets. In other respects, the redemption sale can be viewed as featuring the same advantages and disadvantages as a direct stock sale.

Which method of transfer will be best for you? One factor alone seldom controls the method of transfer, as there are advantages and disadvantages to either a purchase of assets or a purchase of shares of stock. However, one factor may outweigh others and thus dictate how the transaction is ultimately structured.

What factors should you consider before deciding whether to buy assets or corporate shares?

Factors Influencing Method Selection

Liability Protection

The primary consideration is usually the buyer's concern over unknown or contingent liabilities of the seller, should he or she buy the shares of stock of the seller's corporation. A purchase of assets would better insulate the buyer from the seller's liabilities, provided (1) assets were verified to be clear of liens and encumbrances and (2) strict compliance with the Bulk Sales Act was followed. Assuming the sale was for fair consideration and does not constitute a fraudulent transfer under an asset sale, the buyer has no further concern over the seller's liabilities whether actual, unknown, or contingent. This broad protection argues strongly for an asset sale, and in many instances, a buyer's counsel insists upon an asset sale for this one important reason alone.

A buyer's concern over undisclosed liabilities is far greater under a stock sale since undisclosed creditors can later assert their claims against the acquired corporation. The degree of buyer concern will, of course, depend largely on the alternative forms of protection available to the buyer under a stock sale, should unknown creditors later assert claims against the corporation.

When determining the potential risk imposed by undisclosed or contingent liabilities, the buyer must consider not only his or her available recourse but also the likelihood of whether such claims will occur. To help decide, the buyer's attorney may rely on the buyer's accountant to render an opinion as to whether the seller's corporation is "clean" and appears to have a solvent financial condition and adequate accounting records with evidence that obligations are being liquidated in a current and orderly manner.

Once the buyer is satisfied that the possibility of undisclosed liability is remote and the recourse remedies adequate, the purchase of shares can again be considered a reasonable alternative to an asset sale.

Leases

The lease on the business location is another practical consideration. Under a sale of assets, the buyer will normally be required to obtain a new lease unless the seller has the uncommon right to assign the balance of his or her present lease. Under a purchase of shares of stock, the corporation and its lease remain intact, and landlord approval for the sale is ordinarily not required.

With the seller holding a favorable lease, it is advantageous to acquire the corporation instead of assets, which will require negotiating a new lease. In an era when commercial rents are rapidly escalating, rent increases required under a new lease can be a significant factor. A buyer may nevertheless be required to renegotiate a new lease if the existing lease is near expiration, and in this situation, the lease will remain an unimportant issue when structuring the sale.

Financing

Financing arrangements can help determine whether a sale of assets or shares of stock is preferable. If the corporation has high debt, the buyer can, under a purchase of shares, effectively utilize this debt as a credit to the purchase price, thus lowering the necessary down payment. Although the seller's debts can be assumed by a buyer under a transfer of assets, thus creating the same basic financing arrangement, this strategy is more easily accomplished through a stock sale, because creditor approval of the intended sale is not required.

Should assets of the corporation be secured by security interests or other encumbrances to be assumed by the buyer as part of the purchase price, creditor approval is also required, as a seller cannot legally convey assets subject to encumbrance without approval of its lien holders. Upon notice of a proposed sale, secured creditors often insist upon payment or allow the transfer only upon new and less favorable financing terms. Under circumstances of foreseeable creditor interference, the buyer would plan to acquire corporate shares, thus avoiding the need for secured creditor approval.

Contract Rights

The corporation may also hold certain contract rights such as franchises, distributorship agreements, or supplier contracts that are not assignable without consent. The acquisition of corporate stock will leave these contracts intact, whereas an asset transfer will require assignment approval, which may be unavoidable or available only on less favorable terms.

Employee Benefit Plans

Another issue is the compatibility of the selling corporation's employee benefit plans with the buying corporation's benefit plans. If the selling corporation has benefit plans substantially more expensive than the buyer's, it may be worthwhile to buy its shares and maintain the acquisition as a subsidiary, thereby avoiding the need to "merge" the employees of the acquired company into the more costly benefit program of the acquiring company.

Credit Rating

The corporation's credit rating can be either an advantage or a disadvantage when acquiring shares of stock. A good credit rating favors the purchase of shares. Here the buyer obtains the continued benefit of the seller's established rating, as a newly created corporation organized by the buyer will start with very little available credit.

Conversely, a buyer would wisely rely on a new corporation with no credit rating rather than take over a corporation with an adverse rating. Credit can be an important issue, particularly when credit must be relied upon to compensate for lack of initial working capital.

Corporate Charters and Licenses

Still another situation in which a stock transaction will prove a better method of transfer is when preservation of a corporate charter is important. For example, should the corporation hold a banking or insurance charter or perhaps a liquor license, difficult for the buyer to obtain on its own or under assignment, a convincing case can be made for a stock sale.

Partial Sales

If the parties contemplate a sale of only a portion of the business, it is logical to plan a sale of those particular assets, retaining the corporation intact, under which the seller can continue operation with the remaining assets.

Stockholder Approval

Often the selling corporation is owned by a diverse number of stockholders. Therefore, a sale of stock can only be accomplished by agreement of all stockholders, assuming the buyer has bargained for 100 percent ownership, which is generally true with small businesses.

Should some stockholders refuse to sell their shares, a sale of assets becomes the only alternative, as it requires only a two-thirds vote by stockholders to achieve. The seller and buyer, however, each have responsibility to ascertain that both the corporate authority to sell and the sale itself are proper, to avoid future litigation by the dissenting minority stockholders who oppose the sale.

Considering the numerous factors to be weighed, deciding how the business will be transferred is rarely easy. The problem is further magnified when the buyer prefers one method of transfer, and the seller prefers another. Many transactions fail to close only because the parties cannot agree on the method of transfer, despite agreement on all other terms.

UNDERSTAND THE TAX CONSEQUENCES

What are the tax consequences of the proposed method of transfer? The Tax Reform Act (TRA) of 1986 has played a significant role in the structuring of corporate acquisitions, and therefore it is important that the tax consequences of the transaction be considered carefully. To help understand the impact of the new tax law, you should consult an experienced tax accountant and/or a tax attorney.

The TRA considers most corporate acquisitions to be taxable transactions for the seller if the parties structure them as a purchase of either stock or assets in exchange for cash, promissory notes, or other forms of consideration. Mergers often are deemed nontaxable transactions because they involve exchanging the seller's stock or assets for the purchaser's equity securities or a subsidiary created by the purchaser. In order for a sale to be considered a nontaxable transaction, it must fall within one of several reorganization categories contained in Section 368 of the TRA.

Some of the more important aspects of the TRA that you should consider when structuring the sale of a business are

- The restructuring of individual and corporate tax rates.
- The repeal of the favorable treatment for capital gains.
- The special issues regarding the allocation of a purchase price in asset acquisitions. (Prior to 1986, a buyer and a seller could independently negotiate the allocation of the purchase price to the assets being acquired. Negotiations often would focus on how much of the purchase price would be attributed to intangible assets, such as goodwill, and how much would be attributed to depreciable assets. The TRA now requires that you use a specific formula under the residual method of allocation to determine the purchase price in asset acquisitions.)
- The repeal of the "General Utilities" doctrine, which has resulted in the recognition of a gain or a loss at both the corporate level and the shareholder level on liquidating distributions or sales. (Prior to 1986, there was no "double tax" on gains in connection with liquidating distributions except for recaptured taxes and limited related items. Therefore, in an asset acquisition, a seller could distribute the cash and

other consideration received for his or her assets directly to the company's shareholders, who then would be responsible for taxes only at the personal level.)

DRAFTING THE AGREEMENT

The purchase and sales agreement does more than reduce to writing what the parties have already agreed upon. Corporate, tax, and other problems not raised in earlier negotiations may arise once the contract is about to be prepared. Moreover, the contract continues to define the rights and obligations of the parties long after the sale is completed.

A contract to buy or sell a business, like any other important legal document, must be designed to match the transaction. No two are, or should be, identical. The sample contracts found in Appendixes 1 through 5 are representative. However, you will need a carefully prepared agreement to meet your own needs, so remember it's foolish to play lawyer. Buying or selling a business requires professional assistance. You will need your attorney to prepare your agreement if you are to be protected fully. Work closely with your attorney. A well-prepared agreement is a collaborative effort between attorney and client. Your attorney knows the law but doesn't necessarily know the peculiarities of your business or the specific terms or conditions you need or other legal safeguards vital to protect you on operational matters. Finally, *put it in writing*. The general rule is that if it isn't in writing, it isn't enforceable. All terms of the agreement, and later modifications, should be in writing and also approved by your attorney.

CONTRACTS FOR THE SALE OF ASSETS

Asset transfers are more commonly used for the smaller firm. Contracts for the purchase of assets typically cover these points:

Who Are the Parties to the Agreement?

The agreement should include all parties to the agreement. In addition to a corporate seller and buyer, the principals of the respective entities should join in the agreement to the extent that they will be personally bound on indemnifications, notes, agreements not to compete, and similar personal undertakings. Should the transaction involve business brokers or finders due a commission, they, too, should sign for purposes of assenting to commission agreements.

What Assets Are to Be Sold?

The contract must accurately specify the assets to be sold, for many disputes arise from ambiguity on what is to be sold or retained. Seldom will the transaction involve all assets of the business; therefore, assets to be sold and those to be retained by the seller should be itemized. Which of these assets will or will not be sold under your agreement?

- Cash on hand
- Accounts receivable
- Notes receivable
- Securities or interests in other entities
- Prepaid deposits and utilities
- Tax rebates
- Insurance claims
- Litigation claims
- Inventory
- Furniture and fixtures
- Equipment
- Motor vehicles
- Leasehold improvements
- Real estate
- Goodwill
- Business name
- Patents
- Trademarks
- Copyrights
- Customers lists
- Trade secrets
- Franchise or distributorship rights
- Licenses and permits
- Transfer of telephone numbers

Sellers normally retain liquid assets such as cash, receivables, prepaid expenses, and securities. Real estate may also be retained by the seller, as it oftentimes is owned personally. In many instances, the sale will include nothing more than the transfer of inventory, furniture, fixtures, equipment, and the name and goodwill as essential operating assets, although the division of assets always remains the essence of the agreement. Identify, where possible, each major asset to be sold. To avoid later conflict, a detailed description of each major item of equipment and fixtures to be sold should be annexed to the agreement.

What Items Are Excluded from Sale?

Certain pieces of property used in the business may not be owned by the seller and are neither intended to be sold nor retained by the seller. Leased equipment, consigned goods, and similar items, subject to being reclaimed by a third party, are all examples.

Listing these items in the contract is necessary to disclaim any implied warranty of title. The agreement may also provide that the buyer shall return these leased items to their respective owners upon demand and to indemnify the seller for any failure to do so. The seller should also preserve his or her right to return these nonowned items prior to closing unless the buyer previously made arrangements to enter into new leases or consignment contracts.

What Is the Purchase Price?

The purchase price can be formulated several ways.

Fixed Price
In its simplest form, the purchase price can be stated as a fixed dollar amount established prior to contract.

Formula Price
The formula price contemplates the payment of a fixed price whose amount cannot be determined prior to closing. An example might be a price based upon actual inventory, receivables, or assumed liabilities at the time of closing. This may also be treated as a fixed price subject to adjustment. Here the contract

should clearly specify the procedures and formula for establishing the price, the method for determining the amount or value of each item on which the formula is based, and the acceptable range of the formula price.

Contingent Price
Here, price is determined in whole or in part on the basis of the earnings (often called an "earn-out"), volume, or commissions of the acquired business for a specified formula period following the closing. The contingent price becomes payable at stated intervals during or at the end of the stated formula period. The contingent price should clearly define the method of computation and the seller's rights to an accounting to determine compliance. The contingent price may also be combined with a fixed or formula price.

How Will the Purchase Price Be Paid?

Fixed or formula prices may be paid through:

Lump-Sum Payment
The payment of the total purchase price (less deposits) is to be paid fully at closing.

Installment Payments
Here the purchase price is paid in installments over a period of time after closing. The agreement usually provides for a certain down payment at the time of closing, with the balance financed. When a formula price is used, the parties should state whether the adjustments will change the down payment or the amount to be financed. When it will change the financed amount, specify whether it will extend the installment period, allowing payments to remain the same, or whether the installment period will remain the same, increasing payments.

On installment contracts, also define the terms of financing, including the guarantees and the security for the note. Each of the financing documents due to be signed at closing should be approved at time of contract to avoid later dispute as to their terms.

Deposits paid prior to closing would, of course, be reflected as a credit against the total required down payment. The deposit should be sufficiently large to commit the buyer to the transaction. Brokers usually hold the deposit, although in the absence of brokers or an escrow bank, the attorney for the seller may hold the deposit. Large deposits should be placed in an interest-bearing account, with interest to follow principal. The escrow agents should become parties to the agreement, reciting their obligation to release the escrowed deposit and procedures to be followed in the event of a dispute. The parties should also stipulate whether the buyer will forfeit all or part of the deposit as liquidated damages in the event of breach and thus avoid further claims.

How Will Liabilities Be Handled?

If assets are intended to be sold free and clear of all the seller's liabilities, the agreement should so specify. The buyer will need to take all required steps to be protected from the seller's liabilities. This may include compliance with the State Bulk Sales Act (notice to creditors of the intended sale); the issue of indemnifications to the buyer from the seller and its principals; and the right to offset against notes due the seller, should creditor claims arise.

Contracts usually provide that the seller may use sales proceeds to discharge liens or encumbrances at the time of closing. Under this procedure, the buyer coordinates payment, ensuring receipt of the appropriate discharges.

Liabilities may be assumed by the buyer and credited toward the purchase price. The contract should then specify the approximate amount of liabilities to be assumed and the maximum amount allowed. While the specific liabilities to be assumed are usually unknown until closing, the contract should at least define the type of liability. At closing, the seller will provide the actual list of liabilities to be assumed by the buyer, which is then incorporated as part of the contract. Should liabilities be assumed, the buyer may want to reserve the right to compromise or settle liabilities without a subsequent price readjustment and provided the compromise does not create residual liability to the seller. This provision is desirable where liabilities are excessive and a settlement with creditors is appropriate.

The seller will reciprocally want protection on assumed liabilities. This should certainly include indemnification from both the buyer entity and its principals. The contract may also require payment to creditors within a specified time and proof of payment furnished to the seller. Further, the seller may require security agreements, a pledge of the shares of the buyer entity, or other collateral to ensure the buyer's performance under its agreement to pay or discharge the seller's debts.

Oftentimes the parties elect a split approach, with the buyer assuming certain liabilities and the seller others. The seller will, of course, want to pay liabilities directly to which he or she has personal liability such as guaranteed debts and tax obligations.

What Representations and Warranties Should Be Made?

Representations and warranties must be expressly contained within the contract to become the basis for a later claim of misrepresentation, fraud, or deceit. Should the seller corporation be liquidated, or one with negligible assets, the principals should join in the warranty to grant the buyer adequate recourse.

Seller's Warranties

A comprehensive checklist of possible seller warranties include the following:

1. The seller has good and marketable title.
2. The assets are sold free and clear of liens and encumbrances.
3. The seller has full authority to sell and transfer the assets.
4. The seller, as a corporate entity, is in good standing.
5. The seller's financial statements present fairly and accurately the financial position of the company as of its date, and there are no material adverse changes thereafter.
6. Contract rights and leases to be assigned are as represented and in good standing.
7. There is no material litigation pending against the company.
8. All licenses and permits required to conduct the business are in good standing.
9. There are no liabilities other than as represented.
10. The seller's name does not constitute an infringing use on the name of any other entity.

11. All equipment and fixtures shall be sold in good working order.

The parties may elect to define certain assets to be sold under the warranty provisions. For example, the seller may warrant inventory levels or the face value of collectible accounts receivable at the time of takeover. As a practical matter, the seller cannot know in advance their actual values at time of sale, and therefore the warranty may be stated as falling within a range.

The seller should also warrant that certain documents such as financial statements, tax returns, leases, and contracts to be assigned are as represented. Wherever practical, these documents should be annexed to the contract as exhibits.

The agreement should further specify the warranties intended to survive the closing and those considered satisfied upon closing. The buyer will ordinarily insist that all warranties survive closing except for those that can be readily verified at time of closing. An example of the latter may be the warranty that the equipment is in good working order.

Buyer's Warranties
In a cash acquisition, the buyer's warranties are generally limited to those relating to its authority to consumate the transactions under the contract of sale. Where the seller is to provide financing, the warranty should include representations that the buyer's financial condition is as represented. Buyer's warranties can also protect the seller in the event that the purchase is not completed. The buyer, for example, may warrant it will not use the seller's trade secrets, induce employees to leave the seller's employ, or reveal confidential information. To ensure that the buyer will not unfairly compete with the seller in the event that the purchase is canceled, the buyer may covenant not to compete on narrowly defined terms and may further warrant not to enter into a lease for the seller's premises except through acquisition for the seller's business.

Is the Agreement Conditional?

Conditions make performance contingent upon certain events occurring and allows the termination of the contract without penalty, should the conditions not be satisfied. Unlike warranties that are generally within the control of the parties, conditions are ordinarily noncontrollable and usually depend on performance by a third party not a party to the contract.

Most conditions are imposed by the buyer, who must consider every occurrence upon which the transaction should or must be dependent, following this checklist:

1. Seller's warranties and representations shall remain accurate and true at date of closing.
2. No materially adverse change in seller's financial condition occurred prior to closing.
3. The seller has performed all its affirmative and negative obligations under the agreement.
4. The seller provided all required documents contemplated by the agreement, at time of closing.
5. Required opinion letters are obtained at closing.
6. An assignment of lease or new lease on terms acceptable to buyer is obtained.
7. Satisfactory financing for the transaction is obtained.
8. Approval by governmental agencies, if required, is obtained.
9. Licenses and permits can be transferred or obtained.

This list, of course, exemplifies only the more commonly encountered conditions. Possible conditions are limited only by the needs of the particular transaction.

Conditions, when stated in vague terms, serve only as escape clauses for a buyer wrongfully seeking to terminate the contract without penalty. Therefore, conditions should be both reasonable and sufficiently specific to determine whether satisfied. For example, a condition for financing on terms satisfactory to the buyer will easily allow the buyer the opportunity to avoid performance arbitrarily by rejecting even the most favorable financing. A preferred approach would specify financing terms to be obtained. The contract should also require the parties to expend "best efforts" to satisfy their respective conditions.

Should the contract impose conditions over which the seller has no control (financing, satisfactory leases, and the like), the seller must assess the likelihood that the buyer can satisfy the conditions. The seller certainly should not change position in reliance of a sale until all the conditions have been satisfied. The practical approach is for the seller to impose a specific time period for the buyer to satisfy the conditions. On the specified date, the buyer should be bound either to confirm satisfaction of the conditions or to terminate the contract with a return of the deposit. The parties may agree to extend the date for performance, but this should be agreed to only when the seller is convinced the buyer is making satisfactory progress in resolving the conditions. The seller may require the buyer to forfeit a portion of the deposit if the condition is not then satisfied by the extended date, although this greatly depends upon the bargaining positions of the respective parties.

What Activities Are Allowed or Prohibited?

Covenants include both required and prohibited acts by either party pending the closing or thereafter.

Most covenants are to be performed by the seller and relate to the operation of the business pending closing. These covenants are designed to prevent the seller from impairing the goodwill or adversely affecting the financial or legal structure of the business. On asset transfers of a small business, such covenants commonly deal with the maintenance of business hours, inventory levels, credit and service policies, adherence to existing prices, and the continuity of other operational matters designed to retain customers.

Negative covenants during the transition period customarily have the same desired objective of prohibiting acts that would diminish goodwill or impair the value of the business. For example, a seller should agree not to terminate key employees without cause, disrupt favorable relationships with customers, or disclose trade secrets to others.

Covenants will also apply to acts to be performed at closing. Normally, the agreement will specify the respective documents to be delivered by the buyer and seller. The listing will extend not only to closing documents but also to the delivery of specified books and records relating to the conduct of the business.

The covenant not to compete is the most important postclosing covenant. When negotiating the covenant not to compete, the agreement should specify each of the parties required to execute the covenant, and they should become signatories to the agreement. Where employees are expected to execute this covenant, obtain their signatures in advance of the closing.

The covenant not to compete should specifically state its consideration, even if nominal. Unless clearly stated as a separate agreement, the Internal Revenue Service may allocate a portion of the goodwill toward the covenant and thus treat it as ordinary income rather than as capital gains from the sale of the business. The covenant should also be specific as to the prohibited activities and impose reasonable time and geographic limitations. Remedies for breach should also be carefully defined. As with preclosing covenants, the seller may want notice of breach and an opportunity to cure any claimed breach. Thereafter, the buyer will want injunctive relief without a requirement to post bond, in addition to legal remedies for damages. The covenant may also stipulate whether or not the buyer will have the right to delay or set off payments due the seller on a purchase money note, should the seller be in alleged breach of the covenant. Reciprocally, the seller should be released from the covenant upon default by the buyer of any note payments due the seller.

What If There Is Casualty to the Business?

The contract must contemplate the possibility of casualty to the assets prior to closing. A common provision is for the seller to maintain adequate insurance and upon casualty to assign either the claim or proceeds to the buyer—or at the option of the buyer, the agreement may be terminated. Minor casualty, usually casualty to assets comprising less than 5 or 10 percent of the aggregate value of the assets to be sold, may be an exception. Here the buyer should be limited either to accept the insurance proceeds or to accept an adjustment to price. The seller may also reserve the right to replace damaged assets with assets of equivalent value.

Casualty to the premises should give the buyer the same rights as casualty to assets. This may be particularly important where the casualty would terminate the lease or cause business interruption. In this event, the parties may contractually agree to extend the closing for a reasonable time to allow the seller to restore the premises to its prior condition.

Where the business is located within a shopping center or depends on a larger nearby business to create traffic, the buyer may extend the casualty provision to other key tenants or areas of the shopping center, allowing the buyer either to terminate the contract or to defer closing until the designated premises or cotenant have resumed operation.

How Will Brokers Be Paid?

Brokers or finders entitled to commission should become parties to the agreement. Their participation is necessary to confirm the commission arrangement and their obligations as escrow agents where they hold deposits.

Oftentimes, cobrokers are involved, where one broker provided the business listing and the other the buyer. With the division of commissions decided between the cobrokers, the cobroker should join in the agreement.

While brokers are entitled to a commission upon producing a buyer ready, willing, and able to buy on the offered terms or such substitute terms as the seller may accept, the seller may condition payment to brokers to an actual closing. This would avoid a broker's claim against the seller if for any reason the sale does not occur.

The contract should also provide for the allocation of the deposit between seller and broker in the event of buyer breach and deposit forfeiture. By custom, deposit proceeds are evenly divided between seller and broker; however, this remains a matter of agreement. Similarly, the broker may bargain to participate in any recovery against the buyer for damages arising from a buyer's breach. Here the agreement should clarify the proportionate distribution, the maximum payment to the broker, and adjustment for litigation costs.

What Adjustments Will Be Made at Closing?

Most asset transfers require closing adjustments between seller and buyer at time of closing. Common adjustments include rent, payroll, insurance, utilities, service contracts, license and permit fees, and tax obligations.

Prior to drafting the agreement, the parties should review allocable items with their respective attorneys, as often clients are most familiar with operational items that may require adjustment. The agreement should identify each item subject to adjustment and the adjustment formula when a prorated allocation is not suitable.

The adjustments should recognize the possibility that goods ordered by the seller prior to closing may be received by the buyer after closing and therefore not tabulated in the inventory or accounted for in the price. While the buyer should have the option to reject such goods by return to the supplier, acceptance should constitute a postclosing adjustment requiring payment or credit to the seller unless the goods are paid for by the buyer.

The parties may not be in receipt of all entries by which adjustments can be made at closing. The contract may then provide for escrow of funds to satisfy adjustments payable by the seller and a similar escrow by buyer to ensure performance on its obligations.

When Is the Closing Date?

Buyer's and seller's alike are typically anxious to close on the transaction but often unrealistic in their assessment of the time required to complete the legal work, obtain financing, and satisfy other necessary conditions. Plan a realistic closing date and provide flexibility when the closing becomes necessarily delayed for reasons beyond the control of either party.

It is unquestionably best to close as rapidly as possible after agreement is reached because so many problems can develop during the preclosing stage.

On occasion, one or both parties will prefer a delayed closing. For example, the parties may reach agreement in October but for tax reasons negotiate a closing to occur early in January, perhaps to allow the seller the benefit of a heavy selling season. Frequently, a concession that allows one party to capture peak-season sales may greatly influence the price or other terms of the deal.

Unless strict performance for a timely closing is required for some compelling reason, it is best to build flexibility into the closing date. Allowing an automatic extension of 15 to 30 days is reasonable if coupled with a notice requirement, should extension become necessary.

When scheduling the closing, some thought should be given to the most convenient closing date. It is usually best to schedule a closing for the commencement of a new business period, such as the first business day of a month. This makes the calculation of adjustments far easier.

While it is generally true that a scheduled closing date is at best only a target, the parties should execute formal extensions when required. Confirm verbal agreements to extend by letter correspondence.

AGREEMENTS TO TRANSFER SHARES OF STOCK

Many contract terms applicable to asset transfers apply equally to stock transfer agreements; however, the priorities become somewhat different. Asset transfers may be far less complex, as the buyer's primary concern is the assurance of clear title and continuity of the business in a reasonably stable manner pending the closing. Since the stock transfer contemplates the takeover of the seller's corporation, the buyer's objectives include concern over every facet of corporate structure and activity.

A model contract contained in Appendix 1 shows the scope of a relatively simple stock transfer agreement. Stock transfer agreements minimally include these points:

What Stock Is to Be Transferred?

The agreement must specify the stock interest being transferred with certain warranties relating to the shares of stock, including:

- Warranties that the shares to be sold will represent, at time of closing, a stated percentage ownership of the corporation, all classes of stock inclusive
- Warranties that the seller has and shall deliver good title to said shares free of encumbrances, pledge, or other liens
- Warranties that the shares are fully paid and nonassessable

- Warranties that there are no outstanding proxies or other assignment of voting rights attaching to the shares to be sold
- Warranties that all restrictions on transfer imposed by the bylaws or otherwise have been waived, and transfer is thus allowed

How Is the Purchase Price Determined?

Seldom are shares of the closely held corporation sold for a fixed price. Generally, the formula price is used, reflecting the net worth of the corporation at closing.

Although capital assets such as real estate, equipment, and goodwill may have a stipulated value, cash, accounts receivable, and inventory must be determined at closing. Debts will also vary the price. As with asset transfers, the agreement must set forth the method for determining how each will be valued at time of closing.

Larger corporations are oftentimes sold for the book value of the shares at time of closing or based on audited financial statements at an earlier date. This approach has little application to the smaller firm whose assets, including goodwill, are valued as under an asset transfer.

What Warranties Should Apply to the Corporation?

A most important provision in the stock agreement are warranties relating to the legal, financial, and business affairs of the corporation. The buyer will only have these warranties to rely upon if the corporation is discovered to be less than as represented:

- The corporation is in good standing (and in all jurisdictions if a foreign corporation).
- The corporation has good title to all the assets or properties used in connection with the business (except for those delineated as nonowned).
- All required federal and state tax returns have been filed and all monies due paid, and there are no known audits or notices of audit pending.
- All contracts (principal contracts to be specifically identified) are in good standing and not in default or threat of termination.

- All leases are in good standing, without modification or amendment.
- No known proceedings against the corporation by any governmental body or agency exist.
- The corporation is not a party to any litigation (except as may be specified).
- No liens or encumbrances against any asset of the corporation exist (except as may be delineated).
- The corporation is not a party to any contract not subject to termination at will and without penalty (except as may be delineated).
- The corporation has and shall maintain insurance, as specified.
- The corporation has no bonus, profit-sharing, or pension plan, except as specified.
- The financial statements (annexed to the agreement) accurately and fairly represent the financial condition of the corporation as of their date, and no material adverse changes have occurred since.

This list certainly is not all-inclusive, and many other warranties can be considered. Preferably, the buyer's accountant and attorney will identify other warranties appropriate for the transaction, as considerable care should be taken to provide the broadest possible buyer protection.

Two very important additional warranties worthy of discussion refer to liabilities and accounts receivable at time of closing, for both materially determine the purchase price.

Existing liabilities are usually prepared by the seller upon closing and listed as an exhibit to the contract. Nonlisted liabilities or liabilities in excess amounts constitute a breach of the warranty. Under a breach of this warranty, the remedies are normally indemnification, right to set off against notes due the seller, and claims for money damages equivalent to the excess liabilities.

The term *liabilities* under the warranty must be carefully defined and should include: accounts payable; notes payable; expenses payable; taxes accrued to date; rent and occupancy costs accrued to date; loans due officers, directors, stockholders, or any other third party; notes either secured or unsecured; accrued wages; and any other debt or obligation, whether disputed or undisputed, liquidated or unliquidated, contingent or noncontingent, and notwithstanding whether past due, current, or due at a future time, and notwithstanding whether known or unknown.

The seller will equally want protection on indemnified liabilities covered by the warranty. The seller, for example, should have no liability for contingent liabilities adequately insured against. The seller may equally want to limit his or her liability to either the buyer's investment or proceeds derived from the sale by the seller. While not unreasonable, the limitations of liability remain an item for negotiation. At the very least, the seller will want notice of an indemnified liability and the right to defend and settle the claim before the buyer may use self-help to pay or settle the claim and then seek recourse against the seller.

The warranty on accounts receivable and other obligations due the corporation may be handled in a manner similar to liabilities. The closing documents will generally reflect the existing receivables, with the warranty providing for recourse against the seller if receivables remain uncollected within a specified time period. Under this warranty, the buyer will convey to the seller title to the uncollected receivables in exchange for payment. The seller extending financing to the buyer may instead suggest credits to be deducted from the next due installments under the note. Another common approach is for the seller to escrow a reserve against which payment can be made for uncollected receivables.

Since the buyer will ordinarily rely upon certain inventory, liability, and receivable levels to arrive at the contemplated formula price for the shares, it would be appropriate to incorporate a further warranty as to an acceptable range for these assets and liabilities. For example, a depletion of inventory and receivables prior to closing would correspondingly reduce the purchase price but would not be without its adverse impact on future cash flow or ability of the buyer to finance the acquisition.

What Covenants Are Required?

Both affirmative and negative covenants under a stock transfer are largely the same as those found in asset transactions. However, under stock transfers, covenants necessarily expand to protect the buyer from major changes in the financial or legal structure of the corporation to be acquired.

Common additional covenants provide that pending closing the corporation will not undertake or incur

- New indebtedness
- New mortgages
- Extraordinary improvements
- Extraordinary purchases
- Extraordinary disposition of assets
- Defaults on contracts
- Extraordinary contracts
- Redemption of outstanding shares
- Issuance of new shares
- New compensation plans
- Charter or bylaw amendments

How Will Personally Guaranteed Debts Be Handled?

Numerous corporate obligations may impose personal liability upon a selling stockholder. Often, the seller is unaware of previously issued guarantees, only to learn they exist long after the sale when the corporation is in default in its payments. The seller must therefore identify the various personal obligations that will require termination, prior payment, or indemnification under the contract.

Any corporate obligation may be subject to guaranty, and all should be reviewed by the seller. Loans due lending institutions will invariably require the personal guarantees of stockholders. The same is often true of leases on the premises, equipment leases, or other long-term fixed obligations. Nor can it be taken for granted that vendor obligations are without personal guarantees. Suppliers to the small business firm increasingly demand guarantees, which in many instances have been signed years earlier when the business was first started. For this reason, a seller will want to notify vendors that personal guarantees covering future debts are to be terminated upon the closing date. Personal guarantees on utility accounts, money order services, and lottery and other fiduciary accounts must also be extinguished.

The selling stockholder, as a principal corporate officer, will also have statutory liability on federal and state withholding taxes collected from employees, sales and meal tax, unpaid payroll, and in many states, unemployment compensation payments; therefore, these obligations should be fully paid prior to closing.

SUMMING UP

1. Consider carefully whether it is preferable to acquire the seller's assets or corporation.
2. An attorney's representation is essential if your interests are to be protected fully.
3. Make certain the agreement fully reflects the terms of your deal. Verbal terms are generally not binding.
4. An agreement is a blend of legal and business decisions. You and your attorney will need close teamwork.

CHAPTER 10

CLOSING THE TRANSACTION

COORDINATING THE TAKEOVER

The days between signing and closing can be critical. During this period your objectives as a buyer are

- *To identify* previously undiscovered problems with the business requiring either resolution or withdrawal from the deal
- *To learn* the business to ensure an orderly and efficient management transition
- *To verify* that the seller is maintaining the goodwill of the business and complying with contractual terms concerning the operation of the business
- *To coordinate* with the seller all financial and operational activities to position the business for takeover properly

To ensure a smooth ownership transition, the buyer and seller must develop a close and cooperative relationship. Unfortunately, many sellers prefer to insulate the buyer from daily operations for fear of disclosing confidential information on a sale that may not go through or for fear the buyer may withdraw from the deal once exposed to problems that, of course, exist with any business. Because objectives differ, a balanced approach is for the seller and buyer to meet periodically after business hours or at a different location to discuss and review key business developments and coordinate and resolve items of transitional importance.

But transitional complications can be greatly minimized during the transitional period if the buyer and seller work within these guidelines:

1. New or replacement personnel should be approved by the buyer. It's unfair to newly hired employees to discover

that they'll shortly have a new employer who may not need their services and equally unfair to the new employer who may not want their services.

2. Major contracts, bids, and orders accepted by the firm should also be approved by the buyer if the contract is to be performed, in whole or in part, after the closing.

3. Collection procedures on overdue accounts and elimination of credit to existing customers should be approved by and coordinated with the buyer, as an overly aggressive collection policy destroys goodwill.

4. The buyer should identify suppliers with whom he or she doesn't intend to do business and thereby allow the seller to return excess or unsalable items to these suppliers to settle accounts while the seller still has leverage with these suppliers.

5. Inventories should be closely adjusted to the inventory guaranteed to exist at closing. A coordinated "sell down" of excess inventory will identify lines the buyer wants reduced or eliminated.

6. Special orders, merchandising deals, new product lines, or other purchases out of the ordinary course should be first cleared by the buyer.

7. No change in service policies, pricing, or business hours that may adversely affect goodwill should occur without advance buyer approval.

As can be seen from this brief transitional checklist, the objectives of the seller and buyer in operating the business can be quite different. The one best way to avoid transitional problems is to close on the transaction as quickly as possible. The more delayed the closing, the greater the likelihood of problems, since change occurs in any business and not all will meet with the buyer's approval. For his or her part, the seller must watch for signs that the buyer is vacillating or may withdraw from the deal, as a less committed buyer should be allowed less voice and control in the management of the company during the transitional period. Frequently, the buyer will make the contract conditional upon such contingencies as financing or satisfactory leases.

Therefore, the seller does not have a truly committed buyer until all such conditions have been fully satisfied and the buyer has advanced a sufficiently large deposit to be bound to the contract firmly.

Should the seller become convinced that the buyer cannot satisfy the conditions, the seller should exercise his or her right to terminate the contract after the date for satisfaction expires. This does not suggest that the seller should discourage further efforts by the buyer. The approach should be that should the buyer eventually satisfy all conditions and be prepared to close, the contract may be subject to restoration, provided the seller has not entered into agreement with a new buyer. However, in the interim, the seller retains the right to place the business on the market once again. An alternative is to grant the buyer a binding extension in return for a nonrefundable deposit that is subject to forfeiture if the conditions remain unsatisfied and the buyer remains unable to close beyond the extension date.

A seller should never inalterably rely on a closing or change his or her position unless all conditions to the agreement are satisfied. Sellers, for example, frequently advise employees or customers of the pending sale, commit to relocation, or enter into new employment or another business venture relying upon a conditional contract that will never materialize. When the sale does collapse, the committed seller cannot easily reverse plans and is then in an embarrassing and often costly situation. Considering the numerous problems that can destroy a sale, avoid future commitments until the sale goes through.

PREPARING FOR THE CLOSING

Preparation for the closing is largely a matter of attending to countless housekeeping duties.

As rapidly as possible after contract, the parties should meet with their respective attorneys and accountants to prepare a complete work list of legal, accounting, and business actions necessary to close the transaction.

Preclosing action checklists depend on the nature of the transaction and the type of business. However, the following checklist is representative:

Seller's Checklist

1. Update corporate minute book.
2. Obtain seller's stock transfer ledger and stock certificate book.
3. Hold required stockholders or directors meetings to approve or confirm sale.
4. Obtain certified copy of incorporation, certificate of good standing, and state tax waivers.
5. Obtain terminations of lease to be held in escrow, pending closing.
6. Obtain payoff amounts on secured obligations.
7. Obtain terminations and discharges of encumbrances to be held in escrow, pending closing.
8. Obtain documentation for the transfer of distributor and dealer agreements.
9. Prepare assignment of patents, trademarks, and licenses, if applicable.
10. Review actions needed to terminate or assign seller's pension plans, retirement plans, employment agreements, profit-sharing agreements, union contracts, and other matters pertaining to employment.
11. Prepare affidavit of creditors list for buyer's compliance with Bulk Sales Act, if applicable.
12. Assemble financial information for the preparation of final tax returns.
13. Update all financial records, ledgers, and journals, if required, for delivery to buyer.
14. Reconcile bank accounts.
15. Prepare list of creditors for Bulk Sales Act.
16. Prepare list of accounts receivable.
17. Obtain copies of all insurance policies, agreements, and debt instruments to be assumed by buyer.
18 Compile all other accounting, legal, and business records to be delivered to buyer.

19. Reconcile accounts with all suppliers and return goods for credit, where applicable.
20. Remove personally owned items from the premises.

Buyer's Checklist

1. Verify availability of contemplated business name, if applicable.
2. Organize buyer entity (corporation or partnership).
3. Hold necessary stockholders or directors meetings to approve purchase.
4. Notify seller's creditors under the Bulk Sales Act, if applicable.
5. Check liens or encumbrances against property to be acquired.
6. Prepare banking resolutions and open checking account.
7. Conduct title search on real estate, if applicable.
8. Arrange inventory tabulation, if appropriate.
9. Obtain required insurance policies, if seller's insurance not assigned.
10. Review and approve all documents relating to buyer financing, if applicable.
11. Prepare new employments contracts, pension, and profit-sharing plans, if seller's plans not assumed.
12. Review all agreements, liabilities, and debt instruments to be assumed by buyer.
13. Prepare and obtain executed lease or assignment of lease to be held in escrow, pending closing.
14. Obtain federal taxpayer identification number.

FIVE TIPS FOR A SMOOTHER CLOSING

Most closings impose last-minute stumbling blocks that range from mere aggravations to devastating deal-destroying events. What can you do to turn your closing into a harmonious ceremony?

1. Have all closing documents reviewed and approved well in advance. The closing should be a mere signing event, not

an opportunity to have attorneys wrangle over documents that could have been resolved weeks earlier.

2. Make certain all contingencies and arrangements with third parties (financing, leases, and the like) are finalized. The closing should not provide an opportunity for either the buyer or the seller to walk away from the deal because "loose ends" have not been tightly tied earlier.

3. Make certain all parties required to sign will either appear at the closing or have signed in advance. Check with your attorney if you are uncertain as to who should be present at the closing.

4. If the buyer and seller are unfriendly, which is, of course, common considering the numerous disputes that can arise, then it may be best to arrange a closing in absentia, with the attorneys exchanging signed documents in place of a face-to-face meeting between the parties.

5. Arrange the closing for the first day of the month to simplify adjustments. Mondays are best, although the beginning of a new payroll period should be considered. Plan on a morning closing. This allows sufficient time to complete the transaction the same day, should time-consuming problems arise.

THE CLOSING CHECKLIST

The actual closing closely resembles the preclosing flurry of legal, accounting, and operational activities.

Regardless of the size, nature, or complexity of the acquisition, the seller, buyer, and their respective advisers require close coordination to bring the transaction to a successful conclusion. To achieve this objective, the parties should prepare a postclosing agenda, with attention to these items:

Final Title/Lien Check

Although buyer's counsel will check title and the existence of liens and attachments prior to closing, a cloud on title or very recent attachment or lien may arise. For this reason, closing documents and the purchase price should remain in escrow until a final postclosing search is completed, which includes:

- An update on title for real estate acquired under the transaction
- Verification that no liens, attachments, or security interests exist against assets sold

Financial Adjustments

While most adjustments may be handled at closing, postclosing adjustments frequently include:

- Inventory adjusted to the amount guaranteed based on postclosing physical tabulation
- Purchases made on the seller's account but received by the buyer and not included in the inventory valuation or paid by the buyer
- Accounts receivable charge-back on guaranteed but uncollected receivables
- Rents, real estate taxes, and other occupancy costs accrued prior to closing, based upon a final statement submitted by the landlord
- Utility, fuel oil, and telephone charges upon presentation of final statements
- Nonassumed liabilities or claims against the buyer arising subsequent to closing
- Income received by the buyer but due the seller

Cancellations and Terminations

To the extent they are not assumed by the buyer, the seller should arrange for the cancellation and termination of

- Utility and telephone accounts
- Insurance policies (with request for rebate on unused prepaid premium)
- Contracts with service firms, including burglar alarms, security services, maintenance firms, and rubbish removal
- Equipment and personal property leases, with consigned and loaned items returned and receipts obtained

- Retainer agreements with accountants, attorneys, public relations firms, advertising agencies, and other professionals
- Leases and tenancies, including subleases
- Guarantees by principals of the selling corporation under a stock transfer
- Other executory contracts not assumed by buyer

Notifications of Sale

There is an important public relations aspect to every acquisition. The buyer must be introduced by the seller to the various constituencies involved with the business and upon whom the business depends for goodwill. The buyer and seller should together prepare press releases, letters of introduction, or other announcements about the sale to

- Employees
- Present and prior customers
- Distributors
- Dealers
- Sales representatives
- Suppliers
- Professional advisers
- Independent contractors with whom the company dealt
- Depository banks

Transfers

Should the buyer assume contracts of the seller, notification should be provided, and where possible, the seller should be released from any further obligation. Other assets involve simple transfers, including:

- Registration and title to motor vehicles
- Insurance policies, including change of named insured and loss payees
- Cash on deposit
- Licenses, permits and registrations
- Corporate assets to be retained by the seller under a stock transfer agreement

Banking Activities

- Seller to close all accounts under an asset transfer
- Buyer to open new accounts under an asset transfer
- Buyer and seller to revoke existing authorizations and issue new signature authorizations to corporate accounts under a stock transfer

Tax Activities

- Buyer, as a new entity, to apply for federal taxpayer identification number and state Federal Insurance Contributions Act (FICA), and unemployment compensation registration
- Seller to file final federal withholding tax, FICA, state withholding, and sales tax and unemployment compensation returns
- Seller to file final federal and state income tax returns
- Buyer to file short-term tax returns, if applicable
- Seller to prepare for "three-month" or "one-year" dissolution, if applicable

Insurance

If the buyer assumes the seller's insurance policies, the buyer's counsel should carefully review coverage to determine whether it is suitable for the buyer's purposes. When new insurance is obtained, it should be in force prior to closing. Prior to closing, determine whether your business needs these forms of insurance:

- Casualty insurance to the premises
- Public liability (in amounts required under the lease)
- Workmen's compensation coverage
- Business interruption insurance
- Motor vehicle insurance
- Product liability insurance
- Plate glass coverage
- Professional liability insurance
- Surety bonds
- Health insurance for employees

Accounting Activities

Considerable accounting responsibility exists during the transition stage. Prior to closing, the buyer's accountant should review the seller's accounting systems and financial controls to consider whether the buyer should adopt the same system, integrate various accounting and management information systems into its own existing system, or design totally new accounting procedures.

Because so many businesses maintain partially or totally computerized systems, lack of compatibility between a buyer's and a seller's system creates nightmarish transitional problems. If the seller is efficiently computerized, the buyer should certainly consider acquiring the seller's computer system to ensure continuity and efficiency of operations. Reproduction of computer disks allows both the buyer and the seller to retain duplicate copies for their respective postclosing use.

Beyond the traditional financial controls needed for every business, such as payroll, accounts payable, accounts receivable, and general ledger, the new acquisition also requires detailed financial planning and monitoring during its early years. Sound control is particularly important because under new management sales become speculative, whereas costs and expenses must be adjusted continuously to match the fluctuating sales. The buyer is also likely to undertake substantial capital expenditures, further threatening cash flow. For numerous reasons, the newly acquired business will have great financial volatility, unlike the company under more stable, long-term ownership.

To ensure necessary financial stability, the buyer's accountant should prepare and review

- Capital expenditure budgets
- Expense budgets
- Purchases budgets
- Sales budget
- Cost controls
- Cash flow statements, projected monthly over one- and three-year terms

The buyer's accountant should frequently compare actual income and expenditures to that budgeted or forecast to undertake timely corrective action before serious financial problems occur. Many business failures are attributable to lack of close financial navigation following acquisition. An accounting system must therefore be designed to provide meaningful information, and the buyer must be committed to its use.

Corporate Amendments

Several corporate amendments must be drafted if the buyer acquires shares of stock in the corporation. The buyer's counsel should also see to it that the corporation

- Holds required meetings to elect new directors and officers
- Files notice of change of officers and directors in state of incorporation and where operating as a foreign corporation
- Amends its corporate purpose to include any planned change of business activity
- Amends its bylaws to reflect changes required by the buyer
- Updates prior resolutions and corporate minutes

UNDER NEW MANAGEMENT

Congratulations! The business is finally yours, but don't be too anxious to make important changes. It takes time to really know the business and its customers, employees, and competition. It takes even longer to test the strengths and weaknesses of the business. Although you will buy the business with many improvements in mind, you want to make changes based on what you *know* will work, rather than on what you *think* will work. *So move slowly.*

How can you safely turn the business into the success it can be under your new management?

1. Learn the critical aspects of the business quickly. Leave less important details for later.

2. Ask the seller to assist during the transition period. Listen to the seller because the seller has an understanding of the business that comes from years of experience. While the seller may not always be correct, don't automatically assume that he or she is wrong if his or her opinion differs from yours.

3. Speak to employees immediately to relieve their normal concerns about possible terminations. Assess each employee's merit on your own. Invite employee advice but always remain in control over decisions.

4. Contact suppliers early to establish a favorable working relationship but don't hesitate to negotiate more advantageous terms or to shop elsewhere for better deals. Make suppliers prove they deserve *your* business.

5. Build strong customer relationships but don't be pushed into new policies until you know your customers' preferences and the policies that will keep them happy and you competitive and profitable.

6. Change the business name only if the existing name has a poor reputation or a new name offers stronger recognition or a more valued reputation. Even then, delay name changes until the business sports its new format and image and is ready to put its best foot forward.

7. Renovate the premises or remerchandise the business cautiously. It will take at least several months to determine what changes are appropriate.

8. Create a written business plan and timetable for implementation. The newly acquired existing business needs the same careful planning as a start-up.

9. Listen to your customers—they are the ones you *must* please. And don't expect miracles overnight. It takes time to build customer loyalty, and you should expect to lose present customers as well as gain new customers.

10. Expect your new business to offer both unpleasant surprises and welcome discoveries. But these will matter little in what the business will eventually become, because the future depends only on what you can do with the business under your new management.

SUMMING UP

1. The days prior to closing can be critical. A coordinated transition depends upon close buyer-seller involvement.
2. Try to close the deal as quickly as possible to avoid last-minute complications.
3. Go slow in making changes in the business once it's yours. Learn the business first and then you can make decisions with far fewer errors.

CHAPTER 11

WHEN YOU SELL

MAKING THE DECISION

The day will inevitably arrive when the process will turn full cycle and it will become time to sell.

Could there possibly be a business owner who hasn't at one time or another thought of selling his or her troublesome enterprise? Constant pressure from owning a business can be tiring, and the stress of day-to-day problems can at times become overwhelming.

Fortunately, for most owners the urge to sell quickly passes. You eventually find solutions to even stubborn problems, and there is always the fear of the unknown, should you sell. Still, there will inevitably come a time when you can no longer run the business effectively or operate it with the enthusiasm you once had. Then, you instinctively know it's finally time to transfer ownership to more willing hands.

Why do you want to sell? It's important to understand your underlying reasons because there are often options. For example, if the business is operating at a loss or is heavily indebted, the solution may be to retain a consultant to help turn around the firm. Tired or burned out? The answer may be a partner or manager—or perhaps just more time off. A partnership feud, as another example, should not prompt a sale of the entire business but a buyout of the partnership interest. Look for the alternatives with your advisers and family before your commit yourself to a sale. You can always proceed with a sale, but you cannot reverse a completed sale. Since the reasons prompting a sale may be temporary or easily solved, allow yourself at least six months to reach a final decision.

Much like the process of buying, the decision whether to sell and how to sell effectively can also be complex and boggle your mind with a host of questions:

- Should I tell my employees?
- What should I do to dress up the business?
- How can I improve my financial statements?
- Can I legally sell the business?
- What price and terms do I want for the business?
- How can I best "package" the business to sell?

The decision to sell is a major one in the life of a business owner, and each owner has his or her own reasons for reaching that decision. Of the nearly 14 million businesses in the United States, approximately 1 million are actively for sale at any one time, and as the expression goes, "the rest can easily be bought at a high enough price." Just as there are many reasons to buy, there are, of course, also many reasons to sell. Boredom or burnout is the first of four common reasons. After managing their businesses for years, owners tire of the routine and lack of challenge. Many business owners are unwilling to devote themselves to the vigors of growth or to cope with the endless problems or complications that are part and parcel of business life. There is also the desire for liquidity. Business owners frequently see the lion's share of their net worth tied up in their business. Selling allows the buyer to liquidate his or her net worth for retirement purposes or for more rewarding investment. Similarly, the desire to pursue other interests may beckon. In our increasingly fluid society, many business owners sell because they are drawn to other occupations or wish to try new life-styles. Finally, a frustrating lack of capital can take its toll. Hampered by insufficient working capital, many owners realize that they can neither grow nor compete effectively against better capitalized firms. Rather than stagnate, or fail, these owners close up shop or sell to larger companies. Everyday factors such as age, poor health, relocation of a family member, or other personal reasons still account for about half the businesses sold.

DEVELOP YOUR EXIT PLAN

On the very first day you set up your business, you should plan for the day you will leave your business. By formulating an exit plan early in your business's development, you can intelligently structure the business for maximum resale value. A well-designed exit plan allows you to choose among three options:

1. Sell your entire business and exit the business completely.
2. Sell part of your business and stay on in a managerial position. In this situation, the buyer usually seeks a return on investment higher than obtainable through passive investments methods. Of course, you will surrender equity in your business but will in return obtain capital to finance the growth of your business.
3. Continue running the business without selling in whole or in part. However, even in this situation, with an exit plan in place you are prepared to sell, should someone make an irresistible offer you cannot refuse.

Designing an exit plan may be time-consuming, but it pays in increased value for your business, whether today or in the future.

Before you can strategically market your business, you have homework to do. Several months may be needed to position the business correctly, but that is time profitably spent. The well-positioned business sells much faster and for considerably more than does the poorly presented opportunity.

What should your first steps be?

Test the Market

To bring your business to market intelligently, first know how competitive the market is and what comparable businesses are available and sell for. Pretend you're a buyer for two or three months. You'll soon develop an accurate sense of what your business will sell for, once you know how comparable businesses are priced.

Develop a Team Approach

If you have partners, make certain there is agreement not only on the decision to sell but also on the key terms of sale. Actively involve each partner in the buy-sell process by delegating specific responsibilities necessary to position the business.

Consider Employees

Should you tell your employees of your plans? Two choices are yours: Say nothing or reveal exactly what you are planning to do. There are arguments to favor each. If you don't tell your staff and word leaks out, your employees will feel betrayed. On the other hand, early disclosure may create job insecurity, prompting employees to leave prematurely. Therefore, this decision requires judgment. However, many experienced sellers suggest it is best to tell confidentially only key employees and long-term staff members. Consider an attractive bonus plan for key employees who remain. It can prove to be an inexpensive way to solve the ever-present employee problem.

Dress Up the Business

Small but shrewd investments revitalizing the appearance of the business can pay big dividends. But spend sparingly. It is counterproductive to replace or add expensive capital assets, since you probably won't recapture your investment. However, you can inexpensively "dress up" the business with a "paint and cleanup" campaign. To handle the financial impact of the cleanup campaign, set an affordable budget. How much cash can you devote to the project? List and prioritize expenditures based on what will provide the highest visual benefit for the lowest dollar cost.

Operate with Long-Term Goals

The ever-present temptation will be to sacrifice the future for the present. To maximize presale profits, sellers foolishly raise prices, curtail credit, eliminate advertising, slash research and development costs, and curb expenses for long-term projects perceived to be of benefit only to the buyer. Thinking "short term" haunts a seller for three reasons. First, it may take far longer to sell the business than imagined; second, the negative impact of such actions on the business may be felt sooner than anticipated; and finally, a knowledgeable buyer will expect continuity of policy to maintain goodwill and benefit the business after the sale.

FINANCIAL POSITIONING: LOOKING HEALTHY

Although the "window-dressing" steps are important, a coat of paint and a friendly smile can't take the place of solid profits.

The seller and his or her accountant share responsibility to position the business financially so that it looks as much like a money-maker as it legitimately can. Unfortunately, small businesses keep notoriously poor financial records. Many good businesses remain unsold, or are finally sold for a fraction of their true value, because the buyer could not decipher its financial past or project its rosy financial future from its dismally scant records. Many sellers, of course, bless sparse records when the objective is to conceal losses. But the strategy can backfire, as the buyer may assume that far greater losses exist.

Financial positioning will help you achieve three objectives:

- To present past business performance favorably
- To identify changes required in the financial structure necessary best to position the business for sale
- To project most favorably future profitability and cash flow under a buyer's management

Financial positioning demands accurate and current financial statements. Buyers will want to see income statements, tax returns, balance sheets, and cash flow statements. These financial statements should cover at least three to five years of operation and should ideally cover a longer time period when an even more favorable trend can be demonstrated.

Highlight the Profit History

The income statement is clearly the most important financial statement of interest to a buyer, since historical profits help project future profits. Lack of profits is the one major difficulty when attempting to sell small businesses for a respectable price. Seldom are these enterprises as unprofitable as they appear; but profits are usually deeply buried in the income statement. Numerous opportunities exist to conceal profits. Unreported income, extraordinary write-offs, accelerated depreciation, and other "paper" expenses can eradicate profits of even the best income producer. The dilemma created by such sharp accounting practices is that the financial statements inevitably reflect dismal earnings or losses when the seller decides to sell. Armed only with poor statements, the seller can only expect a poor price.

Timing the sale is thus part of preparation. While it is not always possible to plan a sale two or three years in advance, for purposes of showing the most favorable profits possible, it may be possible to defer a sale at least one fiscal year if a stronger profit picture can emerge. At the very least, prepare quarterly statements to reflect maximum profits from the moment the decision is made to sell.

One quick way to correct the financial picture is to reconstruct more favorable financial statements. Highlight extraordinary expenses that distorted profitability. A simple reconstruction deleting extraordinary expenses can quickly turn paper losses into substantial profits—and thus be consistent with the true operational profitability of the enterprise. Similarly, be prepared to show the buyer the various extraordinary or nonrecurring expenses that have diminished profits, particularly when these expenses are not likely to be encountered by the buyer. Remember, buyers of small businesses rarely have adequate managerial experience to interpret actual profitability when
a business shows otherwise. Inexperienced buyers focus only on the bottom line without attempt to reconstruct or to look deeply to find profitability. Reconstructed statements, accompanying the actual financial statements or tax returns, constitute an essential sales tool when trying to sell a business for top dollar.

Small business buyers, while interested in profits, are primarily interested in what they personally can take out of the business. A business may show little or no profit yet may provide its owners substantial income and perks. Separately outlined salaries, fringe benefits, perks, pensions, business-owned automobiles, travel, and the numerous other "personal" items charged off against the business can suddenly make a lackluster business quite interesting.

Buyers are also understandably interested in the sales generated during the immediately preceding few months of operation, to observe whether sales are declining. Buyers justifiably believe that a business is for sale owing to more recent problems seen in reduced current sales. Therefore, the financial presentation should disclose monthly sales for the current months, assuming that current quarterly financial statements are unavailable.

Finally, and most important, anticipate the buyer's many questions concerning the profit history of the business. As with any other sale, a buyer has the right to be skeptical, and it remains for the seller to dispel that skepticism by dressing up the business as attractively and honestly as possible. On the negative side, the seller's accountant may have to explain discrepancies between the financial statements and tax returns or explain away in the most favorable light chronic losses or adverse trends in the performance of the business.

Restructuring the Balance Sheet

The second objective of financial positioning is to adjust the assets and liabilities of the business to facilitate an easier sale.

First, review the balance sheet with the objective of making the company as "lean" as possible.

1. Tabulate your inventory. Sellers frequently do not realize the actual value of their inventory, which may be far above or below the amount imagined. Many small businesses have accrued substantial profits in the form of excessive inventory. Excess inventory should be liquidated to reduce inventory to the lowest acceptable operational level. A reduced inventory not only helps to create profitability but also helps to reduce the price of the business, making it far easier to sell—assuming, of course, that the seller retains the cash.
2. Turn delinquent receivables over for collection and monitor future credit tightly. Again, the objective is to turn idle receivables into cash.
3. Sell excess, obsolete, or unused capital assets such as equipment, furniture, and fixtures at the best price possible. Surplus items will have little or no value to the buyer and will be more advantageously disposed of prior to a sale.
4. Reduce current liabilities and accounts payable to acceptable levels. Many sellers completely pay current bills and thus position the business for sale without debt. This may

be a mistake, as the assumption of liabilities by the buyer can be a convenient way to help finance the buyer.

5. Show *all* liabilities on the balance sheet. Omissions may be later detected by the buyer and throw into question the validity of other financial information or accuracy of representations concerning the business.

6. Review stockholder loans. Loans due to or from the business should be considered for repayment. However, your accountant should help make this decision based on tax considerations.

7. Pay outstanding tax liabilities, accrued expenses, and overdue accounts. These small items, when delinquent, are often magnified by buyers and tarnish the image of even the best company.

Although each of these steps is as applicable to good everyday financial management as it is to the process of favorably positioning a business for sale, the company not on the market can often afford to operate with some financial inefficiency and is forced to put its financial house in order only when a sale is contemplated.

Projecting the Financial Future

Buyers are primarily interested in the future of the business. The seller's past becomes important only to project the buyer's future.

The one most costly error a seller can make is to overlook this point and fail to provide the buyer a clear vision of where the business is headed. The seller's accountant shares this responsibility. The most comprehensive and detailed financial statements have little value in helping to sell the business if the buyer cannot quickly foresee a favorable picture one, two, or five years hence. For example, with sales on an upward trend, why not use a sales graph as a powerful sales tool? Use of graphs to display increased profits or emphasize other financial improvements is a wise strategy. In fact, every indicator emphasizing the true potential of the business *must* be outlined if the business is to be shown in its best light.

Knowledgeable buyers are equally interested in cash flow. A one-year cash flow projection is usually sufficient, but projections should be bolstered by supportable data to justify the income forecasts.

Accurate cash flow projections coupled with a detailed income statement will help the buyer determine the financing the business can safely support and the operating capital required. Therefore, cash flow projections should be conservatively adjusted to reflect the net operating surplus to a buyer, before deduction for debt service.

Present, in a professional manner, financial information and other supporting data. The very fact that such comprehensive information is immediately available and contains the many items of interest to a potential buyer certainly creates greater buyer interest and confidence than will nonexistent or poorly organized financial information.

LEGAL POSITIONING: PLUGGING THE LOOPHOLES

Legal positioning goes hand in hand with financial positioning because they are interrelated and both are of interest to a buyer.

There are numerous legal matters to attend to before offering a business for sale. Legal positioning of the business has two broad objectives:

- To clear legal impediments to a sale
- To anticipate legal matters necessary to ensure an orderly sale and managerial and organizational transition of the business

Clearing the Legal Obstacles

Sellers frequently bring a sale to the point of near completion only to find the sale blocked owing to an unanticipated legal obstacle. An early responsibility of the seller and his or her counsel is to review thoroughly the corporate, contractual, financial, and other legal obstacles that may constrain a sale and, where necessary, to remove the impediments.

A comprehensive legal checklist answers these questions:

1. Does the seller have authority to sell? Where the business is owned by partners or multiple stockholders, verify unanimous agreement to sell or alternatively, the selling stockholder controls sufficient votes to authorize and

implement the sale against the objections of dissenting partners.

2. Is the business owned by an estate? Death of the owner will commonly prompt an immediate sale. Ascertain whether the executor agrees to the sale and whether all probate requirements have been satisfied. Where the sale requires court approval, any agreement to sell should be conditional upon obtaining court approval.

3. Is the business franchised? The franchised business cannot ordinarily be sold without franchisor approval. The conditions of assignment and the buyer requirements must be investigated with the franchisor well in advance.

4. Are there major contracts that may interfere with a sale? When the business depends on production or distributorship agreements or perhaps contracts with a primary customer, such contracts should be checked to determine their assignability.

5. Is a sufficient lease available? This one point is repeated elsewhere because so many small businesses are placed on the market without verifying whether an acceptable lease is available to the buyer. Review the terms and assignability of the present lease or the proposed terms of a new lease.

6. Is the business solvent? Unless it is clear that the anticipated purchase price can fully satisfy creditor claims, determine the likelihood of creditors settling for partial payment or the need for reorganization proceedings or other debtor's remedies to reduce the debt prior to the contemplated sale.

Legal Checklist in Planning a Sale

Numerous other legal details precede placing a business for sale. The primary items subject to review may include:

- Pending litigation, to evaluate their impact on any proposed sale
- Employment contracts, to determine whether they can be assigned or terminated without penalty
- Union contracts, to assess their assignability

- Employee pension plans and profit sharing, to assess their assignability or provisions for termination
- Existing contracts, to assess their assignability or rights to terminate
- Secured loans, conditional sales agreements, and equipment leases, to determine their current status and rights to assign, prepay, or terminate these obligations
- Patents and trademarks, to determine whether properly filed and assignable
- Corporate records, to verify required filings and that corporate minutes are current
- Obligations between the owners and the corporation, to determine whether in effect and the conditions of termination
- Personal guarantees issued by owners of the corporation, to determine rights to terminate such guarantees
- Licenses and permits, to verify whether they can be transferred to a new owner

SETTING THE TERMS OF SALE

With financial and legal positioning completed, the seller will begin to pinpoint with greater precision the terms of sale.

Frequently, a seller places a business on the market without a clear idea of what is to be sold or the price, terms, and other important elements concerning the proposed sale. When the seller cannot specify precisely what is for sale and on what terms, brokers are less inclined to take the listing seriously; and of course, the seller cannot intelligently approach buyers with a firm understanding of what is offered and what is expected in return.

A well-conceived sales approach will feature comprehensive, objective, and flexible terms. *Comprehensive*, it necessarily covers all the essential terms of sale and goes well beyond the rudimentary question of price, which tends to be the one focal point of interest to sellers. Attorneys, accountants, and consultants can certainly be useful in helping the seller explore all the possible items on which any ensuing transaction must be based.

Objectivity is the second hallmark of a well-conceived offering. The seller must set realistic and objectively attainable terms. It accomplishes little to approach the market with a clearly excessive price or other terms not likely to be obtained.

Flexibility is the final element. The seller not only must know his or her "asking" price and most desirable terms possible but must also set minimally acceptable terms, the various possible trade-offs, and the terms that are negotiable and nonnegotiable. Moreover, it is vital for the seller's accountant and attorney to understand the seller's priorities and "bottom line" position if they are to help negotiate or structure the transaction effectively.

You can more easily determine the terms of sale if you consider each of these points:

Assets to Be Sold

What assets will be sold and what assets do you plan to retain? Reduce these to two separate lists to prevent later misunderstandings. A listing of assets that may be either sold or retained include:

- Cash on hand
- Accounts receivable
- Notes receivable or securities in other companies
- Prepaid deposits
- Merchandise inventory
- Furniture and fixtures
- Equipment
- Automobiles and motor vehicles
- Leasehold improvements
- Patents, trademarks, and copyrights
- Customers lists
- Name and goodwill
- Contract rights or distributorships
- Assignments of lease
- Telephone numbers
- Real estate
- Permits or licenses

Price

- What is the asking price for the business?
- Is the price firm or negotiable?

- If the price is negotiable, what is the minimally acceptable price?
- Will price be adjusted based on guaranteed asset values (inventory, receivables)?
- Is the price exclusive or inclusive of liabilities? If liabilities are to be assumed, what amount of assumed liability is the price based on? Will the price be adjusted to actual debt at time of sale?
- Is the price a "net price" after payment of brokerage fees?

Financing

You may insist on an all cash sale or determine whether financing is available. If financing is available:

- What down payment is required?
- What are the interest rate and term of payment on proposed seller financing?
- What collateral is required?
- Can the buyer assume existing debts toward the purchase price?

Structuring of Transfer

Decide whether you contemplate a sale of

- Assets
- Corporate shares

If a merger is considered, will the seller accept shares of stock for the purchase price?

Leases and Tenancies

- Is a lease available?
- What are the rent terms, duration of tenancy, and other important lease terms?
- If the seller is to lease the premises, will the buyer have an option or right of first refusal to buy the real estate? If an option is available, what are the option price and option period?

Employment

Do any principals of the selling corporation require employment as a condition of sale? If so,

- What is the general job description?
- What is the required salary?
- Will the employment be protected by contract or terminable at will?
- If an employment contract is required, what is its duration?
- Will you agree to assist the buyer during the transition period? For how long? At what salary?
- Are other key personnel available to remain with the business after sale?

Noncompetition Agreements

Will all principals of the selling corporation agree to a noncompete agreement? If so,

- What activities will they agree to refrain from?
- What are the acceptable duration and geographic area?

Closing Date

Does the seller have any preference, or requirements, as to closing dates? Will a sale be deferred until after a peak selling season, or are there no time restrictions, with the seller ready to transfer whenever a buyer requests?

Other terms may apply and should be considered. But remain somewhat flexible. You may find it necessary to adjust terms to realistically meet the demands of the marketplace, which can only occur when the business has been reviewed by a number of buyers who, hopefully, are as anxious to buy as you are to sell.

SUMMING UP

1. Don't act too quickly when you have the urge to sell. Business frustrations pass, and you may well decide to stay with the business.

2. Selling a business requires the same careful planning as buying, so plan as far in advance as possible.
3. Be prepared to put the business in the best light. A business—like any other commodity—must be attractively packaged to sell.
4. There are numerous obstacles that can delay or prevent a sale. Review potential problems with your accountant and attorney.

APPENDIX 1

PURCHASE AGREEMENTS

AGREEMENT TO SELL ASSETS

AGREEMENT made and entered into by and between XYZ SUPERMARKET, INC., a Massachusetts corporation with a usual place of business at Main Street, Anytown, Massachusetts ("SELLER"), and BUYER COMPANY, INC., another Massachusetts corporation ("BUYER"), with a usual place of business at the same location, all as their respective interests exist and are herein represented.

WHEREAS, SELLER operates a supermarket business at said aforementioned address and is desirous of selling certain assets of the same to BUYER as a going business concern; and

WHEREAS, BUYER is desirous of purchasing said assets and continuing the operation of the supermarket business on terms as herein contained;

NOW, THEREFORE, it is for good and valuable consideration and in consideration of the covenants, agreements, terms, and provisions as herein contained mutually agreed by and between the parties as follows:

ARTICLE I
SALE OF ASSETS

SELLER agrees to sell, and BUYER agrees to purchase and acquire all the following assets, chattels, and items as owned by, located on, and used in connection with the business of the SELLER known as SELLER SUPERMARKET, Main Street, Anytown, Massachusetts:

a) All the inventory, merchandise, and goods for resale existing as of the date of closing

b) All the furniture, fixtures, equipment, supplies, furnishings, and leasehold improvements, without limiting the generality of the foregoing to include all office equipment, counters, shelves, checkout units, cash registers, heating equipment, air conditioners, wall cases, refrigerated units, lighting fixtures, signs, display units, freezers (walk-in or otherwise), compressors, decorative accessories, tools of the trade, accessories, and appurtenances, provided and only to the extent the same are located within the inside walls, ceiling, and floor of the presently existing ground-floor store

c) All the goodwill of the SELLER, including such exclusive rights to the name "SELLER SUPERMARKET"; together with all policy manuals, price lists, supplier lists, customer lists, and secret formula, recipes, or trade secrets to the extent they exist

d) Transfer of SELLER's right of an existing beer and wine license to BUYER or its nominee as more fully set forth herein; together with such rights to an all-alcoholic license as may exist, if any, at time of closing; or thereafter as hereinafter provided

ARTICLE II
ASSETS TO BE RETAINED BY SELLER

SELLER shall retain all right, title, and interest in and to the following items:

1. All cash on hand or on deposit
2. All notes receivable, accounts receivable, prepaid expenses, utility deposits, tax rebates, insurance claims, choses in action, credits due from suppliers and other allowances
3. Motor vehicles and automobiles, excepting for a certain compactor truck now owned that shall be subject to sale hereunder
4. Any equities in SELLER or any other incorporated or nonincorporated entity

Specifically excluded also from any sale are any fixtures, plumbing, wiring, and/or equipment contained within the walls and/or attached to or upon the exterior walls or roof, whether or not said fixtures, plumbing, wiring, and/or equipment pass through or are connected to the interior walls, ceiling, and/or floor of the presently existing ground-floor store or are fastened or connected to any item being sold to BUYER under this Agreement.

ARTICLE III
PURCHASE PRICE

BUYER agrees to pay to SELLER, and SELLER agrees to accept as the full purchase price for all the singular assets to be sold under Article I, supra, the total purchase price of FIFTY THOUSAND ($50,000.00) DOLLARS plus the cost value of the inventory at the time of closing as hereinafter defined and to be evaluated. At the time of closing, a physical inventory shall be conducted and tabulated by XYZ Inventory Tabulators located at Elm Street, Boston, Massachusetts ("Tabulators"). The cost values shall be defined as retail price less twenty (20%) percent. For illustration only, if an item has a retail price of ONE ($1.00) DOLLAR, its cost value shall be EIGHTY ($0.80) CENTS. SELLER and BUYER shall mutually agree in the rejection or assignment of other partial values to any inventory for reason of questionable salability, marketability, retail value, or its being deteriorated, shopworn, or otherwise not suitable for sale at full retail price; however, it is agreed that any item of inventory that can be returned to the distributor or manufacturer for full credit to BUYER shall not be rejected but rather accepted at cost value, thereby giving BUYER the option of making any return. SELLER may retain title to any goods agreed upon as having no value. SELLER and BUYER each pay one-half (½) of the Tabulator's fee.

For illustration only, if the cost value of the inventory is determined to be FIFTY THOUSAND ($50,000.00) DOLLARS, the total purchase price shall be ONE HUNDRED THOUSAND ($100,000.00) DOLLARS.

ARTICLE IV
ALLOCATION OF PURCHASE PRICE

The purchase price shall be allocated in the manner following:

$ Cost value as may be determined	–For Article I–a) assets
$ 45,000.00	–For Article I–b) assets
$ 2,500.00	–For Article I–c) assets
$ 2,500.00	–For Article I–d) assets

ARTICLE V
PAYMENT OF PURCHASE PRICE

The purchase price as hereinabove to be determined in accordance with Article III, supra, shall be paid in the manner following:

$ 10,000.00   deposit upon execution hereof by certified check to be held in escrow jointly by SELLER and BUYER.

$ 90,000.00   at time of closing by certified check or bank check, provided that said amount shall be decreased pro rata if the total purchase price shall not equal $100,000.00. Any balance due thereafter shall be paid timely twenty-one (21) days from date of closing.

ARTICLE VI
SALE FREE AND CLEAR

SELLER agrees that it shall sell said assets free and of all liens, encumbrances, liabilities, and claims of parties adverse thereto. SELLER agrees that it shall carry out the following:

1. Waive all the conditions and requirements of the Bulk Sales Act, MGL Chapter 106s6; but SELLER shall complete and execute affidavit as annexed as Exhibit A.
2. At time of closing, SELLER shall provide BUYER with a tax waiver from the Department of Revenue, Commonwealth of Massachusetts.

3. That any and all liens, encumbrances, security agreements, tax liens, or attachments of record shall be fully discharged at time of closing.
4. SELLER shall provide BUYER with an indemnity agreement as annexed as Exhibit B, indemnifying BUYER from any asserted claims against assets sold to BUYER.

ARTICLE VII
SELLER'S WARRANTIES

The SELLER warrants and represents to BUYER with knowledge the BUYER shall rely on same to enter into this transaction each and all of the foregoing:

a) That the SELLER owns all and singular the assets being sold hereunder and has full marketable title to same excepting only for items set forth on Exhibit C, "nonowned assets."
b) That the SELLER has full right and authority to enter into this agreement and right to perform and sell hereunder.
c) That there are no known eminent domain or condemnation proceedings affecting the ground-store area containing the supermarket business or any of its common areas.
d) That at the time of the sale all fixtures, equipment, air conditioners, heating equipment, and other apparatus shall be in good working order at the time of passing except those items that upon the date of this Agreement are not functioning. Acceptance of the bill of sale by BUYER shall be conclusive evidence of satisfaction of this warranty. The parties agree that the amount of consideration paid for the above fixtures, equipment, air conditioners, heating equipment, and other apparatus is based upon the fact that these items above are being bought and sold "as is"; and SELLER disclaims any warranty of merchantability for periods beyond the closing, and BUYER accepts the same "as is" and hereby waives forever any rights he or she may have had otherwise.
e) That there are no known governmental or administrative proceedings against SELLER, including, but not limited to, the Board of Health or Building Inspector, that have arisen due to, or in connection with, its conduct of the supermarket business.

ARTICLE VIII
COVENANT NOT TO COMPETE

SELLER agrees and covenants that it shall not compete with the supermarket business being transferred herein pursuant to the terms of the covenant not to compete agreement as annexed as Exhibit D.

ARTICLE IX
SELLER'S OBLIGATION PENDING CLOSING

SELLER agrees, warrants, and covenants that during the pendency of this agreement that

1. SELLER shall maintain customary store hours.
2. SELLER shall maintain its customary and usual pricing and promotional programs.
3. SELLER shall maintain an adequate stock necessary to maintain the goodwill of the business.
4. SELLER shall not conduct any liquidation or so-called close-out sales.
5. SELLER shall maintain the current employees for the benefit of BUYER; however, nothing herein shall prevent a discharge for cause or require BUYER to employ any present employee.

Acceptance of the bill of sale shall be conclusive evidence of satisfaction of this Article IX. In the event of any asserted breach, BUYER shall give SELLER written notice thereto, and SELLER shall cure within three (3) days thereafter. In the event SELLER shall not so cure, then BUYER shall have the option to terminate this Agreement without further recourse to either party thereto.

ARTICLE X
CASUALTY

It is further provided that if there is any casualty, destruction, or loss to the assets described in Article I–b) in an amount equal to or in excess of ten (10%) percent of the total value, then in such instance this Agreement may be terminated at the election of BUYER, unless said assets or premises shall, before the date of closing, be restored or replaced to their former condition.

ARTICLE XI
CONDITIONS PRECEDENT, CONCURRENT, AND SUBSEQUENT

This Agreement and all of BUYER's obligations hereunder shall be fully conditional upon the occurrence of the following:

BUYER's obtaining a lease for the present premises of SELLER, together with certain land purchase options as included therein ("Lease") and as annexed hereto as Exhibit E. It is expressly agreed and understood that this Agreement and the Lease shall be mutually dependent; and BUYER shall not be obligated to perform under this Agreement without benefit of said Lease, and reciprocally BUYER shall have no rights under said Lease unless the sale is concluded under this Agreement. The purchase options are attached as Exhibits F, G, and H.

ARTICLE XII
BROKERS

The parties warrant and represent to each other that there are no brokers to this transaction and none entitled to commission.

ARTICLE XIII
ADJUSTMENTS

The parties agree that at the time of closing they shall prorate and adjust for allocable and other expenses subject to adjustment in the manner following:

1. Merchandise ordered by SELLER prior to closing but received by BUYER subsequent to closing and therefore not tabulated in the inventory shall either be (a) paid for by BUYER or (b) rejected by BUYER and returned to shipper for credit to SELLER. BUYER agrees to indemnify and hold harmless SELLER for BUYER'S failure to comply with this provision. This paragraph shall survive the closing date.
2. There shall be no adjustment for yellow page advertising, electric, telephone, or gas as BUYER shall simultaneously with closing establish its own accounts.
3. There shall be no adjustment for insurance premiums as BUYER shall obtain its own insurance.
4. Payroll (excepting for accrued wages, benefits) shall be adjusted. There shall be an adjustment for fuel oil, rent, burglar alarm rentals, service contracts, and alcoholic licensing fees (provided that nothing herein shall obligate BUYER to assume any executory contracts of SELLER).

ARTICLE XIV
MISCELLANEOUS

1. All Exhibits are hereby incorporated by reference.
2. This constitutes the entire agreement, and there are no other terms, conditions, warranties, representations, or inducements except as are expressly set forth herein.
3. Headings are for convenience only and are not an integral part of this Agreement.
4. This Agreement, executed in duplicate, shall be binding upon and shall inure to the benefit of the parties, their successors, assigns, and personal representatives.
5. The parties shall do, undertake, execute, and perform all acts and documents reasonably required to carry out the tenor and provisions of this Agreement.

ARTICLE XV
CLOSING

The closing shall be on October 1, 1984, at 2:00 P.M. at office of SELLER.
Time is of the essence.
Signed under seal this   day of   , 1984.
SELLER SUPERMARKET, INC.

By:_____
President

BUYER COMPANY, INC.

By:_____
President

AGREEMENT TO PURCHASE SHARES

AGREEMENT made and entered into by and between ABC CORPORATION of Anytown, Massachusetts (hereinafter "SELLER");

XYZ CORPORATION with a usual place of business at Main Street, Anytown, Massachusetts (hereinafter, "CORPORATION"); BUYER CO., another Massachusetts corporation at Central Street, Anytown, Massachusetts (hereinafter "BUYER"); and MICHAEL DOE (hereinafter "DOE") and JOEL SMITH (hereinafter "SMITH"), both of Anytown, Massachusetts; all as their respective interests exist and are herein represented.

WITNESSETH

WHEREAS, SELLER is the owner of all the issued and outstanding shares of stock of the CORPORATION and is desirous of selling and transferring all of said shares to the CORPORATION under a redemption, all as contained hereunder; and

WHEREAS, the CORPORATION is desirous of purchasing and acquiring said shares, redeeming same, and retiring said shares as nonvoting treasury stock, and otherwise fulfilling the terms and conditions as herein contained; and

WHEREAS, the CORPORATION is desirous of issuing new shares to the BUYER and the BUYER is desirous of acquiring said shares from the CORPORATION, with the intent that upon consumation of this agreement the BUYER shall be the sole stockholder of all the issued and outstanding shares of stock of the CORPORATION; and

WHEREAS, as an inducement for the SELLER to enter into this agreement, DOE and SMITH as the principals of BUYER agree to guarantee certain obligations of the CORPORATION hereunder.

WITNESSETH

That for ONE ($1.00) DOLLAR and other good and valuable consideration of the agreements, conditions, terms, provisions, covenants, representations, and inducements as herein contained, it is mutually and reciprocally agreed by and between the parties as follows:

ARTICLE I
SALE OF SHARES BY SELLER

SELLER hereby agrees to sell and transfer, and the CORPORATION agrees to purchase, acquire, and redeem, all the shares of stock in and to the CORPORATION as owned and held by SELLER, said shares being further described as shares of common stock, evidenced by stock certificate number 2, and being further referred to hereinafter as SELLER's shares.

ARTICLE II
SELLER'S REPRESENTATIONS AS TO SELLER'S SHARES

The SELLER expressly warrants and represents to the BUYER each of the following:

1. That the described SELLER's shares represent all the issued and outstanding shares of the CORPORATION, of all classes inclusive, and there are no outstanding subscriptions to sell further shares other than as shall be entered into by BUYER pursuant to this agreement
2. That the SELLER has good and marketable title to the SELLER's shares
3. That said SELLER's shares are fully paid and nonassessable
4. That said SELLER's shares are free from lien, encumbrance, pledge, and sequestration and shall be transferred free of any adverse claim thereto
5. That there are no outstanding proxies, assignment of rights, or other form of stock power transfer arising from SELLER's shares
6. That all required waiver of restrictions on transfer of SELLER's shares have been obtained
7. That upon transfer the CORPORATION shall have good and marketable title to all the presently outstanding shares

ARTICLE III
PURCHASE PRICE

The CORPORATION agrees to pay to the SELLER for the purchase and redemption of the SELLER's shares a price equal to the cost value of the inventory plus $50,000; and to be subtracted from said combined sum shall be all existing liabilities of the CORPORATION at the time of transfer, all as further defined below. (For illustration purposes only, if the cost value of the inventory is $60,000, and liabilities total $40,000, the purchase price shall be $60,000 + $50,000 = $110,000 − $40,000, equaling a purchase price of $70,000.) In addition to the purchase price, as so defined, the CORPORATION shall further transfer to the SELLER certain assets of the CORPORATION as assets of the CORPORATION as set forth in Article VI, infra.

For purposes of determining the cost value of the inventory, the parties shall cause a physical tabulation of all inventory for resale owned by the CORPORATION to be conducted by John Doe Co. ("Tabulators"), immediately prior to sale hereunder. The Tabulators shall value the inventory at cost, inclusive of customarily prevailing trade, cash, or quantity discounts. The Tabulators shall reject from tabulation and inventory that which in their judgment is unmerchantable or unsalable, which may be removed by SELLER. Items of questionable value may have partial values assigned. The determination by the

Tabulators of the cost value shall be binding upon the parties and deemed conclusive. The SELLER and BUYER shall each pay one half of the Tabulators' fee.

The term *existing liabilities* as used herein shall mean and include all debts, obligations, and liabilities of the CORPORATION existing or accrued at time of transfer hereunder, including but not limited to: accounts payable; expenses payable; notes payable; taxes accrued to date; accrued wages, rents, and loans due any party; and obligations of every nature and description, whether secured or unsecured, disputed or undisputed, known or unknown, liquidated or unliquidated, presently due or due at a future time, contingent or noncontingent and notwithstanding whether the CORPORATION's liability is primary or secondary. Exempted from liabilities are contingent claims, known or unknown, for which there is adequate insurance coverage, and further exempted are all interest charges, service fees, penalties, or other like assessments for late payment accrued from date of transfer. The BUYER shall prepare a schedule of liabilities as above defined and annex same at time of transfer as Exhibit A.

ARTICLE IV
RECOURSE FOR UNLISTED LIABILITIES

SELLER represents and warrants to the BUYER that the only debts, obligations, and liabilities of the CORPORATION at time of transfer shall be those scheduled and contained on Exhibit A. In the event any debt, liability, or obligation not scheduled thereinafter arises or be asserted, or asserted by any creditor or claimant in excess of that listed, then in such instance:

1. The CORPORATION and BUYER shall have full rights to indemnify as against the SELLER pursuant to indemnity agreement as set forth as Exhibit B ("indemnity agreement").
2. In the event SELLER shall fail to promptly and fully indemnify under said indemnity agreement, then in such instance, the CORPORATION may as a further cumulative remedy pay or otherwise satisfy or discharge said unscheduled liability and deduct said expended payment from the next due installment(s) due under the promissory note due SELLER as further described in Article V, infra

ARTICLE V
PAYMENT OF PURCHASE PRICE

The purchase price as shall be determined in accordance with Article IV, supra, shall be paid in the manner following, at time of sale:

$10,000.00   By cash or certified check, funded by a payment to the CORPORATION of the subscription price for a new stock issue of corporate shares to BUYER pursuant to stock subscription to be entered into by BUYER under Article VIII

$ (balance to be determined)	Evidenced by a promissory note for said balance amount payable in 72 monthly installments with interest thereon at 14 percent on the unpaid balance, all as set forth in Exhibit C, ("note").

Said note shall be further secured by a senior security interest on all assets of the CORPORATION, all as set forth in Exhibit D, to be fully perfected in accordance with the Uniform Commercial Code.

Said note shall be further secured by a certain guarantee of BUYER, DOE and SMITH, jointly and severally pursuant to guarantee annexed as Exhibit E ("guaranty").

Said guarantee and note shall be further secured by a pledge to SELLER of all the issued and outstanding shares of the CORPORATION pursuant to pledge agreement annexed as Exhibit F.

ARTICLE VI
ADDITIONAL TRANSFERS TO SELLER

As additional compensation and payment to the SELLER, for the purchase and redemption of the SELLER's shares, the CORPORATION shall transfer and convey to SELLER at time of closing:

1. All cash on hand and on account
2. All accounts receivable, including Medicaid receivables accrued to date, to be transferred without recourse
3. 1–197■ Volvo Sedan, sold subject to a lien on said vehicle to be paid and discharged by SELLER

In accordance with the foregoing, the CORPORATION shall execute and deliver to SELLER a Bill of Sale as annexed as Exhibit G.

ARTICLE VII
REDEMPTION BY CORPORATION

The CORPORATION agrees and acknowledges that upon sale and transfer to it of all of SELLER's shares as hereinbefore contained, it shall thereupon cause said shares to be held as nonvoting treasury stock.

ARTICLE VIII
NEW STOCK ISSUE TO BUYER

Simultaneous with the sale and redemption to the CORPORATION of the SELLER's shares, the BUYER shall acquire 10 shares of the CORPORATION, under a new stock issue, all pursuant to a stock subscription agreement annexed as Exhibit H, and the CORPORATION shall accept said subscription and upon payment of the full subscription price issue said shares to the BUYER, the intent being that upon issue, the BUYER shall thereupon own all the issued and outstanding shares of the CORPORATION.

ARTICLE IX
ADDITIONAL WARRANTIES OF SELLER

As an inducement for BUYER to enter into this agreement, and in acknowledgement that BUYER shall rely upon same, the SELLER expressly makes the following warranties and representations to the BUYER relative to the CORPORATION and its affairs:

1. That the CORPORATION is in good standing as a Massachusetts corporation
2. That all tax returns or filings due any taxing authorities have been duly filed and paid
3. That the CORPORATION has good and marketable title to all assets, chattels, or properties on its premises or used in connection with its business excepting only for scheduled nonowned items listed on Exhibit I
4. That the present lease held by the CORPORATION is set forth as Exhibit J, and that said lease is without modification or change, is in full force and effect, is in good standing, and there are no known breaches thereto by the CORPORATION, and there are no known proceedings to evict, terminate said lease, or otherwise curtail or impair the tenancy or the CORPORATION's rights thereunder
5. That the only security interest, conditional sale, lease-option agreement, lien, or encumbrance against any asset of the CORPORATION is scheduled on Exhibit K, and said security interest (or other UCC Article 9 transaction) remains in force without default, and there are no known proceedings to foreclose, terminate, replevy, or repossess any asset so secured
6. That there are no known lawsuits pending against the CORPORATION
7. That there are no known audits pending against the CORPORATION by any governmental body, including any taxing authority or Medicaid agency
8. That there are no known proceedings against the CORPORATION by the Board of Pharmacy or Drug Enforcement Administration, and all required licenses and permits of the CORPORATION to conduct a retail drugstore are current and in good standing
9. That the CORPORATION is not bound on any executory contract other than contracts terminable at will, without penalty or breach (excepting for lease or scheduled security agreements) other than those listed on Exhibit L

10. That to the Seller's best knowledge and reasonable belief, the existing liabilities scheduled on Exhibit A are materially and substantially accurate and all-inclusive
11. That the CORPORATION has full authority to enter into this transaction, acquire SELLER's shares, and enter into all of SELLER's undertakings herein

ARTICLE X
COVENANT NOT TO COMPETE

The SELLER further agrees to execute and deliver to the CORPORATION a covenant not to compete as set forth as Exhibit M. It is understood that the consideration for this covenant shall be $1.00 and not the purchase price for the redeemed shares, in whole or in part.

ARTICLE XI
RESIGNATIONS

The SELLER shall at time of transfer provide BUYER with the resignations of all officers and directors of the CORPORATION as set forth on Exhibit N, and thereafter BUYER as sole stockholder of the CORPORATION shall install new officers and directors and promptly cause notice of change of officers and directors to be filed with the Secretary of State.

ARTICLE XII
ADJUSTMENTS

The parties agree to adjust and prorate certain allocable expenses and other apportionable charges, including

1. Wages and vacation pay
2. Rent
3. Utility charges
4. Prepaid expenses

ARTICLE XIII
TRANSITIONAL OBLIGATIONS

The parties agree to do, undertake, and perform all acts reasonably required or incidental to ensure an orderly transition of ownership control, which shall include but not necessarily be limited to the following:

1. There shall be a tabulation of a controlled substances inventory between SELLER and registered manager designee of BUYER, and reapplication

by BUYER for permits to the Board of Pharmacy and Drug Enforcement Administration.

2. The SELLER shall deliver to BUYER all books, records, documents, invoices, tax returns, insurance policies, corporate records, books, and other written properties of the CORPORATION and shall to the extent reasonably required familiarize BUYER with the operation of the pharmacy.

3. The parties further agree to execute and deliver any further documents reasonably required or incidental to fulfill and perform the tenor of this agreement.

ARTICLE XIV
BROKERS

The parties acknowledge that United Business Brokers, ███████████ Street, ████████, Massachusetts, is the broker to this transaction and is due a broker's fee of $6,000 payable by the SELLER at time of closing.

ARTICLE XV
RELEASES

SELLER and CORPORATION agree to release and discharge one and the other from any and all liabilities and obligations between them (excepting for those obligations created by this agreement intended to survive), pursuant to release annexed as Exhibit O.

ARTICLE XVI
MISCELLANEOUS

1. All exhibits are herein incorporated by specific reference.

2. This constitutes the entire agreement, and there are no other terms, conditions, warranties, representations, or inducements made or relied upon, other than as expressly contained.

3. This agreement shall be binding upon and inure to the benefit of the parties, their successors, assigns, and personal representatives.

4. This agreement is executed with copies, and executed copies shall have the full force of executed originals.

ARTICLE XVII
CLOSING

The date for closing shall be May 30, 1984, at 9:00 A.M., at the office of ██████, ████████████████████████████████████ Street, ████████, Massachusetts.

Signed under seal this 30th day of May, 1984.

_____

By: _____

By: _____

_____

Michael Doe

_____

Joel Smith

APPENDIX 2

FINANCING DOCUMENTS

PROMISSORY NOTE

$100,000.00

Principal Amount

October 15, 1983

FOR VALUE RECEIVED, the undersigned hereby jointly and severally promise to pay to the order of XYZ, INC., Main Street, Anytown, USA, the sum of One Hundred Thousand ($100,000.00) Dollars, together with interest thereon at the rate of 10 percent per annum on the unpaid balance. Said sum shall be paid in the manner following:

In 72 equal, consecutive monthly installments of $ each, with a first payment due 30 days from date hereof.

All payments shall be first applied to interest and the balance to principal.

This note may be prepaid at any time, in whole or in part, without penalty.

This note shall at the option of any holder hereof be immediately due and payable upon the occurrence of any of the following:

1. Failure to make any payment due hereunder within 15 days of its due date
2. Breach of any condition of any security interest, mortgage, pledge agreement, or guarantee granted as collateral security for this note
3. Breach of any condition of any security agreement or mortgage, if any, having a priority over any security agreement or mortgage on collateral granted, in whole or in part, as collateral security for this note
4. Upon the death, dissolution, or liquidation of any of the undersigned, or any endorser, guarantor, or surety hereto
5. Upon the filing by any of the undersigned of an assignment for the benefit of creditors, for bankruptcy, or for relief under any provisions of the Bankruptcy Code; or by suffering an involuntary petition in bankruptcy or receivership not vacated within 30 days

In the event this note shall be in default, and placed with an attorney for collection, then the undersigned agree to pay all reasonable attorney fees and costs of collection. Payments not made within five (5) days of due date shall be subject to a late charge of 5 percent of said payment. All payments hereunder shall be made to such address as may from time to time be designated by any holder hereof.

The undersigned and all other parties to this note, whether as endorsers, guarantors, or sureties, agree to remain fully bound hereunder until this note shall be fully paid and waive demand, presentment, and protest and all notices thereto and further agree to remain bound, notwithstanding any extension, modification, waiver, or other indulgence by any holder or upon the discharge or release of any obligor hereunder or to this note, or upon the exchange, substitution, or release of any collateral granted as security for this note. No modification or indulgence by any holder hereof shall be binding unless in writing; and any indulgence on any one occasion shall not be an indulgence for any other of future occasion. Any modification or change of terms, hereunder granted by any holder hereof, shall be valid and binding upon each of the undersigned, notwithstanding the acknowledgment of any of the undersigned, and each of the undersigned does hereby irrevocably grant to each of the others a power of attorney to enter into any such modification on their behalf. The rights of any holder hereof shall be cumulative and not necessarily successive. This note shall take effect as a sealed instrument and shall be construed, governed, and enforced in accordance with the laws of the Commonwealth of Massachusetts.

By:_____

This note is secured by a security agreement of even date.

GUARANTY AGREEMENT

OBLIGOR: XYZ, INC., a Massachusetts Corporation

OBLIGATION: A certain promissory note issued by Obligor to ABC, INC., dated August 10, 1983, in the original amount of $100,000

For good and valuable consideration, and as an inducement for the parties entering into the above captioned obligation (hereinafter "Obligation"), the undersigned (hereinafter jointly and severally referred to as "Guarantors") do conditionally and absolutely guarantee the full and punctual payment of all monies due from the Obligors under the aforesaid Obligation; and agree that out liability hereunder shall by primary without the requirement of any recourse first being made to any other obligor under said Obligation; or to any collateral under any security agreement that may exist relative to said Obligation; and we do hereby waive all notices of default, presentment, demand, protest, or notices thereto; and agree to remain fully bound and liable hereunder notwithstanding any extensions, waivers, indulgences, modifications, or alterations to said Obligation; or to any security agreement or mortgage granted as collateral security thereto; and notwithstanding the release or substitution of any collateral thereto; or the release or discharge of any obligor under said Obligation or any other guarantor hereunder; and the guarantors hereunder shall have no rights of subrogation until and unless this Obligation is fully paid and discharged; and we acknowledge that there are no representations made to us or relied upon by us for our entering into this guarantee; and we do hereby waive all suretyship defenses and defenses in the nature thereof. This guaranty shall take effect as a sealed instrument this day and year first above written.

_____
John Doe

_____
Mary Doe

GENERAL SECURITY AGREEMENT

AGREEMENT made this 25th day of August 1984 between XYZ, INC. ("Debtor") and ABC CORP. ("Secured Party").

1. *Security interest.* Debtor grants to Secured Party a security interest ("Security Interest") in all personal property and fixtures including inventory, equipment and other goods, documents, instruments, general intangibles, chattel papers, accounts, and contract rights (as such terms are defined by the Uniform Commercial Code as in effect in Massachusetts from time to time [the "Uniform Commercial Code"]) in which Debtor now has or hereafter acquires any right and the proceeds therefrom ("Collateral"). The Security Interest shall secure the payment and performance of Debtor's promissory note dated the date hereof in the principal amount of One Hundred Thousand Dollars ($100,000.00) ("Note"), a certain Loan Agreement dated the date hereof by and between Debtor and Secured Party and the payment and performance of all other liabilities and obligations of Debtor to Secured Party of every kind and description, direct or indirect, absolute or contingent, due or to become due, now existing or hereafter arising (collectively with the Note called the "Obligations").

2. *Financing statements and other action.* Debtor agrees to do all acts that Secured Party deems necessary or desirable to protect the Security Interest or to otherwise carry out the provisions of this Agreement, including, but not limited to, the execution of financing, continuation, amendment, and termination statements and similar instruments and the procurement of waivers and disclaimers of interest in the Collateral by the owners of any real estate on which the Collateral is located. Debtor appoints Secured party as Debtor's attorney irrevocable to do all acts that Debtor may be required to do under this Agreement.

3. *Debtor's place of business.* Debtor warrants that

a) Debtor's principal place of business is located at ▆▆ Main Street, ▆▆ ▆▆, Massachusetts
b) Debtor has no other place of business
c) The records concerning Debtor's accounts and contract rights are located at its principal place of business
d) The record owners of the real estate on which any of the Collateral is located and their addresses are:

_____

Debtor covenants to notify Secured Party of the addition or discontinuance of any place of business or any change in the information contained in this paragraph 3.

4. *Location of collateral.* Debtor warrants and covenants that all of the Collateral shall be located

a) At Debtor's principal place of business specified in paragraph 3a) of this Agreement
b) In a safe deposit box in the Debtor's name at _____

c) In bank accounts in Debtor's name at _____

d) In such other locations as are set forth on Exhibit A hereto

None of the Collateral shall be removed from the locations specified in this paragraph other than in the ordinary course of business.

5. *Encumbrances.* Debtor warrants that Debtor has title to the Collateral and that there are no sums owed or claims, liens, security interests, or other encumbrances against the Collateral. Debtor covenants to notify Secured Party or any claim, lien, security interest, or other encumbrance made against the Collateral and shall defend the Collateral against any claim, lien, security interest, or other encumbrance adverse to Secured Party.

6. *Maintenance of collateral.* Debtor shall preserve the Collateral for the benefit of Secured Party. Without limiting the generality of the foregoing, Debtor shall

a) Make all repairs, replacements, additions, and improvements necessary to maintain any equipment in good working order and condition
b) Maintain an inventory sufficient to meet the needs of its business
c) Preserve all beneficial contract rights
d) Take commercially reasonable steps to collect all accounts
e) Pay all taxes, assessments, or other charges on the Collateral when due

Debtor shall not sell, lease, or otherwise dispose of any item of the Collateral except in the ordinary course of business and shall not use the Collateral in violation of any law.

7. *Maintenance of records.* Debtor covenants to keep accurate and complete records listing and describing the Collateral. When requested by Secured Party, Debtor shall give Secured Party a certificate on a form to be supplied by Secured Party listing and describing the Collateral and setting forth the total value of the inventory, the amounts of the accounts, and the face value of any instruments. Secured Party shall have the right at any time to inspect the Collateral and to audit and make copies of any records or other writings that relate to the Collateral or the general financial condition of Debtor. Secured Party may remove such records and writings for the purpose of having copies made thereof.

8. *Collection of accounts.* Secured Party may communicate with account debtors in order to verify the existence, amount, and terms of any accounts or contract rights. Secured Party may at any time notify account debtors of the Security Interest and require that payments on accounts and returns of goods be made directly to Secured Party. When requested by Secured Party, Debtor shall notify account debtors and indicate on all billings that payments and returns are to be made directly to Secured Party. Secured Party shall have full power to collect, compromise, endorse, sell, or otherwise deal with the accounts or proceeds thereof and to perform the terms of any contract in order to create accounts in Secured Party's name or in the name of Debtor.

If any of Debtor's accounts or contract rights arise out of contracts with a governmental body subject to the Federal Assignment of Claims Act or a similar statute, Debtor shall notify Secured Party thereof in writing and execute any instruments and take any action required by Secured Party to ensure that all monies due and to become due under such contract shall be assigned to Secured Party.

This Agreement may but need not be supplemented by separate assignments of accounts and contract rights; and if such assignments are given, the rights and security interests given thereby shall be in addition to and not in limitation of the rights and Security Interest given by this Agreement.

9. *Insurance.* Debtor shall maintain insurance covering the Collateral against such risks, with such insurers, in such form, and in such amounts as shall from time to time be reasonably required by Secured Party; provided, however, that the amount of said insurance coverage shall at all times equal or exceed the fair market value of the Collateral and in no event be less than $100,000.00. All insurance policies shall be written so as to be payable in the event of loss to Secured Party and shall provide for ten (10) days' written notice to Secured Party of cancellation or modification. At the request of Secured Party, all insurance policies shall be furnished to and held by Secured Party. Debtor hereby assigns to Secured Party return premiums, dividends, and other amounts that may be or become due upon cancellation of any such policies for any reason whatsoever and directs the insurers to pay Secured Party any sums so due. Secured Party is hereby appointed as attorney irrevocable to collect return premiums, dividends, and other amounts due on any insurance policy and the proceeds of such insurance, to settle any claims with the insurers in the event of loss or damage, to endorse settlement drafts and in the event of a default under this Agreement to cancel, assign, or surrender any insurance policies. If while any Obligations are outstanding, any return premiums, dividends, other amounts or proceeds are paid to Secured Party under such policies, Secured Party may at Secured Party's option take either or both of the following actions: (a) apply such return premiums, dividends, other amounts, and proceeds in whole or in part to the payment of the unpaid installments of principal and interest on the Note in the inverse order of maturity or to the payment of satisfaction of any other Obligations; or (b) pay over such return premiums, dividends, other amounts, and proceeds in whole or in part to Debtor for the purpose of repairing or replacing the Collateral destroyed or damaged, any return premiums, dividends, other amounts, and proceeds so paid over by Secured Party to be secured by this Agreement.

10. *Fixtures.* It is the intention of Debtor and Secured Party that none of the Collateral shall become fixtures.

11. *Default.* If while any Obligations are outstanding, any one or more of the following events of default shall occur:

a) Any representation made by Debtor is untrue or any warranty is not fulfilled

b) Debtor fails to pay any amounts due under any of the Obligations when due

c) Debtor fails to observe or perform any covenant, warranty, or agreement to be performed by Debtor (1) under this Agreement or (2) under any other document executed by Debtor in connection with the Obligations

d) Debtor shall be in default under any obligation undertaken by Debtor whose default has a material adverse effect on the financial conditions of Debtor or on the value of the Collateral

e) Debtor or any guarantor of any of the Obligations is involved in any financial difficulty as evidenced by

1. An assignment, composition, or similar device for the benefit of creditors
2. Inability to pay debts when due
3. An attachment or receivership of assets not dissolved within thirty (30) days
4. The filing by Debtor or any guarantor of a petition under any chapter of the Federal Bankruptcy Code or the institution of any other proceeding under any law relating to bankruptcy, bankruptcy reorganization, insolvency, or relief of debtors
5. The filing against Debtor or any guarantor of an involuntary petition under any chapter of the Federal Bankruptcy Code or the institution of any other proceeding under any law relating to bankruptcy, bankruptcy reorganization, insolvency, or relief of debtors where such petition or proceeding is not dismissed within thirty (30) days from the date on which it is filed or instituted

then in each such event Secured Party may declare Debtor in default and exercise the Rights on Default as hereinafter defined.

12. *Rights on default.* In the event of a default under this Agreement, Secured Party may

a) By written notice to Debtor declare the Obligations, or any of them, to be immediately due and payable without presentment, demand, protest, or notice of any kind, all of which are hereby expressly waived
b) Exercise the rights and remedies accorded a secured party by the Uniform Commercial Code or by any document securing the Obligations
c) Perform any warranty, covenant, or agreement that Debtor has failed to perform under this Agreement
d) Take any other action that Secured Party deems necessary or desirable to protect the Collateral or the Security Interest

No course of dealing or delay in accelerating the Obligations or in taking or failing to take any other action with respect to any event of default shall affect Secured Party's right to take such action at a later time. No waiver as to any one default shall affect Secured Party's rights upon any other default.

Secured Party may exercise any or all of its Rights on Default concurrently with or independently of and without regard to the provisions of any other document that secures an Obligation.

After default, Debtor, upon demand by Secured Party, shall assemble the Collateral at Debtor's cost and make it available to Secured Party at a place to be designated by Secured Party.

The requirement of the Uniform Commercial Code that Secured Party give Debtor reasonable notice of any proposed sale or disposition of the Collateral shall be met if such notice is given to Debtor at least five (5) days before the time of such sale or disposition.

13. *Expenses.* Any payment made or expense incurred by Secured Party (including, without limitation, reasonable attorneys' fees and disbursements) in connection with the preparation of this Agreement, any other document executed by Debtor in connection with the Obligations, and any amendment thereto, or in connection with the exercise of any Right on Default, shall be added to the indebtedness of Debtor to Secured Party, shall earn interest at the rate set forth in the Note, shall be payable upon demand, and shall be secured by the Security Interest.

14. *Notices.* Any notice under this Agreement shall be in writing and shall be deemed delivered if mailed, postage prepaid, to a party at the principal place of business specified in this Agreement or such other address as may be specified by notice given after the date hereof.

15. *Successors and assigns.* This Agreement shall inure to the benefit of and shall bind the heirs, executors, administrators, legal representatives, successors, and assigns of the parties. The obligations of Debtor, if more than one, shall be joint and several.

16. *Interpretation.* Reference to the singular or the plural shall be deemed to include the other where the context requires. In particular, the use of the term *Debtor* in the singular shall include all debtors, and the default of any debtor shall be deemed to be a default of all debtors.

17. *Governing law.* This Agreement shall be governed by and construed under the laws of the Commonwealth of Massachusetts.

This Agreement shall have the effect of an instrument under seal.

XYZ, INC.

By: _____

ABC CORP.

By: _____

PLEDGE AGREEMENT

KNOW ALL MEN BY THESE PRESENTS

I, JOHN DOE of Braintree, Massachusetts, for valuable consideration paid, hereby DEPOSIT and PLEDGE with JAMES SMITH as collateral security to secure the payment of a certain promissory note of even date in the original principal amount of $100,000.00 as issued to JAMES SMITH by the undersigned (hereinafter referred to as "DEBT"), and to secure the payment of any other direct or indirect, primary or secondary liability, joint or several, or any renewals thereof, of the undersigned to said Pledgee, due or to become due, or that may hereafter be contracted, and to secure any judgment on any of the foregoing, the following described property:

> 22 shares of the common stock of XYZ, INC. represented by Certificate No. 1 and representing all the shares of said Corporation presently owned by the undersigned

Any addition to or substitutes for the foregoing security shall likewise be deemed pledged with the Pledgee hereof as collateral security for said liabilities and included in the term *security* as used herein.

The Pledgee may assign or transfer said debt to any person, firm, or corporation and deliver said security, or any part thereof, to such assignee or transferee, who shall thereupon become vested with all rights and powers herein given to the Pledgee in respect thereof; and such assignor or transferor shall thereafter be relieved and discharged from any responsibility or liability to the undersigned in respect thereof.

Any deposits or other sums at any time credited by or due from the Pledgee to the undersigned and any securities of other properties of the undersigned in the possession of the Pledgee, whether in safe keeping or otherwise, may at all times be held and treated as collateral security for the payment of the said debt, and any other liabilities of the undersigned to the Pledgee hereof, and such deposits or other sums, may at any time be applied or set off against the amount due or to become due on said debt, or any other liability of the undersigned.

It is acknowledged that during the pendency of this pledge agreement, the Pledgor shall have all rights to vote the stock and shall be entitled to all dividends thereon.

The undersigned represent that they have a controlling interest in the corporation from which said pledged stock is issued, and they shall not vote for any further issue of stock of any class during the pendency of this agreement, or if any further stock be issued, then it shall be delivered to the Pledgee as additional collateral security hereunder.

Undersigned further warrants that during the pendency of this pledge agreement that

1. Undersigned as principal stockholder shall not issue any proxies on said pledged shares
2. Undersigned shall not vote to

   a) Sell, transfer, or convey assets of the Corporation out of the ordinary course of business

b) Remove or relocate the principal business location of the Corporation outside the Commonwealth of Massachusetts.

Upon nonpayment of said debt, or any liability above mentioned whenever due, or in any case, the undersigned shall be adjudged a bankrupt or shall file a voluntary petition in bankruptcy or shall make a general assignment for the benefit of creditors or in case a petition be filed praying that the undersigned be adjudged a bankrupt, or a receiver of the undersigned's property shall be appointed by any court, the Pledgee may immediately sell the whole or any part of the security, with or without notice or advertisement, either at a public or private sale, at the option of the Pledgee. The proceeds of the sale shall be applied (1) toward the payment of all expenses incurred by the Pledgee, including costs and expenses of collections, sale and delivery, and reasonable attorney's fees; (2) toward payment of said debt; (3) toward the payment of any liabilities secured hereby; and (4) any balance then remaining to be paid to the undersigned. The Pledgee may bid and become purchaser at any such public sale, or at any private sale made through a stock exchange or Broker's Board, free from any right of redemption, which the undersigned hereby waives and releases, and no other purchaser shall be responsible for the application of the purchase money. No delay of the Pledgee in exercising any right hereunder shall constitute waiver of such right. The Pledgee shall have the right to enforce any one or more of its remedies, whether or not herein specified, in whole or in part, successively or concurrently.

The Pledgee hereof may pay taxes, charges, assessments, liens, or insurance premiums on the security or any part of it or otherwise protect the value thereof and the property represented thereby, and may charge against the security all expenditures so incurred, but the Pledgee hereof shall be under no duty or liability with respect to the collection of any security held hereunder or of any income thereon nor with respect to the protection or preservation of any rights pertaining thereto beyond the safe custody of such security.

The Pledgee hereof may collect any part of said security by any lawful means. The term *Pledgee* shall mean and include any subsequent holder or transferee.

IN WITNESS WHEREOF, I hereunder set my hand and seal this   day of   , 1985.

John   Doe

APPENDIX 3

TRANSFER DOCUMENTS

BULK SALES AFFIDAVIT

I, John Doe, the undersigned, being President of XYZ, Inc. (Seller), and being of lawful age, being first duly sworn, on oath state:

1. That the undersigned executes this affidavit on behalf of the Seller under a certain contract for the sale of assets from Seller to ABC, Inc. (Buyer), dated August 3, 1983
2. That this affidavit is furnished pursuant to Article 6 of the Uniform Commercial Code and is provided to the above named Buyer in connection with the sale described under said contract
3. That the following is a true, complete, and accurate list of all the creditors of Seller and, to the knowledge of the undersigned, assert or claim to assert one or more claims against the Seller, together with the correct business address of each such creditor or claimant and the amounts due and owing or otherwise claimed (Attach list naming creditors, their address, and claimed amount due.)

Signed under seal this   day of   , 1983.

XYZ, INC.

By: _____
John Doe

Subscribed and sworn to before me this   day of   , 1983.

_____
Notary Public

BULK SALES NOTICE

DATE:

TO:

Please take notice that XYZ, Inc. of Main Street, Anytown, Massachusetts (Seller), shall make a bulk sale or transfer of its goods to ABC, Inc. (Buyer) of Border Street, Anytown, Massachusetts.

To the knowledge of Buyer, the Seller has not done business under any other name during the past three years.

All debts of the Seller shall be paid in full as they fall due as part of this bulk sale.

Creditors are directed to send all bills to:

XYZ, Inc.
Main Street
Anytown, Massachusetts

The sale shall occur ten (10) or more days from the date of receipt of this notice. This notice is provided in accordance with Article 6 (Bulk Sales or Transfers Act, so-called) of the Uniform Commercial Code.

Very truly,
ABC, Inc.

By: _____

INDEMNITY AGREEMENT ON NONASSUMED OBLIGATIONS

TO:

Gentlemen:

As an inducement for your entering into an agreement to acquire assets of ABC, Inc., Main Street, Anytown, Massachusetts (hereinafter "Corporation"), and in further consideration of your waiver of compliance with G.L. 6–106 (The Bulk Sales Act), we the undersigned, as principals of the Corporation, do hereby jointly and severally agree:

1. That we shall cause all known and liquidated debts of the Corporation to be paid from the proceeds of sale by making full payment to all creditors holding nondisputed claims within twenty (20) days of closing date. In accordance therewith, we hereby agree that all proceeds of sale shall be deposited in escrow with your attorney, John Smith, who shall have full authority to issue checks as we may direct.

2. We further acknowledge our agreement to defend against and otherwise fully indemnify and save you harmless from any actual or alleged liability or claim arising from the corporation. In accordance thereto, in the event any such claim is made, then you shall provide us reasonably timely notice of same. We shall thereafter defend against said claim at our own expense. In the event we shall fail to so defend, or you shall otherwise incur any loss, including but not limited to attachment, or other sequestration on any asset sold, then you may upon prior notice to us pay, settle, or otherwise discharge said asserted claim. We shall thereinafter within thirty (30) days fully reimburse you for all sums expended in discharging said claim together with reasonable attorneys fees required in your defending against said claim.

3. In the further event we shall be in breach of this agreement, we agree to pay all reasonable costs and attorneys fees necessary for the enforcement hereunder.

4. This indemnity agreement shall not extend to certain obligations expressly to be assumed by you pursuant to Article 8 of a certain purchase and sale agreement between us and shall not apply to asserted claims for which adequate insurance coverage is available. This agreement, however, shall otherwise be unlimited as to amount and duration.

5. This agreement shall be binding upon and inure to the benefit of the parties, their successors, assigns, and personal representatives.

Signed under seal this   day of August, 1983.

_____

John Doe

_____

Mary Doe

CONFIDENTIALITY AGREEMENT

AGREEMENT and acknowledgment between ABC, Inc. (Company) and John Doe (undersigned).

WHEREAS, the Company agrees to furnish the undersigned certain confidential information relating to the affairs of the Company for purposes of

Evaluating the business of the Company for purposes of prospective purchase and acquisition by the undersigned, and

WHEREAS, the undersigned agrees to review, examine, inspect, or obtain such information only for the purposes described above, and to otherwise hold such information confidential pursuant to the terms of this agreement,

BE IT KNOWN, that the Company has or shall furnish to the undersigned certain confidential information, as set forth on attached list, and may further allow the undersigned the right to inspect the business of the Company and/or interview employees or representatives of the Company, all on the following conditions:

1. The undersigned agrees to hold all confidential or proprietary information or trade secrets ("information") in trust and confidence and agrees that it shall be used only for the contemplated purpose, shall not be used for any other purpose, or disclosed to any third party.

2. No copies will be made or retained of any written information supplied.

3. At the conclusion of our discussions, or upon demand by the Company, all information, including written notes, photographs, memoranda, or notes taken by you, shall be returned to us.

4. This information shall not be disclosed to any employee or consultant unless he or she agrees to execute and be bound by the terms of this agreement.

5. It is understood that the undersigned shall have no obligation with respect to any information that is known by the undersigned or generally known within the industry prior to date of this agreement or that becomes common knowledge within the industry thereafter.

Dated:

ABC, INC.

By: _____
Authorized Officer

_____
John Doe

COVENANT NOT TO COMPETE

For one ($1.00) dollar and other good consideration, we, John Doe and Mary Doe (jointly and severally "undersigned"), do hereby agree that we shall not directly or indirectly compete with the business of XYZ, Inc. with an address at 10 Border Street, Anytown, Massachusetts.

The term *not compete* as herein used shall mean that the undersigned shall not in any capacity, directly or indirectly, engage in the business of a retail hardware store (or any other retail business substantially engaged in the sale of housewares, tools, paints, or hardware), whether as an owner, partner, officer, director, employee, agent, consultant, investor, lender, or stockholder (except as a minority stockholder of a publicly owned corporation).

This covenant shall remain in full force and effect for ten (10) years from date hereof and extend only to a radius of twenty (20) miles from 10 Border Street, Anytown, Massachusetts.

In the event of any alleged breach, the undersigned shall be provided written notice of same and be allowed ten (10) days to cure. Thereafter, and unless fully cured, XYZ, Inc., or its lawful successors and assigns, shall have full legal and equitable relief, without requirement for posting bond as a condition for injunctive relief; the remedies herein being cumulative and not necessarily successive. The breach by one of the undersigned shall equally constitute a breach by the other, and their liability shall be joint and several.

Signed under seal this   day of August, 1983.

_____

John Doe

_____

Mary Doe

CONSULTING AND NONCOMPETITION AGREEMENT

AGREEMENT made as of the 1st day of February, 1984, by and between XYZ, INC., a Massachusetts corporation with offices at 10 Main Street, Boston, Massachusetts (hereinafter called the "Company"), and JOHN DOE of Anytown, Massachusetts (hereinafter called the "Consultant").

WITNESSETH

WHEREAS, pursuant to a letter agreement dated as of February 1, 1984 (hereinafter called the "Letter Agreement"), the Company is acquiring certain of the assets of ABC Corp. (hereinafter "ABC"), of which the Consultant is the President and principal stockholder;

WHEREAS, the Company desires to assure itself of the services of the Consultant, if he is physically able to render the same, until January 31, 1986, and to obtain his agreement not to compete until the same date, and to that end desires to enter into an agreement with him as hereinafter set forth; and

WHEREAS, the Consultant is desirous of entering into such an agreement for the consideration hereinafter set forth;

NOW, THEREFORE, in consideration of the premises and the mutual covenants herein set forth, the parties hereto hereby agree as follows:

1. From the date hereof until January 31, 1986 (the "Term of this Agreement"), the Consultant shall be available to provide consulting services and shall not compete as follows:

a) During the Term of this Agreement, the Consultant shall be available to the extent requested by the Company to provide consulting and advisory services to the Company in connection with its operation of its business. Such services shall be provided when, and for the periods, requested by the Company upon reasonable notice to the Consultant (but subject to the reasonable prior commitments of the Consultant at the time of any such request). In any event, the Consultant shall be available for at least 20 hours of consulting time during each month during the first year of the consulting period and 10 hours during each month thereafter. In addition to the fees provided in Section 2 hereof, the Consultant shall be entitled to reimbursement (upon presentation of satisfactory receipts) by the Company of all reasonable out-of-pocket costs and expenses incurred in connection with providing the consulting services.

b) During the Term of this Agreement, the Consultant will not enter into competition with the Company in any part of New England or New York State. For purposes of this paragraph, the word *competition* shall be deemed to mean association by the Consultant with any enterprise that shall be engaged in the manufacture, distribution, or sale of any products reasonably deemed by the Company to be competitive with any products manufactured or sold by ABC prior to the date hereof, either as the owner of stock in or lender of money or credit to such a competing business, directly or indirectly; or as an officer or director of a corporation, a member of a partnership, or the proprietor of a firm engaged in any such business, or as an employee or agent of or consultant to any such business. The parties agree that ABC sold its products throughout New England and New York State and that the Consultant was primarily responsible for the development and marketing of the products of ABC. Notwithstanding anything hereinbefore contained, the Consultant shall not be prohibited from owning a less than 1 percent interest in the Common or Preferred Stock of any corporation that is listed for trading on any national stock exchange.

2. In consideration for the agreements of the Consultant herein, the Company agrees to pay the Consultant at the rate of $2,000.00 per month on the last day of each month during the Term of this Agreement, provided that the Consultant is not then in breach of his agreements hereunder. In the event of the death of the Consultant during the Term of this Agreement or such mental or physical disability on his part that he cannot discharge his duties under Section 1a) hereof, he shall not be deemed to be in breach of his obligations under such Section 1a), and the payments to be made under this Section 2 shall be made to him or his personal representatives for the balance of the Term of this Agreement, for the services rendered prior to his death or disability, as deferred compensation.

3. The parties hereto agree that the services to be rendered by the Consultant are special, unique, and of an extraordinary character. In the event of the breach by the Consultant of any of the provisions of this Agreement, the Company, in addition and as a supplement to such other rights and remedies as may exist in its favor, may apply to any court having jurisdiction to enforce the specific performance of this Agreement and may apply for injunctive relief against any act that would violate any of the provisions of this Agreement.

4. Any notice to be given by either party hereunder shall be in writing, mailed by certified or registered mail with return receipt requested, shall be addressed to the other party at the address hereinbefore stated or to such other address as may have been furnished by such other party in writing, and shall be deemed to have been given on the date of mailing.

5. No modification, amendment, or waiver of any of the provisions of this Agreement shall be effective unless in writing specifically referring hereto and signed by both parties.

6. This instrument constitutes the entire agreement of the parties hereto with respect to the Consultant's duties and obligations and is compensation therefor.

7. The failure to enforce at any time any of the provisions of this Agreement or to require at any time performance by the other party of any of the provisions hereof shall in no way be construed as a waiver of such provisions or to affect either the validity of this Agreement, or any part hereof, or the right of either party thereafter to enforce each and every such provision in accordance with the terms of this Agreement.

8. All questions pertaining to the validity, construction, execution, and performance of this Agreement shall be construed in accordance with and governed by the laws of the Commonwealth of Massachusetts.

9. The invalidity or unenforceability of any particular provision of this Agreement shall not affect the other provisions hereof, and this Agreement shall be construed in all respects as if such invalid or unenforceable provisions were omitted.

10. This Agreement shall be binding upon and shall inure to the benefit of the Company and any successor to the Company, and any such successor shall be deemed substituted for the Company under the provisions of this Agreement. For the purposes of this Agreement, the term *successor* shall mean any person, firm, corporation, or other business entity that at any time, whether by merger, purchase, liquidation, or otherwise, shall acquire all or substantially all of the assets or business of the Company.

11. The Consultant's obligations hereunder and his rights to receive payment therefor are hereby expressly declared to be nonassignable and nontransferable except in the case of the Consultant's death.

IN WITNESS WHEREOF, the parties hereto have caused this instrument to be duly executed as of the day and year first above written.

XYZ, INC.

_____   By: _____
John Doe   Its President

BILL OF SALE

FOR VALUE RECEIVED, and pursuant to a certain agreement between the parties, BE IT KNOWN that ABC, Inc., a Massachusetts corporation with a usual place of business at Main Street, Anytown, Massachusetts (hereinafter "Seller"), does hereby sell, transfer, convey, and assign forever unto XYZ, Inc., another Massachusetts corporation, and its successors and assigns (hereinafter "Buyer") each and all of the following assets and properties located on, or used in connection with, the Seller's business, being more particularly described as:

1. All merchandise, inventory, goods for resale, and supplies
2. All furniture, fixtures, equipment, leasehold improvements, and appurtenances and accessories thereto as more particularly set forth in Exhibit C, to said purchase and sale agreement, and as otherwise contained
3. All goodwill, rights to the name "ABC," customers lists, trade secrets, and transfer of telephone number

The aforesaid assets are sold subject to such terms, conditions, warranties, and disclaimers as set forth within the agreement between the parties, which provisions are herein incorporated by reference and intended to survive acceptance of this bill of sale.

Provided, nevertheless, that Seller hereby warrants that it has good and sufficient title to said assets, that said assets are being sold free and clear of all liens, encumbrances, liabilities, or adverse claims thereto, and that Seller warrants to Buyer good and marketable title to each and all of said assets and shall defend against and fully indemnify and save harmless Buyer from any claims adverse thereto.

Signed under seal this   day of August, 1983.

ABC, INC.

By: _____
  Authorized Officer

APPENDIX 4

LEASE AGREEMENTS

LEASE AGREEMENT

THIS LEASE AGREEMENT made as of the   day of   , 19   , by and
between   ("Lessor") and   (Lessee").

WITNESSETH

Premises

1. In consideration of the rents and covenants set forth, Landlord hereby
leases to tenant and tenant hereby rents from Landlord the premises shown outlined in red on Schedule A attached hereto (hereinafter referred to as the
"Premises"), located in the portion of the Building known as   (hereinafter
referred to as the "Building"). The Building is located in the City of   . The
Premises are composed of approximately   square feet of rentable area, including a proportionate share of the undivided common areas of the building. The
lease of the Premises shall be for the term, upon the rentals and subject to the
terms and conditions set forth in this Lease Agreement and Schedules hereto.

Use: Quiet Enjoyment

2. The Premises shall be used by Tenant for the purpose of conducting a
restaurant therein and for no other purpose; provided that Tenant shall not use,
permit, or suffer anything to be done in the Premises or anything to be brought
into or kept in the Premises, in either case, that occasions discomfort or annoyance to any other tenants or occupants of the Building, or that in Landlord's
reasonable judgment may tend to impair the reputation or appearance of the
Building or tend to interfere with the proper and economic operation of the
Building by the Landlord.

So long as Tenant is not in default of any covenant or term of this Lease
Agreement, Tenant shall have the right to peaceful and quiet enjoyment of the
Premises during the term hereof.

Term: Termination

3. **A.** The term of this Lease Agreement shall commence on or before , and the initial term shall be for a period of five (5) years.

B. This Lease Agreement shall terminate at the end of the original term hereof, or any extension or renewal thereof, without the necessity of any notice from either Landlord or Tenant to terminate the same, and Tenant hereby waives notice to vacate the Premises and agrees that Landlord shall be entitled to the benefit of all provisions of law respecting the summary recovery of possession of Premises from a tenant holding over to the same extent as if statutory notice had been given. For the period of two (2) months prior to the expiration of the term, or any renewal or extension thereof, Landlord shall have the right to show the premises and all parts thereof to prospective tenants during normal business hours.

C. At the expiration or earlier termination of this Lease Agreement, Tenant shall, at Tenant's expense, remove all of Tenant's personal property and repair all injury done to the Premises, or any part of the property, and surrender the Premises, broom clean and in as good condition as they were at the beginning of their term, reasonable wear and tear excepted. All property of Tenant remaining on the premises after the expiration or earlier termination of this Lease Agreement shall be conclusively deemed abandoned and at Landlord's option may be retained by Landlord, or may be removed by Landlord, and Tenant shall reimburse Landlord for the cost of such removal. Landlord may have any such property stored at Tenant's risk and expense.

Rent

4. **A.** Tenant covenants and agrees to pay to Landlord, as rental for the Premises, Annual Basic Rental payable in advance in equal monthly installments on the first day of each month as stated on Schedule B attached hereto.

B. Except as otherwise specifically provided herein, any sum, amount, item, or charge designated or considered as additional rent in this Lease Agreement shall be paid by Tenant to Landlord on the first day of this month following the date on which Landlord notifies Tenant of the amount payable or on the tenth day after the giving of such notice, whichever shall be later. Any such notice shall specify in reasonable detail the basis of such additional rent.

C. All rentals payable by Tenant to Landlord under this Lease Agreement shall be paid to Landlord at the office of Landlord herein designated for notices. Tenant will promptly pay all rentals herein prescribed when as the same shall become due and payable. If Landlord shall pay any monies or incur any expenses in correction of violations of covenants herein set forth, the amount so paid or incurred shall, at Landlord's option, and on notice to Tenant, be considered additional rentals, payable by Tenant with the first installment of rent thereafter becoming due and payable, and may be collected or enforced as by law provided in respect of rentals.

If the Tenant disputed the additional rental charges by the Landlord, then the dispute will be submitted to the American Arbitration Association, whose decision will be binding on all parties.

Advance Rental

5. Landlord acknowledges receipt from Tenant of   Dollars to be held as advanced rental to be forfeited, without limitation of other remedies, for any defaults hereunder by Tenant occurring prior to the commencement of the term hereof. If no such defaults occur, then such payment shall be applied by Landlord against the rental first falling due hereunder.

Renewal Option

6. This Lease may be renewed at the time option of the Lessee at the expira tion of the original five- (5) year term of this Lease for one (1) additional five- (5) year term, under the same terms and conditions herein, except the rent for the first five- (5) year renewal option will be as set forth on Schedule B.

Improvements

7. Any work to be performed by Tenant in the premises shall be done at Tenant's expense and based upon plans and specifications that shall be subject to Landlord's written approval. Landlord's approval of Tenant's plans shall in no event, unless expressly set forth in such approval, be deemed to create any obligation on the part of Landlord to do any work or make any installations in or about the premises, or to authorize Tenant to make any further additions, improvements, or alterations to the premises. Entry by Tenant or its agents for the purpose of performing work or decoration or for installation of equipment and furnishings in the premises shall be permitted by Landlord.

Common Areas

8. Tenant, during the term of this Lease Agreement, shall have the right to nonexclusive use, in common with others, of corridors, washrooms, stairways, and other facilities as may be constructed and designated in the Building from time to time, by Landlord for use by Tenant of the Building to be subject to the terms and conditions of this Lease Agreement and to the reasonable rules and regulations for use thereof as may be prescribed from time to time by Landlord.

Landlord shall have the right at any time without thereby incurring any liability to Tenant therefor, and without abatement in rent, to make changes or revisions in the common areas of the Building or their portion of the real estate in which the Building is located, for such purposes as Landlord may deem appropriate, so long as said revisions do not impair the use of the premises by the Lessee.

Utilities and Services

9. A. The Landlord shall provide and maintain the necessary mains, ducts, and conduits in order to bring water, electricity, heat, and light to the Building.

B. All means of distribution of water, gas, electricity, heat, light, air conditioning, ventilation, telephone service, or any other service or utility within the Premises shall be supplied and maintained by the Tenant at Tenant's sole expense. Tenant shall pay as and when the same become due and payable all charges for electricity, gas, heat, hot water, and any other utilities supplied to the Premises. Tenant shall pay as and when the same become due and payable all charges for telephone or other communication services used, rendered, or supplied upon or in connection with the Premises. Tenant shall indemnify and save Landlord harmless from and against any liability or damages on such account.

C. Tenant agrees to supply and maintain in the Premises at its own expense any fire prevention equipment required pursuant to any law, ordinance, regulation, or requirement of any public authority or insurance inspection or rating bureau or similar organization.

D. Landlord shall not be liable for full or partial stoppage or interruption of the above services or utilities unless negligence on the part of Landlord shall be shown, and Landlord shall not be liable for consequential damages in any event.

Operating Costs

10. Tenant shall pay all costs and expenses incurred by Tenant in the operation maintenance and management of the Premises and for repairs and replacements, cleaning, and maintenance of the Premises, including, without limiting the generality of the foregoing: (i) maintenance of mechanical, electrical, ventilating, heating, and air-conditioning equipment in the Premises; (ii) the cost of electrical energy for the operation of any machine, appliance, or device used in the operation in the Premises; (iii) maintenance, repair, and replacement of all personal property and fixtures in the Premises; (iv) fire, casualty, liability, and such other insurance as may from time to time be required to be maintained on the Premises by Landlord's mortgagees or ground lessors.

Real Estate Taxes

11. A. As used herein, the following terms wherever initially capitalized shall have the following meanings:

(a) *Taxes* shall mean the portion of any real estate rental receipt or gross receipt tax levied against or in respect of the Building that is allocable to the Building, or any other tax levied against Landlord in substitution for or in lieu of any tax that would otherwise constitute a real estate tax or a specific tax on rentals from the Building, plus the cost, including attorney's and appraiser's fees, of any negotiation, contest, or appeal pursued by Landlord in an effort to reduce the tax or assessment on which any tax provided for in this Section is based.

B. In each *Tax Year,* which expression shall mean each twelve- (12) month period established as the real estate Tax Year by the taxing authorities having lawful jurisdiction over the Building, Tenant shall pay to the Landlord percent of such Taxes, which shall be due and payable within thirty (30) days after delivery of a statement therefor by Landlord, which statement shall set forth in the amount of Taxes payable by Landlord and Tenant's Proportionate share thereof. Simultaneously with the payment of Tenant's Proportionate Share of such Taxes and on the first day of the next succeeding eleven (11) calendar months, Tenant shall remit to Landlord, as additional rent, one–twelfth of such amount. If the total of such monthly remittances is less than or greater than the Tenant's Proportionate Share of the Taxes for the next succeeding Tax year, as set forth in a statement by Landlord to Tenant, the amount of such difference shall be adjusted by Landlord and Tenant, each party hereby agreeing to pay to the other, as the case may be, within thirty (30) days of the mailing of such statement, such amount as may be necessary to effect such adjustment. If the term of this Lease Agreement shall commence or terminate during any Tax Year, Tenant shall be liable only for the portion of the Taxes for such Tax Year as represented by a Fraction, the numerator of which is the number of days of the term that falls within the said Tax Year and the Denominator of which is 365.

Fixtures, Equipment, and Appurtenances

12. All fixtures, equipment, improvements, and appurtenances attached to or built into the Premises prior to or during the term of this Lease Agreement, whether by Landlord at its expense or at the expense of Tenant (either or both) or by Tenant, shall be and remain part of the Premises and shall not be removed by Tenant at the end of the Term unless otherwise expressly provided in the Lease Agreement. All electrical, telephone, communication, radio, vaults, panelling, molding, shelving, ventilating, silencing, air-conditioning, and cooling equipment shall be deemed to be included in such fixtures, equipment, improvements, and appurtenances, whether or not attached to or built into the Premises. Where not built into the Premises, and if furnished and installed by and at the sole expense of Tenant, all removable electrical fixtures, carpets, furniture, trade fixtures, or business equipment shall not be deemed to be included in such fixtures, equipment, improvements, and appurtenances and may be, and upon the request of Landlord shall be, removed by Tenant upon the condition that such removal shall not materially damage the Premises or the Building and that the cost of repairing any damage to the premises or the Building arising from such removal shall be paid by Tenant; provided, however, that any such items for which Landlord shall have granted any allowance or credit to Tenant shall be deemed not to have been furnished and installed in the premises by or at the sole expense of Tenant. If this Lease Agreement shall be terminated by reason of Tenant's breach or default, then, notwithstanding anything to the contrary in this Lease Agreement contained, Landlord shall have a lien against all Tenant's property in the Premises at the time of such termination to secure Landlord's rights hereunder.

Alterations and Improvements by Tenant

13. Tenant shall make no alterations, decorations, installations, removals, additions or improvements in or to the premises after the commencement of the term without Landlord's prior written consent and then only by contractors or mechanics approved by Landlord. No installation or work shall be undertaken or begun by Tenant until Landlord has approved written plans and specifications therefore; and not amendments or additions to such plans and specifications shall be made without the prior written consent of Landlord. Any such work, alterations or decorations, installations, removals, additions and improvements shall be done at Tenant's sole expense and at such time and in such manner as Landlord may from time to time designate. If tenant shall make any alterations, decorations, installations, or removals, additions or improvements, then Landlord may elect to require Tenant at the expiration of this Lease Agreement to restore the premises to substantially the same conditions as existed at the commencement of the term hereof.

In the event any lien shall at any time be filed against the Premises or against any part of the Building by reason of work, labor or services performed or alleged to have been performed, or materials furnished or alleged to have been furnished by, for or to Tenant or to anyone holding the Premises through or under Tenant, Tenant shall forthwith cause the same to be discharged of record or bonded to the satisfaction of Landlord. If Tenant shall fail to cause such lien forthwith to be so discharged or bonded after being notified of the filing thereof, then, in addition to any other right or remedy of Landlord, Landlord may discharge the same by paying the amount claimed to be due, and the amount so paid by Landlord and all costs and expenses, including reasonable attorney's fees incurred by Landlord in procuring the discharge of such lien, shall be due and payable by Tenant to Landlord as additional rent on the first day of the next following month.

Signs and Advertising

14. Tenant will not place or suffer to be placed or maintained on the premises any signs or advertising matter except as follows:

A. Main Marquee

1) Maximum height of sign to be placed in the assigned area will be ____ feet and ____ feet.

2) The sign will be illuminated from within.

B. Sign to be attached to building

1) Maximum height of sign to be attached to building will be inches and will be harmonious with the other signs on the building.

2) The sign attached to the building shall consist of individual letters that shall be illuminated and adhered to the building.

C. All expenses incurred for the construction, installation, and maintenance of the signs will be the sole expense of the Lessee.

D. The Lessor will approve all signs before installation.

Repairs by Landlord: Inspection

15. A. Landlord shall (i) keep the structure and exterior of the Building in serviceable condition and repair; (ii) comply with the applicable governmental rules, regulations, laws, and ordinances affecting the Building. Landlord reserves the rights to interrupt, curtail, stop, and suspend the furnishing of any services and the operation of the plumbing, electrical, heating, ventilating, and air-conditioning systems when necessary by reason of accident or emergency or for repairs, alterations, replacements, or improvements that may become necessary or when it cannot secure supplies or labor, or by reason of any other cause beyond its control without liability therefore or any abatement of Annual Basic Rental being due thereby. The obligations of Landlord contained in this Section 15A shall be performed at the expense of Landlord, except to the extent that any such obligation arises from the negligence or wrongful act or failure to act of Tenant, its officers, agents, employees, contractors, or subcontractors, or from act or failure to act of Tenant that is contrary to the terms and provisions of this Lease Agreement, in either of which case, Tenant shall bear the expense of the performance of such obligation by Landlord.

B. Landlord, its agents, employees, and contractors shall have the right to enter the Premises at all reasonable times for the purpose of mechanical, plumbing, heating, ventilating, and air-conditioning equipment and agrees that, to the extent reasonably possible, such inspections, installations, maintenance, repairs, or replacements shall be made at such times and in such manner as not to disrupt unreasonably tenant's normal business operations.

Repairs by Tenant: Floor Load

16. A. Tenant shall keep the Premises clean and neat and in good order and repair and will surrender the premises in as good condition as when received, excepting depreciation caused by ordinary wear and tear and damage by fire, unavoidable accident, or act of God. Tenant shall not overload the electrical wiring within the Premises or serving the Premises and will install at its own expense, but only after obtaining Landlord's written approval, any additional electrical wiring that may be required in connection with Tenant's apparatus.

B. Tenant shall not place a load upon the floor of the Premises exceeding the floor load per square foot, which such machines and mechanical equipment shall be placed and maintained by Tenant at Tenant's expense in settings sufficient to absorb and prevent vibration, noise, and annoyance. Any moving of such equipment shall be at the sole risk and hazard of Tenant, and Tenant will indemnify and save Landlord harmless against and from any liability loss, injury, claim, or suit resulting directly or indirectly from such moving. Tenant will comply with all laws, ordinances, rules, and regulations of governmental authorities and all regulations as Landlord may prescribe by written notice to Tenant with respect to the use or occupancy of the Premises or the Building.

C. Tenant shall keep the plumbing, electrical, heating, ventilating, and air-conditioning systems and service lines in serviceable condition and repair and will keep the lobby, common corridors, and other means of ingress and egress to the Premises in a clean and safe condition.

Insurance

17. Tenant will keep in force at its expense as long as this Lease Agreement remains in effect during such other time as Tenant occupies the Premises or any part thereof: public liability insurance, including contractual liability, with respect to the premises in companies and in form acceptable to Landlord with minimum limits of Five Hundred Thousand ($500,000.00) Dollars on account of bodily injuries to or death of one person and One Million ($1,000,000.00) Dollars on account of bodily injuries to or death of more than one person as a result of any one accident or disaster; property damage insurance with minimum limits of Two Hundred Thousand ($200,000.00) Dollars; and fire and extended coverage insurance on Tenant's personal property, including trade fixtures, floor coverings, furniture, and other property removable by Tenant. Tenant will further deposit the policy or policies of such insurance or certificates thereof with Landlord, which policies shall name Landlord or its designee an additional named insured, and shall also contain a provision stating that such policy or policies shall not be canceled except after ten (10) days' written notice to Landlord. If the nature of Tenant's business is such as to place all or any of its employees under the coverage of local workmen's compensation or similar statutes, Tenant shall also keep in force, at its expense, so long as this Lease Agreement remains in effect and during such other times as Tenant occupies the Premises or any part thereof, workman's compensation or similar insurance affording statutory coverage and containing statutory limits. If Tenant shall not comply with its covenants made in this Section 17, Landlord may cause insurance as aforesaid to be issued, and in such event Tenant agrees to pay, as additional rent, the premium for such insurance upon Landlord's demand.

Indemnity by Tenant: Exoneration

18. A. Tenant will indemnify Landlord and save Landlord harmless from and against any and all claims, actions, damages, liability, and expenses, including attorney's fees and other professional fees in connection with loss of life, per-

sonal injury, and/or damage to property arising from or out of the occupancy or use by Tenant of the Premises or any part thereof or any other part of the Building, or the Building occasioned wholly or in part by any act or omission of tenant, its officers, employees, agents, or contractors.

B. To the maximum extent permitted by law, Tenant agrees to use and occupy the premises and such other portions of the Building as Tenant is permitted to use at Tenant's own risk; and Landlord shall have no responsibility for any injury to persons, or loss of or damage to property, sustained or occurring in or on the premises, or occurring elsewhere (other than in the Premises) in or about the Building; and in particular, not limiting the generality of the foregoing, Landlord shall have no responsibility for injury to persons or loss of or damage to property sustained or occurring on or about the stairways, public corridors, sidewalks, or other appurtenances and facilities used in connection with the Building or the Premises arising out of the use and occupancy of the Building or the premises by Tenant, or by any person claiming by, through, or under Tenant, on account or based upon the act, omission, fault, negligence, or misconduct of any person or persons other than Landlord and those for whose conduct Landlord is legally responsible.

C. Landlord shall not be liable for any injury or damage to persons or property resulting from fire, explosion, falling plaster, steam, gas, electricity, electrical disturbance, water, rain or snow, or leaks from any part of Building or from the pipes, appliances, or plumbing works or from the roof, street, or subsurface or from any other place or caused by dampness or by any other cause of whatever nature, unless caused by or due to the negligence of Landlord, its officers, employees, agents, or contractors, and then only after (i) notice to Landlord of the conditions claimed to constitute negligence; (ii) the expiration of a reasonable time after such notice has been received by Landlord without such conditions having been cured or corrected; and in no event shall Landlord be liable for any loss, the risk of which is covered by Tenant's insurance; nor shall Landlord or its agents be liable for any such damage caused by other tenants or persons in Building or caused by operations in construction of any private, public, or quasi-public work; nor shall Landlord be liable for any latent defect in the Premises or in the Building.

Increase in Insurance Premiums: Waiver of Subrogation

19. A. Tenant will not do or suffer to be done or keep or suffer to be kept anything in, upon, or about the premises that will contravene Landlord's policies insuring against loss or damage by fire or other hazards (including, without limitation, public liability) or that will prevent Landlord from procuring such policies in companies acceptable to Landlord. If anything done, omitted to be done, or suffered by Tenant to be kept in, upon, or about the premises shall cause the rate of fire or other insurance on the premises or on other property of Landlord or of others in the Building to be increased beyond the minimum rate from time to time applicable to the Premises or to any such property for the use or uses made thereof, Tenant shall pay, as additional rent, the amount of any such increase upon Landlord's demand.

B. Landlord shall cause each insurance policy carried by it insuring the Building against loss by fire or any of the casualties covered by standard extended coverage to be written in such a manner as to provide that the insurer waives all right of recovery by way of subrogation against Tenant in connection with any loss or damage covered by the policy. Tenant will cause each insurance policy carried by it insuring the Premises as well as the contents thereof, including trade fixtures and personal property, against loss by fire or any of the casualties covered by standard extended coverage to be written in such a manner as to provide that the insurer waives all right of recovery by way of subrogation against Landlord in connection with any loss or damage covered by the policy. Neither party hereto shall be liable to the other for any loss or damage caused by fire or any of the casualties covered by standard extended coverage, which loss or damage is covered by the insurance policies maintained by the other party, provided that such policies are not invalidated by such waiver; and provided, further, that if either party shall be unable to obtain the waiver of subrogation required by this section without additional premiums therefore, then unless the party claiming the benefit of such waiver shall agree to pay such party for the cost of such additional premium within thirty (30) days after notice of the statement setting forth such requirement and the amount of additional premium, such waiver shall be of no force and effect between such party and the claiming party. It is agreed that should either party fail to procure such waiver, if available without additional cost (or if available at additional cost and the other party has agreed to pay such additional cost), it will pay to the other in liquidated damages all monies to which any subrogor hereunder becomes entitled and the cost of reasonable legal defense of any claims for subrogating.

Fire or Other Casualty

20. A. If the Premises shall be damaged by fire, the elements, accident, or the casualty for which Landlord is required to insure pursuant to this Lease Agreement ("Casualty"), but the premises are not thereby rendered untenantable in whole or in part, Landlord shall promptly at its expense cause such damage occurred, Annual Basic Rental, and other charges to be abated proportionately as to the portion of the Premises rendered thereof are rendered tenantable. If, as a result of Casualty, the Premises are rendered wholly untenantable, subject to the provisions of Section 20B, Landlord shall at its expense cause such damage to be repaired, and the Annual Basic Rental and other charges shall be abated from the date of such Casualty until the Premises have been rendered tenantable, in which case the proportionate abatement in Annual Basic Rental and other charges shall be made as determined above for partial damage.

In no event shall Landlord be liable for interruption to Tenant's business or for damage to or replacement or repair of Tenant's personal property, including trade fixtures, floor coverings, furniture, and other property removable by Tenant under the provision of this Lease Agreement, or Tenant's leasehold improvements.

B. If the premises are (i) rendered wholly untenantable or (ii) damaged as a result of any cause that is not covered by Landlord's insurance or (iii) damaged in whole or in part during the last year of the term (or an extension thereof, if any), or if Building is damaged to the extent of fifty (50%) percent or more of the total rentable floor area thereof, whether or not the Premises are damaged, then in any of such events, Landlord may terminate this Lease Agreement by giving to Tenant notice within ninety (90) days after the occurrence of such event. Annual Basic Rental and other charges shall be adjusted as of the date of such cancellation.

C. If the Building is so substantially damaged that it is reasonably necessary, in Landlord's judgment to demolish the Building including the Premises for the purpose of reconstruction, Landlord may demolish the same, in which event the Annual Basic Rental and other charges shall be abated as if the Premises were rendered untenantable by the Casualty.

Condemnation

21. If the whole or any part of the Premises shall be taken under the power of eminent domain, this Lease Agreement shall terminate as to the part so taken on the date Tenant is required to yield possession thereof to the condemning authority. Landlord shall make such repairs and alteration as may be necessary in order to restore the part not taken to useful condition, and the Annual Basic Rental shall be reduced proportionately as to the portion of the Premises so taken. If the portion of the Premises so taken renders the balance of the Premises untenantable, taking into account the nature of Tenant's business, either party may terminate this Lease Agreement as of the date when Tenant is required to yield possession. If twenty-five (25%) percent or more of the total rentable floor area of the Building is taken as aforesaid, the Landlord may terminate this Lease Agreement as of the date of the taking. All compensation awarded for any taking of the leasehold and/or the improvements thereon shall belong to and be the property of Landlord; provided, however, that nothing contained herein shall prevent Tenant from applying for reimbursement from the condemning authority (if permitted by law) for moving expenses or removal of Tenant's furniture, business equipment, and such fixtures as Tenant is permitted to remove hereunder, but if and only if such action shall not reduce the amount of compensation otherwise recoverable by Landlord from the condemning authority.

Assignment, Mortgaging, and Subletting

22. Tenant covenants and agrees that neither this Lease Agreement nor the terms and estate hereby granted, nor any interest herein or therein, will be assigned, mortgaged, pledged, encumbered, or otherwise transferred, and that neither the Premises, or any part thereof, will be encumbered in any manner by reason of any act or omission on the part of Tenant, or used or occupied, or permitted to be used or occupied, or utilized for desk space or for mailing privileges by anyone other than Tenant, or for any useful purpose other than as stated in Section 2, hereof, or be sublet, or offered or advertised for subletting, without the prior written consent of Landlord in every case. Consent by Landlord to any

assignment, mortgaging- or subletting shall not constitute a waiver of the necessity for such consent for any subsequent assignment, mortgaging, or subletting that would otherwise occur by operation of law, merger, consolidation, reorganization, transfer, or other change of Tenant's corporate or proprietary structure.

No assignment, subletting, or licensing shall affect or reduce the liability of Tenant for their performance of the terms and provisions hereof.

Performance by Tenant

23. A. Tenant covenants and agrees to perform all obligations herein expressed on its part to be performed or observed by it. If Landlord should send notice specifying action desired by Landlord in connection with any such obligations, Tenant agrees to promptly comply with the terms of such notice. If Tenant shall not commence and proceed diligently to comply with such notice to the satisfaction of Landlord within three (3) days after delivery thereof, Landlord may, in addition to any rights or remedies provided hereunder or at law, enter upon the Premises without terminating this Lease Agreement and do the things specified in said notice. Landlord shall have no liability to Tenant for any loss or damages resulting in any way from such action by Landlord, and Tenant agrees to pay promptly upon demand any expense incurred by Landlord in taking such action.

B. Notwithstanding anything in this Lease Agreement to the contrary, Landlord shall have the right to enter immediately the Premises to correct any situation that, in the sole discretion of Landlord, is deemed to be of an emergency nature. Landlord shall have no liability to Tenant for any loss or damages resulting in any way from such action by Landlord, and Tenant agrees to pay promptly upon demand any expenses incurred by Landlord in taking such action.

Bankruptcy

24. If any sale of Tenant's interest in the Premises created by this Lease Agreement shall be made under execution or similar legal process; or if a voluntary or involuntary petition or answer proposing the adjudication of Tenant as a bankrupt or the reorganization of Tenant pursuant to the federal or state proceeding filed against Tenant and such petition or answer is not discharged or denied within thirty (30) days of the date of the filing thereof; or if Tenant shall be adjudicated a bankrupt or insolvent and such adjudication is not vacated within ten (10) days; or if a receiver or trustee shall be appointed for its business or property and such appointment of Tenant or any arrangement with its creditors shall be approved by a court under the Federal Bankruptcy Act or any state bankruptcy law; or if Tenant shall make as assignment for the benefit of creditors; or if in any other manner Tenant's interest under this Lease Agreement shall pass to another by operation of law, Tenant shall be deemed to have breached a material covenant and Landlord may reenter the Premises and/or declare this Lease Agreement and the tenancy hereby created terminated. Notwithstanding such termination, Tenant shall remain liable for all rent and damages that may be due at the time of such termination and shall be liable for the damages set forth in Section 2.

Default: Remedies

25. A. If the Tenant shall fail to pay when due any rental or other charges required to be paid by Tenant hereunder or shall fail to perform or comply with any of the other terms, covenants, agreements, or conditions of this Lease Agreement, or if Tenant vacates or abandons the Premises, such act or omission shall constitute a default under this Lease Agreement. In the event of a default by Tenant, Landlord may give written notice to the Tenant in the manner hereinafter provided for giving notices, and if Tenant thereafter fails to cure any such default involving the payment of money within ten (10) days after the date on which such notice was given, or if the default involves some act or omission other than the payment of money and shall not be cured within ten (10) days after the date on which such notice was given, or if the default involves some act or omission other than the payment of money that cannot be cured within ten (10) days after the date on which such notice was given and the cure thereof is not undertaken promptly within such period and thereafter expeditiously completed, then in any such event, upon Landlord's, at its option, serving a written notice of cancellation to Tenant specifying the nature of said default and the date of such cancellation, this Lease Agreement and the term hereof shall terminate and come to an end on the date specified in such notice of cancellation, and Tenant shall quit and surrender the Premises to Landlord as if the term hereunder ended by the expiration of the time fixed herein, but Tenant shall remain liable as hereinafter provided.

Upon any such expiration or termination of this Lease Agreement, Tenant shall quit and peacefully surrender the Premises to Landlord, and Landlord, upon or at any such expiration or termination, may without further notice enter upon and reenter the Premises and possess and repossess itself thereof, by summary proceedings, ejectment or otherwise, and may dispossess Tenant and remove Tenant and all other persons and property from the Premises (and such property may be removed and stored in a public warehouse or elsewhere at the cost of and for the account of Tenant without resort to legal process and without being deemed guilty of trespass, or becoming liable for any loss or damage that may be occasioned thereby) and may have, hold, and enjoy the Premises and the right to receive all rental income of and from the same.

If this Lease Agreement shall be terminated pursuant to this Section 25 or by summary proceedings or otherwise, or if the Premises or any part thereof shall be abandoned by Tenant, or shall become vacant during the term hereof, or if Landlord enters or reenters the premises under the provisions hereof or pursuant but as agent for Tenant if this Lease Agreement not to be terminated, or if this Lease Agreement be terminated, in its own behalf, relet the Premises or any part thereof, or said Premises with additional premises for such term or terms (which may be greater or less than the period that would otherwise have constituted or constitute the balance of the term of this Lease Agreement) and on such conditions (which may include concessions or free rent and alterations of the Premises) as Landlord, in its uncontrolled discretion, may determine and may collect and receive the rent therefor. Landlord shall in no way be responsible or liable for any failure to relet the Premises or any part thereof, or for any failure to collect any rent due upon such reletting.

If this Lease Agreement is not terminated and if the net proceeds or avails received from such reletting during any month be less than the rental or other charges that are payable under this Lease Agreement by Tenant, Tenant shall pay any such deficiency to Landlord. Such deficiency shall be calculated and paid monthly. The aforesaid net proceeds or avails shall be computed after deducting, without limitation, all repossession costs, brokerage and management commissions, operating expenses, legal expenses, reasonable attorney's fees, alterations and repair costs, and expenses of preparation for such reletting.

No such default by Tenant under this Lease Agreement, expiration or termination of this Lease Agreement, or summary proceeding, abandonment or vacancy, reentry by Landlord, or dispossession of Tenant shall relieve Tenant of its liability and obligations under this Lease Agreement, whether or not this Lease Agreement may have been terminated and whether or not the premises shall be relet. In any such event, Tenant shall pay Landlord the rent and all other charges required to be paid by Tenant up to the time of such event. Thereafter:

(i) Tenant, until the end of the term of this Lease Agreement, or what would have been such term in the absence of any such event, shall be liable to Landlord as damages for Tenant's default the equivalent of the amount of the rent and other rent and charges that would be payable under this Lease Agreement by Tenant if this Lease Agreement were still in effect, less the net proceeds or avails of any reletting effected pursuant to the provisions of this Section 25 after deducting all Landlord's expenses in connection with such reletting, including, without limitation, all repossession costs, brokerage and management commissions, operating expenses, legal expenses, reasonable attorney's fees, alterations and repair costs, and expenses of preparation for such reletting.

(ii) Without notice or other action by Landlord, Landlord shall become entitled to recover from Tenant, as damages for such breach, in addition to any damages becoming due under subparagraphs (iv) and (v) of this Section 25, an amount equal to the difference between the rent and additional rent reserved in this Lease Agreement from the date of such breach to the date of the expiration of the original term demised and the then fair rental value of the Premises for the same period. Said damages shall become due and payable to landlord immediately upon such breach of this Lease Agreement and without regard to whether this Lease Agreement be terminated or not.

(iii) If the Premises or any part thereof be relet by Landlord for the unexpired term of this Lease Agreement, or any part thereof, before presentation of proof of such liquidated damages to any court, commission, or tribunal, the amount of rent reserved upon such reletting shall prima facie be the fair rental value for the part or the whole of the Premises so relet during the term of reletting. Nothing herein contained shall limit or prejudice the right of Landlord to prove for and obtain as liquidated damages by reason of such termination an amount equal to the maximum allowed by any statute or rule of law in effect at the time when, and governing the proceedings in which, such damages are to be proved, whether or not such amount be greater, equal to, or less than the amount of the difference referred to above.

(iv) If this Lease Agreement be terminated by summary proceedings or otherwise, or if the Premises are abandoned or become vacant, and whether or not the Premises be relet, Landlord shall be entitled to recover from Tenant, and Tenant shall pay to Landlord, in addition to any damages becoming due under this Section 25, the following: an amount equal to all expenses, if any, including reasonable counsel fees, incurred by Landlord in recovering possession of the Premises, and all reasonable costs and charges for the care of said Premises while vacant, which damages shall be due and payable by Tenant to Landlord at such time or times as such expenses are incurred by Landlord.

(v) If this Lease Agreement be terminated in any manner whatsoever, Tenant covenants and agrees, any other covenant in this Lease notwithstanding:

(a) That the Premises shall be in the same condition as that in which Tenant has agreed to surrender them to Landlord at the expiration of the term hereof.

(b) That Tenant on or before the occurrence of any such event shall perform any covenant contained in this lease Agreement for the making of any improvement, alteration, or betterment to the Premises, or for restoring or rebuilding any part thereof

(c) That, for the breach of any covenant above stated in this subparagraph, Landlord shall be entitled to recover and Tenant shall pay to Landlord the then cost of performing such covenant

B. Tenant, for and on behalf of itself and all persons claiming through or under Tenant, also waives any and all right of redemption or reentry or repossession in case Tenant shall be dispossessed by a judgment or by warrant of any court or judge or in case of reentry or repossession or dispossession by Landlord or in case of any expiration or termination of this Lease Agreement. The terms *enter, reenter, entry, reentry, repossession, dispossession, possess,* and *repossess,* as used in this Lease Agreement, are not restricted to their technical legal meanings.

C. No failure by Landlord to insist upon the strict performance of any agreement, term, covenant, or condition hereof or to exercise any right to remedy consequent upon a breach thereof, and no acceptance of full or partial rent during the continuance of any such breach, shall constitute a waiver of any such breach or of such agreement, term, covenant, or condition. No agreement, term, covenant, or condition hereof to be performed or compiled with by Tenant, and no breach thereof, shall be waived, altered, or modified except by a written instrument executed by Landlord. No waiver of any breach shall affect or alter this Lease Agreement, but each and every agreement, term, covenant, and condition hereof shall continue in full force and effect with respect to any other then existing or subsequent breach thereof.

D. In the event of any breach or threatened breach by Tenant or any of the agreements, terms, covenants, or conditions contained in this Lease Agreement, Landlord shall be entitled to enjoin such breach or threatened breach and shall have the right to invoke any right and remedy allowed at law or in equity or by statute or otherwise as though reentry, summary proceeding, and other remedies were not provided for in this Lease Agreement.

E. Tenant shall pay a "late charge" not in excess of seven (7%) percent of any installment of Annual Basic Rental (or any other charge or payment as may be considered additional rental under this Lease Agreement) when paid more than seven (7) days after the due date thereof, to cover the administrative expense involved in handling delinquent payments.

Remedies Cumulative

26. Each right and remedy provided for in this Lease Agreement shall be cumulative and shall be in addition to every other right or remedy provided for in this Lease Agreement or now or hereafter existing at law or in equity or by statute or otherwise, and the exercise or beginning of the exercise by Landlord or Tenant of any one or more of the rights or remedies provided for in this Lease Agreement or now or hereafter existing at law or in equity or by statute or otherwise shall not preclude the simultaneous or later exercise by the party in question of any or all other rights or remedies provided for in this Lease Agreement or now or hereafter existing at law or in equity or by statute or otherwise.

Subordination: Attornment

27. A. Tenant's rights under this Lease Agreement are and shall always be subordinate to the operation and effect of any lease of land only or of land and buildings in a sale-leaseback transaction, any mortgage, deed of trust, or other security instrument now or hereafter placed upon the Building, or any part or parts thereof by Landlord. This cause shall be self-operative, and no further instrument of subordination shall be required. In confirmation thereof, Tenant shall execute such further assurances as may be requisite. In addition to the obligations set forth in Section 27A above, Tenant agrees to attorn to any successor in interest to Landlord whether by purchase, foreclosure, sale in lieu of foreclosure, power of sale, termination of any lease of land only, of land and buildings in a sale-leaseback transaction or otherwise, if so requested or required by such successor in interest, and Tenant agrees, upon demand, to execute such agreement or agreements in confirmation of such attornment.

Landlord or its mortgagee, or other similar secured party, may, at their option, make this Lease Agreement superior to any such mortgage, ground lease, or other security instrument by giving Tenant ten (10) days prior written notice. No other documentation shall be necessary to effect such change.

B. If any person shall succeed to all or part of Landlord's interest in the Premises upon the exercise of any remedy provided for in any mortgage of the Premises now or hereafter recorded to which this Lease Agreement is prior as provided in Section 27A above, (i) Tenant shall attorn and recognize such person as Tenant's Landlord as above provided and this Lease Agreement shall continue in full force and effect as a direct lease between such person and Tenant as fully and with the same force and effect as if this Lease Agreement had originally been entered into by such person and Tenant, except that such person shall not be liable for any act or omission of Landlord prior to such person's succession to title, nor be subject to any offset, defense, or counterclaim accruing prior to such person's succession to title, nor be bound by any payment prior to such person's succession to title of rent or any other sum for more than one month in advance or by any modification of this Lease Agreement or any waiver, compromise, release, or discharge of any obligation of Tenant hereunder, unless such modification, waiver, compromise, release, or discharge shall have been specifically consented to in writing by the mortgagee under said mortgage, and (ii) such person and each person succeeding to its interest in the Premises shall not be liable for any warranty or guaranty of Landlord under the Lease Agreement and shall be liable for the performance and observance of the other covenants and conditions to be performed and observed by Landlord under this Lease Agreement only with respect to the period during which such person shall own such interest.

C. Tenant agrees that at any time and from time to time at reasonable intervals, within ten (10) days after written request by Landlord, Tenant will execute, acknowledge, and deliver to Landlord and/or to such assignee, mortgagee, or other similar secured party as may be designated by Landlord, a certificate stating that this Lease Agreement is unmodified and in full force and effect (or that the same is in full force and effect as modified, listing the instruments of modification), the dates to which rent and other charges have been paid, and whether or not to the best of Tenant's knowledge Landlord is in default hereunder (and if so, specifying the nature of the default). It is being intended that any such statement delivered pursuant to this paragraph may be relied upon by a mortgage, ground lessor assignee of Landlord's interest in the Building.

The failure of Tenant to execute and deliver such certificate shall constitute a default hereunder, in which event Landlord is hereby authorized as attorney and agent of Tenant to execute such certificate and in such event Tenant hereby confirms and ratifies any such certificate executed by virtue of the power of attorney hereby granted.

Successors and Assigns

28. This Lease Agreement and the covenants and conditions herein contained shall inure to the benefit of and be binding upon Landlord, its successors, and assigns, and shall be binding upon Tenant, its successors, and assigns and shall inure to the benefit of Tenant and only such assigns of Tenant to whom the assignment of Tenant had been consented to in writing by Landlord as herein provided.

29. All notices from Tenant to Landlord shall be in writing directed to Landlord, Attention: . All notices from Landlord to Tenant shall be in writing directed to Tenant at   . Either party may designate in writing a substitute address for notices, and thereafter notices shall be directed to such substitute address.

Applicable Law

30. This Lease Agreement shall be construed under the laws of the Commonwealth of Massachusetts.

Captions and Headings

31. Captions and headings are for convenience and reference only.

Joint and Several Liability

32. If two or more individuals, corporations, partnerships, or other business associations (or any combination of two or more thereof) shall sign this Lease Agreement as Tenant, the liability of each such individual, corporation, partnership, or other business association to pay rent and perform all other obligations hereunder shall be deemed to be joint and several. In like manner, if the Tenant named in this Lease Agreement shall be a partnership or other business association, the members of which are, by virtue of statute or general law, subject to personal liability, the liability of each such member shall be joint and several.

Broker's Commission

33. There are no brokers to this transaction and none entitled to commission.

No Option

34. The submission of this Lease Agreement to Tenant for examination does not constitute a reservation of or option for the Premises, and this Lease Agreement becomes effective only upon execution and delivery thereof by Landlord.

No Modification

35. This Lease Agreement and the Schedules attached hereto are intended by the parties as a final expression of their agreement and as a complete and exclusive statement of the terms thereof, all negotiations, considerations, and representations between the parties having been incorporated herein. No course of prior dealings between the parties or their affiliates shall be relevant or admissible to supplement, explain, or vary any of the terms of the Lease Agreement. Acceptance of, or acquiescence in, a course of performance rendered under this or any prior agreement between the parties or their officers, employees, agents, or affiliates shall not be relevant or admissible to determine the meaning of any of the terms of this Lease Agreement. No representations, understandings, or agreements have been made or relied upon in the making of this Lease Agreement other than those specifically set forth herein. This Lease Agreement can only be modified by a writing signed by all of the parties hereto or their duly authorized agents.

Severability

36. If any term or provision, or any portion thereof, of this Lease Agreement, or the application thereof to any person or circumstances shall, to any extent, be invalid or unenforceable, the remainder of this Lease Agreement, or the application of such term or provision to persons or circumstances other than those as to which it is held invalid or unenforceable, shall not be affected thereby, and each term and provision of this Lease Agreement shall be valid and be enforced to the fullest extent permitted by law.

Third-Party Beneficiary

37. Nothing contained in this Lease Agreement shall be construed so as to confer upon any other party the rights of a third-party beneficiary as to any provisions contained herein.

Rents

38. Such terms as rent, rentals, additional rent, or contributions, wherever used throughout this Lease Agreement, shall be deemed to be rent as between a landlord and tenant.

Memorandum of Lease

39. This Lease Agreement shall not be recorded. Landlord and Tenant shall, at the option of either party, execute and deliver a memorandum of the Lease Agreement, or a "Notice of Lease," so-called, in proper form for the purpose of recording, but said memorandum shall not in any circumstances be deemed to modify or change any of the provisions of the Lease Agreement, the provisions of which shall in all instances prevail.

IN WITNESS WHEREOF, Landlord and Tenant, intending to be legally bound hereby, have each duly executed this Lease Agreement under their respective seals as of the day and year first above written.

Attest:

_____   By:_____

                                    By:_____

ASSIGNMENT OF LEASE

ASSIGNMENT of lease by and between   (Tenant), and
(Subtenant), and   (Landlord).

For good consideration, it is agreed by and between the parties that

1. Tenant hereby assigns, transfers, and delivers to subtenant all of Tenant's rights in and to a certain lease between Tenant and Landlord for certain premises known as (Describe)

, under lease dated

19   (Lease).

2. Subtenant agrees to accept said Lease, pay all rents, and punctually perform all of Tenant's obligations under said Lease accruing on and after the date of delivery of possession to the Subtenant as contained herein. Subtenant further agrees to indemnify and save harmless the Tenant from any breach of Subtenant's obligations hereunder.

3. The parties acknowledge that Tenant shall deliver possession of the leased premises to Subtenant on   , 19   ; time being of the essence. All rents and other charges accrued under the Lease prior to said date shall be fully paid by Tenant and thereafter by the Subtenant.

4. Landlord hereby assents to the assignment of lease, provided that:

a) Assent to the assignment shall not discharge Tenant of its obligations under the Lease in the event of breach by Subtenant.

b) In the event of breach by Subtenant, Landlord shall provide Tenant with written notice of same, and Tenant shall have full rights to commence all actions to recover possession of the leased premises (in the name of Landlord, if necessary) and retain all rights for the duration of said Lease, provided it shall pay all accrued rents and cure any other default.

c) There shall be no further assignment of lease without prior written consent of Landlord.

5. This agreement shall be binding upon and inure to the benefit of the parties, their successors, assigns, and personal representative.

Signed under seal this   day of   , 19

_____

Tenant

_____

Subtenant

_____

Landlord

APPENDIX 5

FRANCHISE AGREEMENT

FRANCHISE AGREEMENT

THIS AGREEMENT, made and entered into this　　day of　　, 19　, by and between　　, a Massachusetts corporation, hereinafter referred to as Company, and　　, hereinafter referred to as Franchisee.

PREAMBLE

WHEREAS, Company is the owner of certain trademarks, including　, which have or may be registered with the Patent Office of the United States of America or with the Secretary of the Commonwealth of Massachusetts Office of Corporations Trademark Division, including all proprietory rights and goodwill thereto; and

WHEREAS, Company is engaged in the business of franchising optometry centers and, in connection therewith, licensing the use of trademarks, which said optometry centers are herein referred to as　　and hereinafter referred to as "Optometry Offices"; and

WHEREAS, Company has established a high reputation with the public as to the quality of products and services available, which said high reputation and goodwill have been and continues to be a unique benefit to Company and its franchisees; and

WHEREAS, Franchisee recognizes the benefits to be derived from being identified with and licensed by Company, and being able to utilize the system names and marks that Company makes available to its franchisees; and

WHEREAS, Franchisee desires to be franchised to operate a Optometry Office pursuant to the provisions hereof and at the location specified herein, and Franchisee has had a full and adequate opportunity to be thoroughly advised of the terms and conditions of this Franchise Agreement by counsel of its own choosing,

NOW, THEREFORE, in consideration of the mutual covenants herein contained, the parties agree as follows:

271

I. FRANCHISE PAYMENT: SERVICES BY COMPANY

A. Franchise Payment. The Company acknowledges payment to it by Franchisee of the total sum of $5,000, consisting of $4,500 as and for a franchise fee; $500 for initial assistance essential to the Franchisee consisting of the training and the services detailed at Paragraph B, Subparagraphs 2, 3, and 4 below. Franchisee acknowledges that the grant of the franchise constitutes the sole consideration for the payment of the franchise fee and that said sum shall be fully earned by the Company upon execution and delivery hereof. No further franchise fee shall be payable during the term hereof; in the event a promissory note or other evidence of indebtedness is accepted by Company as partial payment, then the prompt and faithful discharge of such obligation shall be a material consideration. Failure of Franchisee to pay such obligation on its due date shall constitute a material default of this Franchise Agreement, and Company shall not be obligated to give notice of such default, anything in Article XII hereof to the contrary notwithstanding.

B. Services by Company. Company agrees during the term of this Franchise Agreement to use its best efforts to maintain the high reputation of the Optometry Offices and in connection therewith to make available to Franchisee:
1. Consultation regarding specifications and plans for the building, equipment, furnishings, decor, layout, and signs identified with Optometry Offices, together with advice and consultation concerning them
2. A preopening training program conducted at Company's training center, or location of its choice
3. Opening consultation for representative of Company at Franchisee's premises
4. Opening promotion programs conducted under the direction of Company's Market Department
5. The Company's confidential standard business policies and operations data instruction manuals (hereinafter collectively called "Manual"), a copy of which is (or will be) delivered and loaned to Franchisee for the term hereof
6. Such merchandising, marketing, and advertising research data and advice as may be from time to time developed by the Company and deemed by it to be helpful in the operation of Optometry Offices
7. Consultation and advice by Company's representatives, either by personal visit, telephone, mail or otherwise, as may from time to time be reasonably required by Franchisee
8. Such special techniques, instructions, services, and other operational developments as may be from time to time developed by the company and deemed by it to be helpful in the operation of Optometry Offices.

II. FRANCHISE GRANT : AREA : TERM

A. Franchise Grant. Subject to the terms and conditions of this Franchise Agreement and the continuing good faith performance thereof by Franchisee, Company grants to Franchisee the franchise to operate an Optometry Office at the location of the premises; and in consideration of the payment by Franchisee of the license fees and advertising and sales promotion contribution hereinafter specified, Company's licenses to Franchisee for the term hereof, the Company's right to use at the premises and in the operation of such the name ████████ Eye Associates together with such other insignia, symbols, and trademarks that may be approved and authorized by Company from time to time in connection with Optometry Offices, and the goodwill derived from such previous use by Company.

B. Term. The term of this Franchise Agreement shall commence on the date of agreement hereof and shall expire at midnight on the day preceding the tenth (10th) anniversary, unless sooner terminated in accordance with the terms and conditions hereof.

III. PREMISES

A. The premises at which Franchisee shall operate an Optometry Office are fully described in the control sheet attached hereto. It shall be the obligation of the Franchisee to procure, on its own terms, a suitable location for the operation of an Optometry Office and submit same to Company for approval. The Company shall make the final decision as to the desirability and viability of any proposed Optometry Office location.

B. Franchisee shall conduct business from said location only if and when the premises have been improved, decorated, furnished, and equipped with Optometry Office equipment, furnishings, and supplies that meet Company's specifications.

C. During the term of this agreement, the premises shall be used only by the Optometry Office pursuant to the terms of this agreement.

IV. TRAINING

Franchisee will designate itself or another person approved by the Company as a trainee to attend Company's training program. All expenses of travel, room, board, and wages of trainee shall be paid by Franchisee. A portion of trainee's schooling will consist of in-office training at an Optometry Office approved by Company. If at any time trainee shall voluntarily withdraw from training, or shall be unable to complete training, or shall fail to demonstrate to the satisfaction of Company an aptitude, spirit, or ability to comprehend and carry out the course of study, methods, and procedures being taught, then in such event Company shall have the right to require Franchisee to appoint another trainee to undertake and successfully complete the training course.

V. LICENSE FEES AND ADVERTISING CONTRIBUTION

A. License Fees. Franchisee agrees in consideration of Company's licensing its use of the name ████████ Eye Associates, together with such other trademarks and service marks as may be authorized for use by Company, to pay a monthly royalty in the amount of five percent (5%) of Franchisee's gross revenues. License fees shall be paid on or before the tenth (10th) day of each month and shall be based upon gross revenues for the preceding calendar month.

B. Advertising and Sales Promotion. The Franchisee agrees, as partial consideration for the grant of this franchise, to pay to Company a monthly advertising and sales promotion contribution. This sum shall be equal to five percent (5%) of Franchisee's gross revenues. The advertising and sales promotion contribution shall be paid on or before the tenth (10th) day of each month and shall be based upon Franchisee's gross sales for the preceding calendar month. The advertising and sales promotion contribution shall be expended by Company at its discretion for advertising and sales promotion both in Franchisee's market area and on a regional basis, including creative and production costs of advertising and sales promotion elements, and for those market research expenditures that are directly related to the development and evaluation of the effectiveness of advertising and sales promotion.

C. The term *revenues* as used above shall include all income derived from professional services and the sale of eyeglasses, contact lenses, and all other eye care products of every nature and description, including service policies but excluding any sales tax applicable thereto.

D. Accounting Procedures: Right of Audit.

1. Accounting. Franchisee agrees to keep complete records of its business. Franchisee shall furnish monthly profit and loss statements for the preceding month and a profit and loss statement from the beginning of Franchisee's fiscal year to the end of the preceding month. Franchisee shall also submit to Company annual balance sheets, the first of which shall be for the Franchisee's first full fiscal year. All profit and loss statements and balance sheets shall be in accordance with generally accepted principles of accounting and shall be submitted to Company not later than the thirtieth (30th) day of the month following the period for which the written statement shall be submitted.

2. Financial Statements.

   (a) A Franchisee shall submit an annual financial statement as to gross sales, which statement shall be certified to by a certified public accountant within ninety (90) days after the close of its fiscal year.

   (b) In the event Franchisee wishes to apply for an additional franchise, or in the event Franchisee applies to the Company for financial assistance or relief, or seeks a financial arrangement with the Company that differs substantially from existing Company policies, then, in any such event, Franchisee shall be required to submit a complete financial statement that shall be prepared by a certified public accountant. The extent to certification shall be determined by the Treasury Department of the Company.

3. Audits. Franchisee agrees that Company or its agents shall, at all reasonable times, have the right to examine or audit the books and accounts of Franchisee to verify the gross revenues as reported by Franchisee.

VI. STANDARDS AND UNIFORMITY OF OPERATION

Franchisee agrees that Company's special standardized design and decor of buildings and uniformity of equipment and layout, and adherence to the Manual, are essential to the image of an Optometry Office. In recognition of the mutual benefits accruing from maintaining uniformity or appearance, service, products, and marketing procedures, it is mutually covenanted and agreed:

A. Building and Premises. Except as specifically authorized by Company, Franchisee shall not alter the appearance of the improvements or the premises. Franchisee will promptly make all repairs and alterations to the Optometry Office and to the premises as may be determined by Company to be reasonably necessary. Franchisee will paint its Optometry Office when Company, in the exercise of reasonable discretion, determines it advisable, and paint colors will be in accordance with specifications of Company.

B. Signs. Franchisee agrees to display Company's names and trademarks at the premises, in the manner authorized by Company. Franchisee agrees to maintain and display signs reflecting the current image of Company. The color, size, design, and location of said signs shall be as specified by Company. Franchisee shall not place additional signs or posters on the premises without the written consent of Company.

C. Equipment. Franchisee may acquire through Company and other approved sources, by purchase or lease, machinery, equipment, furnishings, signs, and other personal property (hereinafter collectively called "equipment"). Appended hereto as Exhibit B is a list of equipment that must be used by Franchisee in the operation of its business. Franchisee agrees to maintain such equipment in excellent working condition. As items of equipment become obsolete or mechanically impaired to the extent that they require replacement, Franchisee will replace such items with either the same or substantially the same types and kinds of equipment as are being installed in Optometry Offices at the time replacement becomes necessary. All equipment used in Franchisee's Optometry Office, whether purchased from Company or other approved suppliers pursuant to Paragraph F herein, shall meet Company specifications.

D. Eye Care Programs and Services. Franchisee agrees to establish, provide, and offer Optometric Eye Care programs specified by Company to follow all specifications, methods, and formulae of Company as to standards, procedure, content, and use of the Optometric Eye Care programs provided, and to use no other programs, methods, or other like devices of any kind without the prior written approval of Company.

Franchisee agrees that it will operate its Optometry Office in accordance with the standards, specifications, and procedures set forth in the Manual. Franchisee agrees further that changes, revisions, or modifications in such standards, specifications, and procedures may become necessary from time to time and agrees to accept as reasonable such modifications, revisions, and additions to the aforementioned that Company believes, in the good faith exercise of its judgment, to be necessary. Franchisee agrees not to deviate from the standards as set and maintained by Company in the operation of Optometry Office.

Franchise shall remain open for business a minimum of 40 hours weekly and in conformity of all state "Blue Laws" and/or local ordinances restricting days of operation, unless Company consents to other hours or days at the request of Franchisee. Company recognizes that considerations peculiar to the location of Franchisee's premises may make it desirable to alter the aforesaid hours of operation, and Company will not unreasonably withhold its consent to modify the aforesaid hours of operation.

E. Alternate Suppliers. Irrespective of any other provision hereof, if Franchisee gives Company notice sufficiently in advance to permit supplier and specification verification and testing, that it wishes to purchase equipment or products for the Optometry Office from reputable, dependable sources other than Company or its designated or previously approved sources of supply, Company will not unreasonably withhold the prompt approval of such purchases, provided said purchases conform to the appearance, quality, size, and uniformity standards and other specifications of Company.

F. Right to Entry and Inspection. Company or its authorized agent and representative shall have the right to enter and inspect the premises and examine the operation of the franchise for the purpose of ascertaining that Franchisee is operating the Eye Care Center in accordance with the terms of this agreement and the Manual. Inspection shall be conducted during normal business hours. Company shall notify Franchisee of any deficiencies detected during inspection, and Franchisee shall diligently correct any such deficiencies. Upon notification by Company that any equipment or aspect of the operations does not meet the specifications, standards, and requirements of Company, Franchisee shall immediately desist and refrain from the further use thereof.

VII. INSURANCE INDEMNIFICATION

Franchisee is responsible for all loss or damage and contractual liabilities to third persons originating in or in connection with the operation of the Optometry Office and for all claims or demands for damages to property or for injury, illness, or death of persons directly or indirectly resulting therefrom; and Franchisee agrees to defend, indemnify, and save Company harmless of, from, and with respect to any such claims, loss, or damage.

VIII. TAXES

Franchisee shall promptly pay when due all taxes levied or assessed by reason of its operation and performance under this agreement. Franchisee further agrees to secure and pay premiums on a Worker's Compensation policy covering all its employees and, if applicable, to pay state unemployment tax, state sales tax (including any sales or use tax on equipment purchased or leased), and all other taxes and expenses of operating the Optometry Office on the premises. In the event of any bona fide dispute as to the liability for the taxes assessed against Franchisee, Franchisee may contest the validity or the amount of the tax in accordance with procedures of the taxing authority. In no event, however, shall Franchisee permit a tax sale or seizure by levy of execution or similar writ or warrant to occur against the premises or equipment.

IX. OPTION AT END OF TERM

Provided that Franchisee shall have substantially complied with all of the terms and conditions of this agreement between Franchisee and Company, and shall have substantially complied with the operating standards and criteria established for Optometry Office, then at the expiration of the term hereof Company will offer Franchisee the opportunity to remain a Franchisee for one additional period of ten (10) years, provided that:

A. Franchisee shall not be in default on any obligation due Company, and if said default shall not be cured sixty (60) days prior to the renewal, Company may elect to refuse a renewal, by giving notice of such intent to Franchisee thirty (30) days prior to renewal date.

B. Franchisee shall agree to make such capital expenditures as may be reasonably required to renovate and modernize the premises, signs, and equipment, so as to reflect the then current image of Company.

C. Franchisee must have the right to remain in possession of the premises, or other premises acceptable to Company, for the new term. If Franchisee elects (or is required) to relocate, then Franchisee shall pay Company's reasonable expenses for relocating, developing, or evaluating the new premises. Company shall not be required to extend its credit or resources in obtaining financing for premises or equipment.

D. Franchisee shall execute a new franchise agreement on the form then being used by Company, which may differ as to royalty and advertising contributions.

E. Franchisee shall pay the then current royalty and advertising fee as established by Company and shall reimburse Company for the costs and other expenses incurred incident to the exercise of Franchisee's option.

F. Franchisee shall give Company written notice of its desire to exercise its option to continue as a franchisee not less than twelve (12) months prior to the expiration of the term of this agreement.

X. ASSIGNMENT: CONDITIONS AND LIMITATIONS

A. Franchisee shall neither sell, assign, transfer, nor encumber this agreement or any right or interest therein or thereunder, nor suffer or permit any such assignment, transfer, or encumbrance to occur by operation of law unless the written consent of Company be first had and obtained. The assignment of any interest, other than as provided in this article, shall constitute a material breach of this franchise agreement.

B. In the event of the death or disability of a Franchisee, Company shall consent to the transfer of the interest to Franchisee's spouse, heirs, or relatives, by blood or by marriage, whether such a transfer is made by Will or by operation of law if, at the sole discretion and judgment of Company, such person or persons obtaining said interest shall be capable of conducting said business in a manner satisfactory to Company.

C. Franchisee, its heirs, or personal representatives may sell and assign its rights under this agreement to a bona fide purchaser as hereinafter set forth, providing Franchisee shall first offer to sell to Company upon the same terms and conditions as offered to other prospective purchasers. All offers shall be fully set forth in writing and Company shall have ten (10) days within which to accept any offer. If Company has not accepted the offer within ten (10) days, Franchisee may conclude the sale to the prospective purchaser provided that Franchisee is not in default hereunder and further provided that Company may impose reasonable conditions on any assignment permitted hereunder, which may include, without limitation, the following:

1. Assignor must satisfy fully all obligations to Company or others arising out of the operation of the Optometry Office, or Assignee must agree to assume and discharge all obligations to Company or others arising out of the operation of the Optometry Office.

2. Assignee must satisfactorily demonstrate to Company that it meets at least the same financial and managerial criteria required of the Franchisee in qualifying for this agreement.

3. Assignee shall have sufficient equity capital in the business to

result in a debt-to-equity ratio as may be approved by the chief financial officer of Company.

4. Assignee must agree to meet with Company's staff personnel and agree to take the personnel tests to determine his or her aptitude and ability to own and operate an Optometry Office.

5. Assignee must agree to avail itself of the training required of new franchisees and pay Company's then current charges therefor.

6. Assignee, prior to effectiveness of the assignment, shall pay to Company the sum of $2,000 as an assignment expense. If more than one Optometry Office is assigned, there is a charge of $1,000 for each additional Optometry Office included in the same transaction.

D. If Franchisee desires to conduct business in a corporate capacity, Company will consent to the assignment of this agreement to a corporation approved by Company provided Franchisee complies with the provisions hereinafter specified and any other condition that Company may require, including a limitation on the number of stockholders of the assignee corporation. Such assignee corporation shall be closely held and shall not engage in any business activity other than those directly related to the operation of Optometry Offices pursuant to the terms and conditions of franchise agreements with Company. There shall be no transfer charge imposed by Company if such assignment is made within ninety (90) days after the execution of this agreement.

If the rights of the Franchisee are assigned to a corporation, the Franchisee shall be the legal and beneficial owner of the stock of the assignee corporation and shall act as such corporation's principal officer. Provided Franchisee retains controlling interest of the assignee corporation, it may sell, transfer, or assign stock in such assignee corporation to members of its immediate family or to a trustee in trust for same, to its operating managers, or to other franchisees of Company if the franchisee to whom such stock interest is assigned is not then in default of any of the terms of other franchise agreements with Company, Franchisee may sell, assign, or transfer the controlling interest of such assignee corporation under the provisions of Paragraph C of this Article. The sale, transfer, or assignment of any stock interest of such assignee corporation, other than as herein provided, without the written consent of Company, shall constitute a material breach of this Franchise Agreement permitting Company, at its sole option, to terminate same forthwith. The Articles of Incorporation and the Bylaws of the assignee corporation shall reflect that the issuance and transfer of shares of stock are restricted, and all stock certificates shall bear said legend, which shall be printed legibly and conspicuously on the face of each stock certificate.

Franchisee acknowledges that the purpose of the aforesaid restriction is to protect Company's trademarks, service marks, and trade and operating procedures as well as Company's general high reputation and image and is for the mutual benefit of Company, Franchisee, and other franchisees and that violation of this provision shall be cause for cancellation of this Agreement and termination of the Franchise granted herein.

E. The Company may, at any time during the duration of this agreement, assign, transfer, or convey its interest in and to the franchise to a party of its choosing. Any such assignment is without limitation. In the event of an assignment of Company's interest, the obligations and duties of the Franchisee shall remain the same.

XI. LIMITATIONS OF FRANCHISE

A. 1. The Franchisee acknowledges the Franchisor's sole and exclusive right (except for certain rights granted under existing and future license agreements) to use the Franchisor's trademarks in connection with the products, accessories, and services to which they are or may be applied by the Franchisor and represents, warrants, and agrees that neither during the term of this Agreement nor after the expiration or other termination hereof shall the Franchisee directly or indirectly contest or aid in contesting the validity or ownership of the Company's trademarks and trade names and the goodwill now or hereafter associated therewith. Any and all goodwill associated with or identified by the Company's ▬▬▬ Eye Associates trademarks and any successor trade names shall inure directly and exclusively to the benefit and is the property of the Franchisor.

2. No Franchisee advertising or other use of the Franchisor's trademarks and trade names shall contain any statement or material that may, in the judgment of the Franchisor, be inconsistent with the Franchisor's public image, or use, the trademarks or trade names or any advertising material that has been disapproved by the Franchisor for the reasons set forth in this paragraph.

3. The Franchisee shall adopt and use the Company's trademarks only in the manner expressly approved by the Franchisor. The Franchisee shall advertise and promote the Eye Care Center only under the Company's ▬▬▬ Eye Associates trademarks and trade names or any successor trade name or trademark without any accompanying words or symbols except as otherwise required by law and approved in writing by the Franchisor.

4. The Franchisee acknowledges and agrees that the Franchisor is the owner of all proprietary rights in and to the Optometry Office programs, systems, and methods and all other products, services, and materials related thereto as described in the Franchisor's Manual, training guides, and informational materials, and that the program formulae and Optometry Office systems and methods in their entirety constitute trade secrets of the

Franchisor that are revealed to the Franchisee in confidence, and that no right is given to or acquired by the Franchisee to disclose, duplicate, license, sell, or reveal any portion thereof to any person other than an employee of the Franchisee required by his or her work to be familiar with relevant portions thereof. The Franchisee further acknowledges that the program formulae, Standards, and other similar materials furnished to Franchisee hereunder are and will remain the property of the Franchisor and must be returned to the Franchisor immediately upon the termination of this Agreement.

B. No Agency.

1. Nothing contained in this Agreement shall constitute the Franchisee as an agent, legal representative, partner, subsidiary, joint venturer, or employee of Company. Franchisee shall have no right or power to, and shall not bind or obligate Company in any way, manner, or thing whatsoever, nor represent that it has any right to do so.

2. In all public records and in its relationship with other persons, on letterheads and business forms, Franchisee shall indicate its independent ownership of said business and that it is only a franchisee of Company. Franchisee agrees to exhibit on the premises in a place designated by Company a notification that it is a franchisee of Company.

XII. DEFAULT: TERMINATION

A. Default. The occurrence of any of the following events shall constitute good cause for Company, at its option and without prejudice to any other rights or remedies provided for hereunder or by law or equity, to terminate this agreement.

1. If Franchisee shall become insolvent, or if a receiver (permanent or temporary) of its property or any part thereof is appointed by a court of competent authority; if it makes a general assignment for the benefit of creditors, or if a final judgment remains unsatisfied of record for thirty (30) days or longer (unless supersedeas bond is filed), or if execution is levied against Franchisee's business or property, or if suit to foreclose any lien or mortgage against the premises or equipment is instituted against Franchisee and not dismissed within thirty (30) days; or if Franchisee defaults in the performance of any term, condition, or obligation in payment of any indebtedness to Company, its suppliers, or others arising out of the purchase of supplies or purchase or lease of equipment for operation of its said Optometry Office, and if any such default is not cured within thirty (30) days after written notice by Company to Franchisee.

2. If Franchisee defaults in the payment of license fees or advertising due hereunder or fails to submit profit and loss statements or other financial statements or data or reports on gross sales as

provided herein, and fails to cure said default within thirty (30) days after notification thereof, or if Franchisee makes any false statement in connection therewith.

3. If Franchisee fails to maintain the standards as set forth in this agreement and as may be supplemented by the Manual as to cleanliness, health and sanitation, and uniformity (including without limitation, the quality of the Company's Eye Care program) and said failure or default shall continue after notification; or if Franchisee repeatedly commits violations of such provisions.

4. If Franchisee suffers a violation of any law, ordinance, rule, or regulation of a governmental agency in connection with the operation of the Optometry Office and permits the same to go uncorrected after notification thereof, unless there is a bona fide dispute as to the violation or legality of such law, ordinance, rule, or regulation, and Franchisee promptly resorts to courts or forums of appropriate jurisdiction to contest such violation or legality.

5. If Franchisee ceases to do business at the premises or defaults under any lease or sublease or loses its right to the possession of the premises, provided, however, that if the loss of possession is attributed to the proper governmental exercise of eminent domain, or if the premises are damaged or destroyed by a disaster of such nature that the premises cannot be reasonably restored, then Franchisee may relocate to other premises approved by Company for the balance of the term hereof.

6. If Franchisee violates any other term or condition of this agreement and Franchisee fails to cure such violation within thirty (30) days after written notice from Company to cure same.

7. The Franchisee may not, at any time during the duration of this agreement, terminate this agreement without prior written approval of Company.

B. Effect of Termination.

1. Upon termination of this agreement by lapse of time or upon occasion of default, Franchisee's right to use in any manner the trademark ████████ Eye Associates or any other mark registered by Company or insignia or slogan used in connection therewith, or any confusingly similar trademark, service mark, trade name, or insignia, shall terminate forthwith. Franchisee shall not thereafter, directly or indirectly, identify itself in any manner as a ████████ Eye Associates franchisee or publicly identify itself as a former ████████ Eye Associates franchisee or use any of Company's trade secret, signs, symbols, devices, equipment, programs, procedures, or other materials constituting part of the franchise system. Franchisee grants to Company the option to purchase all equipment and any and all insignia bearing Company's trade name or marks thereon at the lower of cost or fair market value at the time of termination.

2. Franchisee agrees that, upon termination of this agreement by lapse of time or default, it will immediately make such removals or changes in signs and colors of buildings and structures as Company shall reasonably request so as to distinguish effectively said premises from their former appearance and from any other Optometry Office. If Franchisee shall fail to make such changes forthwith, then Company may peaceably or by use of legal process enter upon Franchisee's premises and make such changes at Franchisee's expense.

3. In the event of termination for any default of Franchisee, the extent of all damage that Company has suffered by virtue of such default shall be and remain a lien in favor of Company against any and all of the personal property, machinery, fixtures, and equipment owned by Franchisee on the premises at the time of such default.

XIII. ARBITRATION

A. If this agreement shall be terminated by Company and Franchisee shall dispute Company's right of termination or the reasonableness thereof, the parties shall submit said dispute for binding arbitration as hereinafter set forth:

1. Each party shall select one arbitrator, and the two shall select a third; and failing selection of an arbitrator by either or by the two selected by the parties, the third arbitrator shall be selected by the American Arbitration Association or any successor thereof. The arbitration proceeding shall be conducted in accordance with the rules of the American Arbitration Association or any successor thereof. Judgment upon an award of the majority of arbitrators filed in a court of competent jurisdiction shall be binding.

2. If Company or Franchisee shall operate the Optometry Office pending the adjudication of the matter in dispute, said party shall be considered the trustee of the prevailing party and shall be required to make a full and complete accounting of such trusteeship.

B. In the event that any other dispute arises between the parties hereto in connection with the terms or provisions of this agreement, either party, by written notice to the other party, may elect to submit the dispute to binding arbitration in accordance with the foregoing procedure. Such right shall not be exclusive of any other rights that a party may have to pursue a course of legal action in an appropriate forum.

XIV. MISCELLANEOUS: GENERAL CONDITIONS

A. Interpretation. The Preamble recitals are incorporated in and made a part of this agreement. Titles of articles and paragraphs are used for convenience only and are not a part of the text. All terms used in any one number or gender shall be construed to include any other number of gender as the context may require. All exhibits attached hereto are specifically incorporated into this agreement by reference and are made an integral part hereof.

B. Entire Agreement. This agreement constitutes the entire agreement of the parties and supersedes all prior negotiations, commitments, representations, and undertakings of the parties with respect to the subject matter hereof. Franchisee agrees that Company has made no representations, including execution of this agreement, that are not included herein.

C. Nonwaiver. The failure of Company to exercise any right, power, or option given to it hereunder, or to insist upon strict compliance with the terms hereof by Franchisee, shall not constitute a waiver of the terms and conditions of this agreement with respect to any other or subsequent breach thereof, nor a waiver by Company of its rights at any time thereafter to require exact and strict compliance with all terms hereof. The rights or remedies hereunder are cumulative to any other rights or remedies that may be granted by law.

D. Governing Law.

1. This agreement shall become valid when executed and accepted by Company at Waltham, Massachusetts, and it shall be governed and construed under and in accordance with the laws of the Commonwealth of Massachusetts.

2. Notwithstanding anything herein to the contrary, Franchisee shall conduct its business in a lawful manner; and it will faithfully comply with all applicable laws or regulations of the state, city, or other political subdivisions in which it conducts its said business.

E. Severability. If any provision of this agreement is held invalid by arbitration or court decree, such finding shall not invalidate the remainder of this agreement.

F. Notices.

1. All notices to the Company shall be in writing and shall be delivered or sent by registered mail, postage fully prepaid, addressed to its offices at ▬▬▬▬ Street, ▬▬▬▬, MA ▬▬▬ or at such other address as Company shall from time to time designate in writing.

G. Employees. Company shall have no control over employees of Franchisee, including the terms and conditions of their employment.

H. Interference with Employment Relations of Others. Franchisee shall not attempt to attain an unfair advantage over other Company franchisees or Company by soliciting for employment any person who is, at the time of such solicitation, employed by other Company franchisees or Company, nor shall Franchisee directly or indirectly induce any such person to leave his or her employment as aforesaid.

I Liability of Multiple Franchisees. If the Franchisee consists of more than one natural person, their liability under this contract shall be deemed to be joint and several.

J. Modification. This agreement may only be modified or amended by a written document. The Company shall undertake no modifications of this agreement without the prior written approval of Franchisee, and Franchisee shall undertake no modifications of this agreement without the prior written approval of Company.

K. Execution. This agreement is executed in triplicate originals, any one of which may be introduced into evidence as conclusive proof of the context thereof. The agreement shall be binding upon the parties, their heirs, executors, personal representatives, successors, or assigns.

IN WITNESS WHEREOF, Company has caused this agreement to be executed in its name and on its behalf by its proper corporate officers, and Franchisee has hereunto affixed its hand and seal all on the day and year first above written.

Franchisee

By: _____   By: _____

INDEX